THE ROYAL HOUSE OF SCOTLAND

Eric Linklater

Eric Linklater was born in 1899 and
educated at Aberdeen Grammar School and
Aberdeen University. In 1925 he became
Assistant Editor of *The Times* of India and
in 1927 Assistant to the Professor of
English Literature at the University of
Aberdeen. In 1945 he became Rector of
Aberdeen University, for two years. He is
the author of over forty books and he can
trace his own family tree back to the
Norse invaders of Scotland. His literary
career has spanned almost half a century.

The Royal Stewarts took their surname from the office and duties of remote ancestors who were the hereditary High Stewards of Scotland, and stood second in authority only to the monarch. In the times of Mary, Queen of Scots, the name acquired a new spelling and became Stuart. For a little while Mary had been Queen of France, and it seems probable that her French friends found it impossible to pronounce Stewart, but Stuart was within their linguistic capacity. So the royal name Stuart became the accepted form; and it is pleasant to record that it's adoption was dictated by courtesy.

The Royal House of Scotland

ERIC LINKLATER

SPHERE BOOKS LIMITED
30/32 Gray's Inn Road, London, WC1X 8JL

First published in Great Britain in 1970 by
Macmillan & Co. Ltd.
© Eric Linklater, 1970
First Sphere Books edition, 1972

TRADE
MARK

Printed in Great Britain by
Hazell Watson & Viney Ltd,
Aylesbury, Bucks

Contents

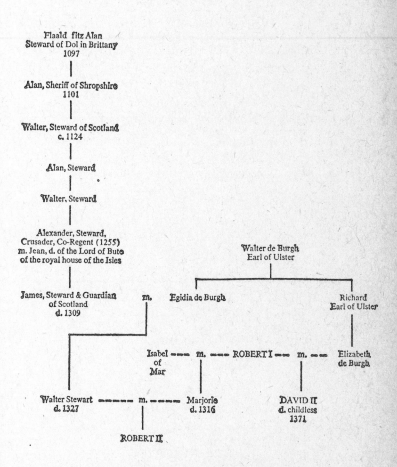

Flaald fitz Alan
Steward of Dol in Brittany
1097

Alan, Sheriff of Shropshire
1101

Walter, Steward of Scotland
c. 1124

Alan, Steward

Walter, Steward

Alexander, Steward,
Crusader, Co-Regent (1255)
m. Jean, d. of the Lord of Bute
of the royal house of the Isles

Walter de Burgh
Earl of Ulster

James, Steward & Guardian   m.   Egidia de Burgh   Richard
of Scotland   Earl of Ulster
d. 1309

Isabel —— m. —— ROBERT I —— m. —— Elizabeth
of   de Burgh
Mar

Walter Stewart —————— m. —————— Marjorie   DAVID II
d. 1327   d. 1316   d. childless
                                                            1371

ROBERT II

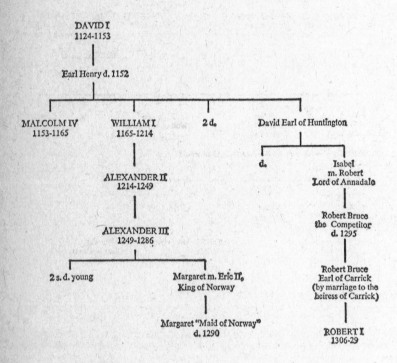

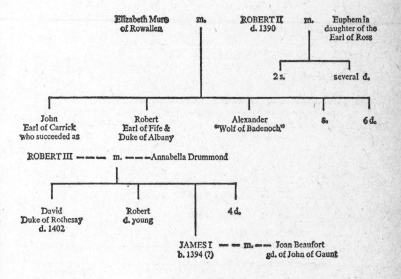

Elizabeth Mure of Rowallen — m. — ROBERT II d. 1390 — m. — Euphemia daughter of the Earl of Ross

2 s.   several d.

John Earl of Carrick who succeeded as   Robert Earl of Fife & Duke of Albany   Alexander "Wolf of Badenoch"   s.   6 d.

ROBERT III — — — m. — — — Annabella Drummond

David Duke of Rothesay d. 1402   Robert d. young   4 d.

JAMES I — — m. — — Joan Beaufort b. 1394 (?)   gd. of John of Gaunt

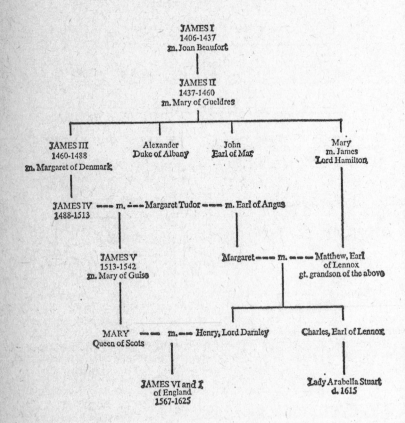

JAMES I
1406-1437
m. Joan Beaufort

JAMES II
1437-1460
m. Mary of Gueldres

JAMES III
1460-1488
m. Margaret of Denmark

Alexander
Duke of Albany

John
Earl of Mar

Mary
m. James
Lord Hamilton

JAMES IV ——— m. ——— Margaret Tudor ——— m. Earl of Angus
1488-1513

JAMES V
1513-1542
m. Mary of Guise

Margaret ——— m. ——— Matthew, Earl
of Lennox
gt. grandson of the above

MARY ——— m. ——— Henry, Lord Darnley
Queen of Scots

Charles, Earl of Lennox

JAMES VI and I
of England
1567-1625

Lady Arabella Stuart
d. 1615

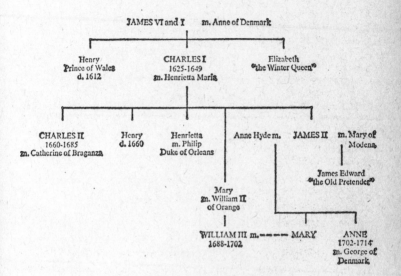

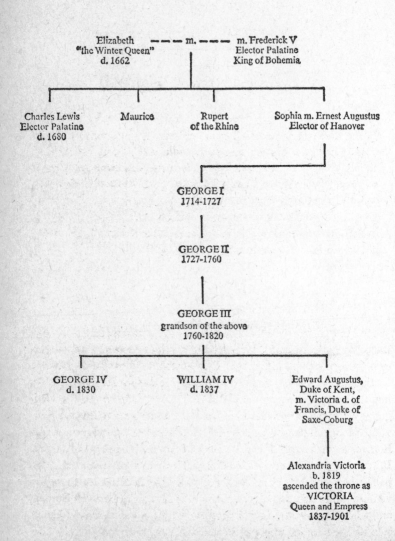

Elizabeth — — — m. — — — m. Frederick V
"the Winter Queen" Elector Palatine
d. 1662 King of Bohemia

Charles Lewis   Maurice   Rupert   Sophia m. Ernest Augustus
Elector Palatine   of the Rhine   Elector of Hanover
d. 1680

GEORGE I
1714-1727

GEORGE II
1727-1760

GEORGE III
grandson of the above
1760-1820

GEORGE IV   WILLIAM IV   Edward Augustus,
d. 1830   d. 1837   Duke of Kent,
                               m. Victoria d. of
                               Francis, Duke of
                               Saxe-Coburg

Alexandria Victoria
b. 1819
ascended the throne as
VICTORIA
Queen and Empress
1837-1901

Introduction: the background

In the Eleventh Century a Breton nobleman, of a minor sort, went over to England. His son became friendly with David, heir to the throne of Scotland, and with him rode north to acquire great possessions. The Breton incomer settled down and prospered. Like an acorn planted in friendly soil he put forth growth, and out of him grew one of the great family trees of Europe. It was a royal tree, and of his seed came the Kings of Scotland and many lesser people. This is how the family and its story began.

1

When the Romans first saw the dolmens and sombre moors of Brittany, the glittering coast and stone circles of a country already brooding its everlasting legends, the people they encountered spoke a primitive Celtic tongue common to much of Europe. It did not survive the Latin impact, but a few hundred years later a variant form of the older language was brought in by invaders from the nearer parts of England.

In the dissolution of their empire England was abandoned by the Romans and menaced by the incursion of Saxon barbarians. Among the Britons—of the sort now called "ancient"—there were those who, appalled by the decay of an alien but protective civilization, chose adventure rather than submission to the rude savages of northern Europe; and from their related homeland attacked the great westward peninsula of France that meets at Ushant the monstrous tides of the narrowed Atlantic. They, who were also a Celtic people—somewhat adulterated by time and their recent neighbours—took possession of the peninsula in the Fifth or Sixth Century of this era, and called it Brittany. To their own mothering island they gave the distinguishing appellation of Great Britain.

The incomers had to fight for their existence. They repelled their Frankish neighbours, the long-haired Merovingian kings, and the Carolingians. In the last quarter of the Ninth Century the Bretons from Great Britain defeated a powerful Norse or Danish army, but a generation or two later there were Vikings on their shores again. Robert, Count of Normandy, sometimes called Robert the Devil, made war against his cousin, Alan of Brittany, the last ruler of all the Breton lands; and in the Twelfth Century Brittany acknowledged Norman suzerainty.

At Dol, on the south shore of the Gulf of St. Malo, there was a family which held the hereditary office of Steward or Seneschal to the Counts of Dol and Dinan, and in 1097 the head of the family joined the First Crusade, and died on it. He was succeeded, in lands and office, by his brother Flaald, whose son Alan apparently went to England with its King, Henry I, son of William the Conqueror; by whom, in 1101, he was appointed to high office in the emergent feudalism of the time as Sheriff of Shropshire. He had a son, Walter, who became friendly with David, the heir or heir-presumptive to the Scottish throne and brother-in-law of King Henry. When David, having succeeded to the throne in 1124, went north to rule his kingdom, Walter fitz Alan went with him.

By David of Scotland—first of that name—Walter was given large estates in the southwestern Lowlands, and made High Steward of the kingdom. David's successor, Malcolm IV, ratified Walter in his office and enlarged his estates. Walter had a son, Alan, who succeeded him; when Alan's son, another Walter, became High Steward in his turn, he took for his own the name of his office, and so determined the dynastic name of all the kings of Scotland from 1371 to 1603.

After Walter the Second's death in 1241 a hundred and thirty years passed before the first of the royal Stewarts found a waiting throne, but the Breton family had become firmly rooted, and was unshaken by the tempests and perils of that long century. It had come from a land whose life had twice been coloured by the native thoughts of a Celtic language, and of the leading men, the chiefs or kinglets of the ancient Britons who had conquered it, some, presumably, had re-established an old hereditary power in new surroundings. That the Counts of Dol and their Stewards were descendants of those chiefs is not impossible—it is, indeed, most probable—and the talent for ruling, and maintaining their rule, which the High Stewards of Scotland so clearly showed in the northern half of Britain may well have been inherited from ancestors in the south and western parts of England.

There is, however, nothing to be told of those ancient fathers of a royal family. They were, beyond question, redoubtable men whose strength of hand and body was matched by a very sturdy and practical intelligence; for never a family ruled, and maintained its rule over great domains for nearly two and a half centuries, without a remarkable genetic inheritance. They lived, of course, in richness and luxury—luxury, not comfort—that set them apart from the anonymous many over whom their rule was absolute; but the basic condition of their life was indistinguishable from the background of their surrounding peasants, fishermen, and fighting men; and a native community of interest mitigated the differences of wealth. They were not illiterate, untutored men, and their peasantry had traditions of their own. Peasant and noble lived in a sort of symbiosis. Poverty and luxury, the strength of the poor and the authority of their rulers, were complementary rather than antagonistic; but to maintain such a relationship the rulers must have been endowed with great intelligence, with a comprehensive sympathy and understanding of the disabilities inherent in a fixed society. One wishes—but vainly—for more knowledge, not only of the daily life, but of the daily thought and emotions of the High Stewards and their dependants.

Alexander, the fourth High Steward, was a Crusader and a Regent of Scotland in the minority of King Alexander III. James, son of Alexander the Steward, became a Guardian of the realm after the King's death, and opposed the aggressive policy of Edward I of England. Edward, whose purpose was to dominate and unify all Britain, conquered Wales and in Scotland provoked the long, destructive War of Independence. James the Steward fought beside William Wallace at the battle of Stirling Bridge; he married Egidia, sister of Richard de Burgh, Earl of Ulster; and died in 1309, leaving a son, Walter, to succeed him.

That Walter, though only a beardless boy, was with Sir James Douglas's division at Bannockburn, and in 1315 married the Lady Marjorie, daughter of Robert the Bruce by his first wife, Isabel of Mar. He played a spirited part in the war, but died, still a young man, in 1326. By Marjorie he had an only son, who at an advanced age became Robert II.

It was the Lady Marjorie, the founding mother of a new dynasty, who seems to have bequeathed to its successive sovereigns a heritage of disaster which none escaped. She and her stepmother were with the Bruce in the disastrous autumn of 1306 when Robert, newly crowned, was in headlong flight from the English and their Highland allies. While Robert sought refuge in the west, the women of his party, with an escort led by the Earl of Atholl and Nigel Bruce, fled through the hills to the strong castle of Kildrummy in Aberdeenshire. Kildrummy, though its walls were thick, was vulnerable to treachery, and the royal women were forced to take flight again. Their apparent hope was to reach the Norwegian islands of Orkney, but they got no farther than Tain on the Dornoch Firth, where they looked for safety in the sanctuary of St. Duthac. But the Earl of Ross, the local potentate, had no respect for St. Duthac, and by him they were sent south for imprisonment.

Edward of England, in a senile fury because the Scots had again defeated him, imprisoned the Countess of Buchan and Robert's sister Mary in cages, constructed for their visible confinement, at Berwick and Roxburgh; and gave orders that another cage should be made for Marjorie in the Tower of London. But Marjorie was still a child, Edward relented, and let her be sent instead to a nunnery in Yorkshire. There she remained until after the battle of Bannockburn, where the Scots took so many distinguished prisoners that Robert, by exchange, was able to procure the release of his Queen and her stepdaughter. A year later she married Walter Stewart, and in 1316, when heavily pregnant, fell from her horse, gave premature birth to a male child, and died. She may have been nineteen or twenty.

When she was given in marriage to Walter Stewart she was King Robert's only legitimate child, and the question of who should succeed, if her father died in battle, could not be deferred. In that hazardous year, though a major battle had been won, the outcome of the war was still in doubt, and Marjorie was not declared heir-apparent but only heir-eventual. Should King Robert, reunited with his second wife after her eight years' imprisonment, beget a male child, the succession would be vested in him. If Robert died without a male heir, the crown would pass to his vigorous but reckless brother Edward: that was decided, with Marjorie's consent, at a parliament sitting in Ayr. Then Edward Bruce went off to venture for the crown of Ireland, which a minor king of Tyrone had offered him, and got no reward but death for his audacity. So, to ensure undisputed succession, a new arrangement had to be made.

Marjorie was dead, but the infant Robert had survived. A parliament at Scone declared him heir to the throne should King Robert die and leave no son, the infant's guardian to be one of those paladins of the war, Randolph, Earl of Moray, or Sir James Douglas. But after their long separation King Robert and Elizabeth his Queen found energy and affection enough to beget and bear four children, two boys and two girls. One of the boys died in infancy; the other, called David, unfortunately lived. And Robert, the child of Marjorie Bruce and Walter Stewart, had to wait a long time before he became the first of the Stewart kings and a monarch of dignified appearance, of intemperate sensuality, and lamentable ineptitude.

2

Neither in history, which records the deeds and achievements of conspicuous men, nor in common knowledge, which remembers the life and disappointments of our neighbours, is it unusual to find that men of large ability, of moral or intellectual stature far above the ordinary, are followed by sons who, as conspicuously as their parents, fall below the average of decency or success. But few men, as great as Robert the Bruce, have been succeeded by so contemptible a son as David II. His shameful career must be considered—and will be considered very briefly—before it is possible to explain and assess the pathetic discomfiture of the earliest Stewart kings, Robert II and Robert III.

Robert I, called Robert the Bruce, had inspired and directed the epic tale of Scotland's War of Independence. His imaginative purpose had been matched by unfailing energy, his military genius by a statesmanship that was elastic at need but adamant at heart. After many years of resolute and determined fighting—fighting, that is, determined by strategy and an unyielding spirit—he achieved everything for which he and his people had striven; and within a few years his kingdom disintegrated, and his successor was ready to throw away, as if it had been a forgotten toy, the gaunt bequest of independence.

Let it be admitted that David II was not to blame for the disasters of his early years: he was only five when he succeeded in 1329, and it was his misfortune that Douglas and Randolph, the paladins of his father's war, were dead already or within sight of death. Scotland's administrative system had almost collapsed, and there was no one strong enough, in will and character, to impose a defensive unity on barons whose innate anarchy had been reinforced by the wealth of the lands with which the late King had extravagantly rewarded them. When Edward III of England renewed the war, Scotland appeared to suffer total defeat except for its stubborn refusal to admit defeat.

David fled to France, and Scotland found relief from its neighbour's savage pressure when Edward III, in pursuit of fame and a richer prize, followed him to claim the throne of France and precipitate the Hundred Years' War. Scotland showed signs of revival, but was again humiliated when its King returned and led an invasion of northern England. He was taken prisoner at Neville's Cross, and remained in captivity for eleven years. He was ransomed for 100,000 marks, and wasted the revenues of his impoverished country on witless folly. His nobles rebelled, but were pacified, and David rode to London with a scandalous proposal to surrender to Edward the succession to the Scottish throne in return for cancellation of his ransom.

A parliament summoned to Scone in 1364 angrily refused approval of that shameful bargain. It was a parliament notable not only for its independence, but for the fact that it represented, for the first time, the Three Estates of the realm: with nobles and prelates sat members from the royal burghs. In the slowly rising mercantile class were the only moneymakers of the kingdom, and it is conceivable that David himself, in the hope of personal profit, was responsible for elevation of the Third Estate, and so permitted the first faint rays of a yet distant democratic dawn to lighten the political darkness of his age. There seems nothing else to be said in his favour, and few can have mourned him when he died in 1371.

3

Though twice married, David II died childless and was succeeded by his nephew, Robert II, son of Marjorie Bruce and Walter the Steward. Older than the late King, Robert had acted as Regent during David's captivity in England, and thereafter led the barons' opposition to him. With some extravagance he repaired his predecessor's lack of family. He married, in 1349, Elizabeth, daughter of Sir Robert Mure of Rowallan, and by her had four sons and six daughters, most of whom, if not all, had been born before their parents' marriage, but were probably legitimized by it. His second wife was Euphemia, daughter of the Earl of Ross, who gave him two sons and several daughters; and among his illegitimate children were at least eight sons. He was a tall and handsome man, of stately appearance, but he was fifty-five when he succeeded, and ten years later his increasing disabilities compelled him to delegate the executive work of government to his eldest son John, Earl of Carrick. Then Carrick was lamed by a kicking horse and became a chronic invalid; the task of government passed to his younger brother, Robert, Earl of Fife, who by a policy of *laissez faire* and lenient or no taxation made himself popular, and for a period of about thirty-five years, with one brief interval, was the only real source of power in Scotland, and of such government as he thought necessary.

The reign of Robert II lasted nineteen years, and was marked and marred by the usual bickering with England, and a renewal of the alliance with France. John of Gaunt—Shakespeare's "time-honoured Lancaster"—made history by marching as far as Edinburgh, and retiring without burning it; and a French force handsomely subsidised and commanded by Jean de Vienne, Admiral of France, provoked by their riches great resentment among their Scottish allies, and were frustrated by them when they wanted to engage in open battle with their English enemies. The only military encounter, of memorable quality, was the battle of Otterburn in 1388: Harry Percy, known as Hotspur, was defeated, but James, the second Earl of Douglas, was killed; and both were immortalised in the well-known ballad.'

Robert II, having reigned inconspicuously but with apparent good-will, died in 1390 and was succeeded by his son John, Earl of Carrick, who had been kicked by a horse and had never recovered from his injuries. The name John was regarded as unlucky, and the new King preferred to be called Robert III. The legitimacy of Robert and his two surviving brothers, seemingly established by the papal dispensation that allowed the marriage of their father and Elizabeth Mure, was not accepted by all who were interested in the succession; and though, by Act of Parliament in 1373, the order of succession was carefully prescribed—after Robert III to his male heirs; failing whom to his brother the Earl of Fife and his heirs; then to the sons of Robert II's marriage to Euphemia Ross—that enactment was a further source of embarrassment to the eventual heir.

Robert III, a gentle, kindly man, was unfitted for the tasks of government, and his brother, the Earl of Fife, still sustained the burden of his semiregency and enjoyed the authority to which he had grown accustomed. Disorder was widespread, and within a few months of Robert's accession his other brother, Alexander, Earl of Buchan and known as the Wolf of Badenoch, led a Highland host to burn the burgh of Elgin and its noble cathedral. That he did to revenge himself on the Bishop of Moray, who had ordered him to return to a deserted wife. Buchan was persuaded to do penance for his crime, but suffered no other punishment because the King had no power to punish him; and when, in retaliation for the penance inflicted on his father, an illegitimate son of the Wolf led a punitive raid into Angus, he too went unpunished.

The most spectacular domestic event—if such it can be called—of a reign characterised by abstention from rule, was the notorious battle, tournament, or trial by ordeal on the North Inch at Perth. In the presence of the King, and a great concourse of spectators, thirty men of Clan Chattan fought against thirty of Clan Kay till less than a dozen survived. The cause of the quarrel is unknown, but its outcome is said to have been beneficial: the slaughter of so many local champions ensured long peace in the central Highlands. Tournaments were of fairly frequent occurrence, but none other was so murderous as the affair on the North Inch, nor had any recorded consequence.

In 1398 dukedoms—the first in Scotland—were conferred on David, the King's elder son, and on his brother the Earl of Fife. The latter became Duke of Albany, the former was created Duke of Rothesay and did not live long to enjoy his title. He appears to have been not only a wild and dissolute young man, but ill-advisedly ambitious. He became involved with young women whose relations he offended, and challenged his uncle's well-established authority. The King was persuaded to order his arrest, and young Rothesay was made prisoner and taken to his uncle's castle at Falkland; where he died. It is not known if Albany was responsible for his death, but there was widespread suspicion that Rothesay had been murdered, or allowed to die of starvation.

Now, between Albany and succession to the throne, stood only Robert's younger son James, a boy of seven. Albany, whose authority as Warden or Lieutenant of the realm had been so unsuccessfully challenged, resumed his former power, and there was a new war with England in which, in 1402, a large Scottish army, led by Albany's son. Murdoch and Archibald, the young Earl of Douglas, was resoundingly defeated at Homildon Hill in Northumberland by Harry Percy, called Hotspur. Archibald Douglas was a cousin of James Douglas whom Hotspur had killed at the battle of Otterburn; but on the Borders, in the Debatable Lands, that slight mischance was no obstacle to friendship. Young Archibald was made prisoner, and became so warmly attached to Hotspur that when the latter rose in rebellion against Henry IV, his King, Archibald rode with him to battle at Shrewsbury. There Percy was killed, and young Archibald, after killing the Earl of Stafford, was again taken prisoner. Percy, it is said, was mourned in both England and Scotland.

Passive, patient, but ambitious, Albany still ruled in Scotland, and the old King grew uneasy. He had not forgotten Rothesay's death, and with good reason he felt that for James, his surviving son and heir, there was no safety in his own land. Born in Dunfermline in 1394, the youngest son of Robert III and Annabella his Queen, very little is known of James's boyhood, but in February 1406, in circumstances of great secrecy, he was taken by Sir David Fleming, with a strong escort, to North Berwick, and there put aboard a rowing boat which carried him to the Bass Rock. Fleming was one of the old King's most faithful counsellors, and as if to demonstrate the soundness of Robert's judgment—the judgment of a man too frail to rule—Fleming and his people, on their return from North Berwick, were surprised by enemies whose motive remains obscure, and in a small but hard-fought battle he was killed. Albany may have heard—too late to intercept him—of James's projected flight, and mere revenge—but that again is conjecture—may have inspired the battle.

The Bass Rock is a bullet-like island, a mile and a quarter from the Lothian shore, about a mile in circumference and three hundred and fifty feet high. A home for great flocks of solan geese, it can pasture a few sheep, but is a rough and comfortless home for human beings. There, however, for about a month, young James remained until a new escort could be brought together under command of Henry Sinclair, Earl of Orkney, and a bishop. A merchant ship from Danzig was loaded, in Leith, with wool and hides and woolfells, James went aboard to join his retinue, and the ship put to sea. The intention was to take him to some foreign port from which he might travel easily to France, and at the French court he could be brought up in safety. But on the 22nd March, off Flamborough Head, the Danzig ship was captured by English pirates, and James and his retinue were taken to Westminster and Henry IV, the English King.

The capture of the ship may have been due to simple accident, such as pirates have always depended on for their benefit. The English, however, may have been warned of its sailing, either by Albany or some anonymous, mercenary agent. Whatever the cause, the consequence was that James remained an English captive for eighteen years, and his unhappy father died within a few weeks of hearing what had happened. He is said to have spoken his own epitaph—"Here lies the worst of kings and most miserable of men"—and, like Robert II, to have been a man of majestic stature, white-bearded, of benign expression and benign of temper. In the Middle Ages benignity was no king-maker.

Men of Action Defeated

1

James was about twelve years old when the pirates took him captive, and Henry IV, his host and gaoler, received him with notable good humour. "Assuredly," he said, "if the Scots had been polite, they would have sent the young man to me for his education. I also know French."

Officially, or nominally, Scotland and England appear to have been in a state of truce; but that did not impair Henry's intention to keep possession of the boy. He needed every advantage that luck might send him, for his title to the English throne was not beyond challenge, and much violence had perplexed his reign.

In the first year of his captivity James lived in the Tower of London, where he did not lack company. The Duke of Albany's son Murdoch was also a prisoner, as was Griffith, son of the Welsh prince, Owen Glendower; and for their amusement there were, in smaller cages, both lions and leopards. James had his own household, he was treated as a prince, and when plague made the air of London dangerous he and his fellow prisoners were removed to Nottingham. In later years he seems to have lived at court, and he grew up under tutelage that may have been both stricter and more secure than he could have been given in Scotland. But he resented his captivity, and sought means for release. In Scotland, however, Albany ruled and had no wish for the return of a prince who was already beginning to show his energy and ability.

Henry IV died in 1413, and was succeeded by Henry V, whose

genius was robust, whose cultured tastes had been nursed in his father's household. James and his cousin Murdoch were again taken to the Tower, and held there for more than a year; their safety may have been threatened by the Lollards, whose piety had a revolutionary bias and whose discontent was Henry's gravest domestic problem. But Henry was firm, and having imposed peace at home, prepared for war in France. That put an end to James's hope of early release, but Murdoch was allowed to return to Scotland and his father in exchange for Henry Percy, Earl of Northumberland. Relations between Scotland and England grew worse as Henry made ready to invade France, but scuffling on the Border did not prevent diplomatic negotiation nor hinder Henry's capture of Harfleur, his brilliant victory at Agincourt.

Freed from the Tower, James lived occasionally at Kenilworth, sometimes at Windsor, and seems never to have been denied communication with his friends. His greatest embarrassment, apart from loss of liberty, was probably lack of money, a disability common to all Scotland's monarchs; but the rigours of captivity appear to have been mitigated by his growing friendship with Henry. When Henry renewed his war in France, he took James with him, and for that he had good reason.

Albany's second son, John, and Archibald, heir to the Earl of Douglas, had led about six thousand Scottish soldiers into Brittany for service under the Dauphin of France; and with the King of Scots at his elbow, . Henry could denounce them as rebels. It is quite improbable that James went unwillingly. A sullen, resentful companion would, in the circumstances, have been no help to Henry. It is more than likely that James was persuaded to go by his friendship with the ardent King, and by a natural desire for the excitement of foreign travel and a campaign.

By the Treaty of Troyes, in 1420, Henry V of England was recognised as heir and regent of France, and James was present at his marriage to Catherine de Valois, the French King's daughter. A month later, in July, he was with Henry when siege was laid to Melun, where he issued a command to Scots in the army of the Dauphin, to lay down their arms. Buchan, who led the Scottish contingent, refused to acknowledge the order, but when Melun fell a score or so of Scots, accused of taking arms against their sovereign, were hanged.

When Henry made his formal entry into Paris, James was probably with him, and certainly accompanied him on his return to England in

February 1421: at the banquet following Queen Catherine's coronation he sat at her left hand. He spent Easter with Henry and his Queen, he went with them on a royal progress, and at Windsor on St. George's Day he was knighted by Henry.

In the meanwhile, at Baugé between Tours and Angers, the Earl of Buchan and his Scots had defeated an English army, killing the Duke of Clarence, Henry's brother and heir-presumptive, and killing or taking prisoner five English earls. Strategically of no importance, the moral effect of victory was considerable, and Henry's return to France became imperative. Again James went with him, and assisted at the siege of Dreux, of Beaugency, and Meaux. But Henry, exhausted by dysentery and the strain of five years' campaigning, died at Vincennes, at the end of August 1422, and a royal friendship came to an end when James, a chief mourner, returned with the dead King's body for its interment in Westminster Abbey.

2

It was not until some nineteen months after Henry's death that James returned to Scotland. There was long and elaborate negotiation before terms for his release were decided, a treaty completed, and his marriage to Joan Beaufort solemnized.

The marriage was of exceptional interest because as well as a daughter, born punctually before the end of the year, James fathered a poem that revealed the solace he had found, during his captivity, in the works of Geoffrey Chaucer. It is a long poem—a hundred and ninety-seven stanzas, each of seven lines—and the influence of Chaucer is evident through it all.

Over *The King's Quhair*—the King's book, that is—there has hovered much learned debate, but there is no serious doubt that it was written, as it purports to be, by the King himself. It is a literary work, however, and James's description of his first acquaintance with Joan Beaufort—of how, from his room in a tower, he looked down and saw her walking with her women—may have been dictated by literary convention. It may, on the other hand, be true to life; for in the summer of 1423 he was probably at Windsor, where Henry's French widow and her son, Henry VI, often lived, and where Joan might well have been visiting. In the infancy of Henry VI England's government was a council dominated by two sons of John of Gaunt: Henry Beaufort, Bishop of Winchester, and his brother Thomas, Duke of Exeter; Joan's father was their elder brother John, Earl of Somerset, dead a dozen years before.

On the evidence of the poem:[*]

"And therwith kest I doun myn eye ageyne,
        Quhare as I sawe, walking under the tour,
Full secretly new cummyn her to pleyne,
        The fairest or the freschest yong floure
        That ever I sawe, me thoght, before that houre,
For quhich sodayn abate, anon astert,
The blude of all my body to my herte.

And though I stude abaisit tho a lyte
        No wonder was, forquhy my wittis all
Were so ouercom with pleasance and delyte,
        Onely throo latting of myn eyen fall,
        That sudaynly my hert become hir thrall
For ever of free wyll; for of manace
There was no takyn in hir suete face.

And in my hede I drewe ryght hastily,
        And eftsones I lent it forth ageyne,
And sawe hir walk, that verray womanly,
        With no wight mo bot onely women tueyne.
        Then gan I studye in myself and seyne,
'Al suete, ar ye a warldly creature,
Or hevinly thing in likeness of nature?

Or ar ye god Cupidis owin princesse,
        And cummyn ar to lous me out of band?
Or ar ye verray nature the goddess,
        That have depaynted with your hevinly hand
        This gardyn full of flouris, as they stand?
Quhat sall I think, allace! quhat reverence
Sall I minster to your excellence?

Gif ye a goddess be, and that ye like
        To do me payne, I may it noght astert;
Gif ye be warldly wight, that dooth me sike,

Quhy lest God mak you so, my derrest hert,
To do a sely prisoner thus smert,
That lufis yow all, and wote of noght bot wo?
And therfore, merci, suete! sen it is so.'"

Then, after a poetic fashion of the time, he begs Venus for her
favour, calls to a nightingale for song, and bemoans the pain of love.
In a dream he visits the Court of Love, seeks wisdom from Minerva,
and in search of Fortune travels through an enchanted land:

"Quhare, in a lusty plane, tuke I my way
    Endlang a ryver, plesant to behold,
Enbroudin all with fresche flouris gay,
    Quhare, throu the gravel, bryght as only gold,
    The cristall water ran so clere and cold,
That in myn ere maid contynualy
A maner soun, mellit with armony;

That full of lytill fischis by the brym,
    Now here, now there, with bakkis blew as lede,
Lap and playit, and in a rout can swym
    So prattily, and dressit tham to sprede
    Thair curall fynnis, as the ruby rede,
That in the sonne on thair scalis bryght
As gesserant ay glitterit in my sight:

And by this ilke ryversyde alawe
    Ane hye way fand I like to bene,
On quhich, on every syde, a long rawe
    Off treis saw I, full of levis grene,
    That full of fruyte delitable were to sene.
And also, as it come unto my mind,
Off bestis sawe I mony divers kynd:

The lyoun king, and his fere lyonesse;
    The pantere, like unto the smaragdyne;
The lytill squerell, full of besyness;
    The slawe as, the druggar beste of pyne;
    The nyce ape; the werely porpapyne;
The percyng lynx; the lufare unicorne,
That voidis venym with his evour horne.

> There sawe I dress him new out of haunt
>   The fery tiger, full of felonye;
> The dromydare; the standar oliphant;
>   The wyly fox the wedowis inemye;
>   The clymbare gayte; the elk for alblastrye;
> The herknere bore; the holsum grey for hortis;
> The hair also, that oft gooth to the wortis."

The bestiary continues, carried by mere exuberance. It is a poem made from delight, and preserving delight; and all its conventions find new life because the royal captive has decorated them with "fresche flouris gay." Nowhere else can we see so clearly, and in such curious detail, the mind and its mechanism of a mediaeval king who could fall asleep with Chaucer on his pillow, and wake to impose with ruthless determination his royal will and the iron necessities of law on a land sullied by daily bloodshed and loose with anarchy.

The King's Quhair is an honest declaration of James's love for Joan Beaufort: let that be accepted. There remain, for consideration and entertainment, her uncles and their policy. It is not at all improbable that pretty Joan was deliberately displayed to excite James's interest; and when that had been achieved, the Beauforts told him what freedom and a wife would cost.

The people of Scotland have often been accused of avarice, and derided for their devotional interest in money; but nothing in their history exceeds the cupidity of the lordly Beauforts. They demanded, from Scotland, £4000 for James's maintenance during the eighteen years of his captivity. He had been taken prisoner by English pirates, he had been held a prisoner to further English interest; and now he had to pay for his lodging in the Tower, for his service at the siege of Dreux, of Beaugency, and of Meaux. The money was to be paid in six annual instalments—but the first would be remitted as a marriage dowry.

The Beauforts squeezed the poverty of Scotland to increase the profit they had won from their royal *détenu,* and provided a dowry for Joan out of public funds. Seldom have cynicism and rapacity been so nicely mated, even in a marriage contract.

3

James returned to a kingdom that had suffered, in succession, under the fatuities of David II, the ineptitude of Robert II and Robert III, the purposive inactivity of Albany, and the impotence of his son Murdoch. Albany, hoping for the throne, had shown strength only in his determination to give no offence: in the north the Earl of Mar, on the Borders the Earl of Douglas, had maintained a semblance of rule, but in the centre Albany let the administration of justice and the collection of revenue wither away, lest anyone of importance should be hurt in pride or pocket. When his son Murdoch was released from captivity in England, Albany, as if he were king indeed, bestowed on him the right of succession to an undefined regency; and Murdoch, whose will may have been paralysed by years of inactivity, did nothing at all. King James I, with his English bride, succeeded to a realm that retained a national sentiment, but had almost lost its national structure.

James, at the age of twenty-nine or thirty, was a thick-set, strongly built man who, though he had not inherited the imposing stature of his father and grandfather, was endowed with physical and mental vigour such as neither of them had known. He was a good wrestler, he excelled at such earthy pastimes as putting the shot and throwing the hammer—which, from their royal provenance, still survive as popular attractions at Highland gatherings—and as well as his poetic skill, his devotion to Chaucer, he had a singing voice and played the harp. The ransom which the English demanded could, in some degree, be excused as the price of a good education, for his accomplishments were not restricted to poetry, music, and hammer-throwing. He had learnt —perhaps from Henry V—the basic duties of a king. The tradition is old, and may well be true, that his return to Scotland was the occasion for an immediate declaration of his purpose and his policy. "If God grant me but the life of a dog," he said—or is credibly reported to have said—"I will make the key keep the castle, and the bracken-bush the cow."

It seems, moreover, that he wasted no more time on words, but quickly put policy into practice. He crossed the Border in early April 1424, and a few weeks later arrested Sir Walter Stewart, Malcolm

Fleming of Cumbernauld, and Thomas Boyd the younger of Kilmarnock. Their offences are not known, but their arrest was evidence that the lordlings and grandees of the land were no longer immune from the processes of law and exempt from punishment. Boyd was soon set free, Fleming suffered a term of imprisonment, and Walter Stewart was committed to the safety and isolation of the Bass Rock. He was the eldest son of Murdoch, the inept and idle second Duke of Albany, and a young man whose uncontrollable temper may not have excluded some thought of rebellion.

At Scone, on the 21st May, James among his prelates and nobles was crowned King of Scotland. Bishop Wardlaw of St. Andrews, his tutor and guardian when James was a boy, set the crown on his head, and Murdoch—who, as Earl of Fife, had that hereditary right—led him to the throne. On the same day Joan Beaufort was crowned Queen.

A few days later there was a parliament in Perth, and on all classes of the community and on most of their goods taxes were imposed. After years of *laissez faire* the exactions were resented, but revenue was collected, and many were the measures taken to preserve the country's natural wealth. There was to be a closed season for salmon; rooks must be destroyed to save the corn; from April till after harvest no heather should be burnt; duties were imposed on the export of horses, sheep, and herrings; customs and town rents were reserved for the King, and rebellion would be punished by forfeiture of the rebel's lands and goods; the practice of archery was encouraged, the playing of football prohibited. It was a busy parliament, and the acts it passed were sound and comprehensive.

In the summer of 1424 James began to enquire into the legal titles to their estates of some who held land that had formerly belonged to the Crown; and seemingly in consequence of such enquiry he commanded the arrest of two more grandees. One was the Earl of Lennox, Albany's father-in-law; the other Sir Robert Graham, who is said to have denounced the King as a tyrant, was imprisoned at Dunbar, but escaped to the Highlands. There was, as yet, no quarrel between James and Albany; no apparent ill-will between the King and his surviving uncle, the Earl of Atholl.

Despite a seven years' truce with England, the Scottish army in France, that the Earl of Buchan had led to victory at Baugé, was reinforced—perhaps before the truce became effective—by several new companies under the Earl of Douglas. Though the Scots were fighting for France against a common enemy, they were no more popular than other foreign troops, in similar circumstances, who have gone to help endangered allies; the ungrateful French complained of their gluttony and called them *sacs à vin*. In 1424 they were heavily defeated at Verneuil, where Buchan, Douglas, and many notable men were killed. No other Scottish army went to France until Scots began to wear a British uniform, but the "Auld Alliance" was restored, more tenuously, when James's infant daughter Margaret was promised in marriage, at the age of four, to the Dauphin of France who lived to become that ruthless neurotic, Louis XI.

At his second parliament James caused enquiry to be made into the effectiveness of laws previously enacted, and supported measures for the protection of the church and church property; for the extension of its social services, and for the suppression of heresy. There was new legislation for the maintenance of civil peace, the preservation of natural resources, and the provision of more revenue from customs and other duties. Poor men involved in litigation were to be given help in presenting their defence; and some rich men were surprised by James's sudden declaration of hostility.

Albany, his youngest son Alexander, and two of their principal supporters were arrested. The latter were soon released, but Albany and his son lay in prison to await their trial, and James took possession of Murdoch's castles of Falkland and Doune. There was immediate rebellion in the west, led by James Stewart—a son of Murdoch who had contrived to keep his liberty—and the Bishop of Argyll. The rebels attacked and burnt Dunbarton, killing its garrison and an elderly, semiroyal Stewart who was the King's uncle; but James acted promptly, the rebellion collapsed, and its leaders fled to Ireland.

Parliament reassembled, and before an assize of nobles Murdoch, Albany and others were arraigned on charges long since forgotten. Old Albany, Murdoch's father, had certainly hoped and tried to win the throne for himself and his successors; to what extent Murdoch, that seemingly futile man, had maintained his father's purpose is now beyond calculation. He and his sons may have united in passive resistance to the King, or they may have been plotting active rebellion, of which the attack on Dunbarton was an ill-judged and premature demonstration. Before the King himself, the defendants—whose defence is no more known than the charges against them—were all condemned and sentenced to death. Walter Stewart, Murdoch's eldest son, who had been in prison for a year or more, was the first to die. Under the grey walls of Stirling castle he was beheaded on the 24th May, 1425. The old Earl of Lennox, Murdoch's father-in-law, had been a prisoner since the previous summer, and on the 25th he and Murdoch and Alexander, Murdoch's youngest son, were executed.

It seems probable that justice was done, but justice so merciless is dreadful to contemplate, and James has been much blamed for a ruthlessness that made his justice look like vengeance, and for the advantage he derived from the death of men whose vast estates he then acquired. The revenues of Fife, Menteith, and Lennox passed to him, and there have been those who called his justice a mask for cupidity. But when one looks again at the long years of misrule, and negation of rule, from David II to Albany's greedy ambition, the possibility cannot be denied that in Murdoch and his kinsmen James saw an obstacle which had to be removed before he could give Scotland such peace that the key could keep the castle and the bracken-bush the cow. It is difficult to recognise, in the gentle poet of *The King's Quhair*, a man capable of resolution so fierce and determined; but in minds of our own age there is more that men of the Fifteenth Century would find incomprehensible, than we can discern in theirs.

During his captivity in England James had shown interest in the creation of a university at St. Andrews, and supported a petition to Pope Benedict XIII for a bull of foundation. But when he saw for himself the little town on its wind-swept promontory, he seems to have thought it too exposed to the danger of seaborne attack, and suggested that Perth would be a better site for the propagation of learning. There is, too, some evidence that James preferred Perth to Edinburgh as the capital city of his kingdom; and he may well have been right.

Edinburgh lay too near the Border, too far from the Highlands. It grew up as a frontier town, and for a long time before it established itself as the effective centre of government it lay open to reprisal, vulnerable to English enjoyment of incendiarism. Its second disadvantage was perhaps even graver. Edinburgh was remote in sympathy from the northern parts of Scotland, from the Celtic ethos and a social system that was apt for war, indifferent to material benefit, and spiritually satisfying to the clansmen who lived in mutual distrust but in the happy association of their own immediate kind. If Perth had become Scotland's capital, it could have lived and grown without the recurrent punishment that Edinburgh suffered; and a government lodged on the Highland Line might have acquired some sympathy with the splendid savages who shared its country, and realised the advantage of uniting them in interest with Lowlanders who were as turbulent as Clan Donald, but increasingly aware of a changing world and the profit to be wrung from peaceful commerce.

Parliament, summoned again, was active as before. The King's authority and the administration of justice were again stiffened and strengthened, the country's emergent economy was prudently encouraged. With the Papacy there began a long struggle for clerical independence that Scotland wanted, that Rome resented; with the Low Countries there was negotiation for increased trade; with England there was recurrent argument about the payment, overdue, of the next instalment of James's ransom. The King tried, but unsuccessfully, to broaden the influence of parliament by the creation of what could loosely be called a lower chamber; and with some discretion the old alliance with France was renewed.

To counter a Highland foray, that had been temporarily successful, the King marched to Inverness and dealt leniently with dissident chiefs: of the many who were arrested, only two were beheaded and one hanged. James had already shown some sympathy with the clans and their leaders, and admitted that the law could not be applied, in all its severity, to men whose habit of life—so a Scottish parliament believed—included, as common practices, both robbery and murder. Among those whom the King reprieved were the young Lord of the Isles and his mother, the Countess of Ross. But before long James had reason to regret his clemency.

The Lord of the Isles, after brief imprisonment, went to live at court, and liked it less than prison. The Lowland lords, it is said, mocked his uncouth ways, and young Alexander, escaping to his own country, took revenge for the incivilities to which he had been subjected by burning Inverness.

The King made immediate reply. With instant decision and exemplary speed he mustered an army and marched into Lochaber. There he found a formidable opposition. The clans had risen in support of Alexander, and there seems to have been a possibility of massive rebellion. But on the field of battle—a marshy plain—the sight of the royal standard divided the rebels, and Camerons and Macphersons, Macintoshes and Macleans of the north, and Farquharsons of Invercauld submitted to the King. They were moved, perhaps, by a latent or incipient loyalty to the throne; or, more simply, they may have seen the folly of fighting against a better equipped and more numerous foe.

The Lord of the Isles was again made prisoner, and in the summer of 1429 he offered his public submission in somewhat theatrical circumstances. Before the high altar in the chapel of Holyroodhouse, naked but for shirt and drawers, he knelt and presented his sword to the King; while the Queen—presumably by arrangement—pleaded for his life. Again the King showed clemency, and was rewarded for it. Alexander and his mother were sentenced to short terms of imprisonment, and Alexander gave no more trouble.

4

Active parliaments and stubborn diplomacy dominated the scene. Negotiations with the Papacy resulted in a drawn game, with some slight advantages accruing to Scotland; and a wrangling peace was maintained with England, where James was described as a fierce foreseeing man of great experience. Defence of the realm was furthered by statutes that commanded nobles in the west to build oared galleys, and prescribed the proper style of armour for the several orders of society. Another act offers a partial and narrow view of the country's prosperity, for it dictates the sort of clothing that different classes might wear.

Silks and furs were permitted only to knights and lords worth at least two hundred marks a year; in burghs the councillors and bailies might wear fur; wives were to dress according to their husbands' rank and estates. Commoners and their wives were forbidden such luxuries as elaborate hoods and flowing sleeves, neckcloths of lawn, and coats of many colours. There was, it appears, a modest prosperity which prompted a happy tendency to extravagance; and, for the general good, that had to be repressed.

In October 1430 twin sons were born to the Queen, and soon after baptism were knighted. Alexander, the elder, died in infancy, but James, Duke of Rothesay, lived to reign as James II. Very little—and that not illuminating—is known of his childhood.

With England a new truce was concluded, but negotiations for a more lasting peace came to nothing; and no more instalments of the King's ransom were paid. The Highlands again erupted, and rebels commanded by Donald Balloch, of Clan Donald, defeated the Earls of Mar and Caithness at Inverlochy. James attempted to raise money for a new campaign, but there is no record of further adventure in the north, and it may be that the clans' ingrained dislike of union saved the situation for him. It is known that a chief called Angus Duff met in battle Angus Murray, each in command of a considerable army, and so fierce was the fight that few survived it.

A new Pope, Eugenius IV, pressed for the restoration of lost papal authority; but when James resisted, Eugenius became conciliatory. The King, who had thought ill of St. Andrews as a site for a university, withdrew his objections and confirmed its charters. He reinforced his measures to ensure domestic peace, showed his repugnance to manslaughter, and encouraged the suppression of Lollards and other heretics. While France discreetly worked for a breakdown of Anglo-Scottish friendship, James pretended to believe in the possibility of marrying one of his daughters to the Dauphin, the other to Henry VI of England. He found, too, a new occasion for demonstrating the royal authority over nobles of dubious loyalty, and having imprisoned the Earl of March—whose father had been a traitor—took possession of his estates but compensated him with a pension.

Patrick Dunbar, son of the forfeited Earl, found help in England and led a Border raid which was defeated without significant loss on either side. The truce with England expired on the 1st May, 1436, and was not renewed. England was in difficulties in France, where the Burgundians, whose alliance had been the mainstay of English power, transferred their allegiance to Charles VII. France was growing in strength, and after prolonged, anxious, and pettifogging negotiation James's elder daughter Margaret set sail, from Dunbarton, with a great and splendid retinue, for an unhappy destination in La Rochelle and marriage to the Dauphin who became King as Louis XI. Neglected by that detestable young man, she died untimely before she was twenty-one. The expense of her escort, and the fleet which accompanied her, may have been borne by a forced levy on the nobles and richer merchants of the kingdom: a measure which could have done nothing to enhance their affection for James.

As England was in difficulties abroad, the time seemed ripe for an attempt to reconquer the Border strongholds of Berwick and Roxburgh —those long-disputed citadels of No Man's Land—and in August 1436, James mustered a large army to lay siege to Roxburgh. But his army was divided by faction, there was growing opposition to a King who dared to rule, and the knowledge of war that he had learnt from Henry V availed him nothing. The siege was abandoned.

A truce, of sorts, was renewed; and there was more legislation to enforce law and order, to protect—at some cost to personal liberty—the natural wealth of Scotland. The general council of 1436 gave James a final opportunity to declare his faith and reiterate a policy designed for the well-being—though less for the comfort—of his kingdom. It was a policy that now brought him into violent collision with those who had most to lose by it; but before the tragical consequences of his belief in law, his insistence on the throne's authority, became apparent, there was room for an interlude that won its own small place in history.

The continued interest of the Papacy in Scottish affairs was responsible for the arrival, after a tempestuous voyage, of Aeneas Sylvius Piccolomini, who subsequently became famous as Pope Pius II. Aeneas Sylvius came ashore at Aberlady in East Lothian, and promptly made a barefooted pilgrimage, through the snows of winter, to Whitekirk ten miles away. He suffered for his piety, and took a dislike to Scotland. He found it a poor, treeless country—the Highlands were thickly forested, but he did not travel far—and was surprised to see towns unfortified and many houses roofed with turf. The King, whom he thought too fat, received him graciously, paid all his expenses and gave him two good horses; but Aeneas saw proof of the country's degrading poverty in the fact that beggars at the church door were given, as alms, quantities of a black and sulphurous mineral, dug from the ground, which they used as fuel. Scotland had already begun to burn coal.

Aeneas, in disguise, crossed the Border, and found the north of England as poor as Scotland. But Scotland was about to suffer worse impoverishment, and one of the most disabling calamities in its history. While beggars at the church door got their bags of coal, a hotter fire had long been smouldering in the hearts and minds of the King's enemies; and now that fire burst into flame, and James was surprised by murderous insurrection.

He who led the assault was Sir Robert Graham, whom James had confined to prison—from which he escaped—twelve years before. Graham had not concealed his hostility to the King, but had denounced him as a tyrant. In February 1437 James was a guest at the monastery of the Black Friars in Perth. His domestic chamberlain was Sir Robert

Stewart, a grandson of the Earl of Atholl. Atholl, an old man and the King's uncle, was the legitimate son of Robert II by his wife Euphemia Ross. James, the grandson of Robert II and Elizabeth Mure, was the son of a father whose legitimacy could be questioned. Atholl's claim to the throne was, therefore, not without substance; and his grandson was ambitious.

Robert Stewart, turned traitor, dismissed the guards, and unbolted the monastery doors. Graham and others—eight or ten, perhaps—broke in and found the King in his nightgown, and no one with him but the Queen. She bravely opposed the invaders, and was badly wounded. The King, though Aeneas Sylvius thought him too fat, was an active man, and fought hard. But the odds against him were too heavy, and he fell beneath savage and repeated swordthrusts. Twenty-eight wounds were counted on his body, says one account; sixteen in his breast alone, says another.

In his zeal for reform he may have been intemperate, but his death was an unmitigated disaster. Authority and the rule of law were what Scotland needed, and James I, with heroic energy and noble persistence, did much to repair the chaos he inherited. But there were those who preferred chaos to order, and as so often in Scotland's history the strength of chaos exceeded the power of the throne. There is some, but insufficient satisfaction, in the knowledge that his English Queen—granddaughter of John of Gaunt—survived her wound and lived to be revenged on her husband's murderers.

5

Dying under torture, Sir Robert Graham is said to have declared that posterity would justify his murder of King James as the destruction of a tyrant. Posterity, however, has chosen to regard James as the most able and energetic of monarchs after David I and Robert I; and the immediate consequence of his murder was a springtide of revulsion against the assassins who, within a few weeks, were all captured and, with old Atholl, appallingly tormented before being put to death. The Queen herself, a woman of considerable character, was determined that they should not escape justice. She had been, it seems, a loving wife as well as an active and helpful consort. She was the mother, not only of the boy James, but of six daughters, of whom four were married abroad and two in Scotland.

James II was only six when, in 1437, he was crowned King at Holyroodhouse, and detestation of his father's murder did not create for him a climate of comfort and security. For a dozen years Scotland had lived under discipline, and when the disciplinarian died, anarchy succeeded him. Parliament decreed that, until the boy was twenty-one, there should be no alienation of royal lands or property; ambassadors were sent to England to secure a nine years' truce; and Archibald, Earl of Douglas, was named the King's Lieutenant. But those orderly enactments were quickly followed by violent competition for possession of the King's person, the contenders being Sir Alexander Livingstone, the Keeper of Stirling Castle, and Sir William Crichton, Keeper of Edinburgh Castle. And several years later, on the heels of that dispute, came a dangerous challenge to the throne—a bid for supreme power— from the great family of Douglas: the Black Douglases, heirs and successors of the good Sir James who had fought so nobly beside Robert the Bruce.

Scotland, however, was not the only country where anarchy threatened law and hindered the orderly development of administration. England lost all her possessions in France except Calais, and in 1455, when James II was in his early twenties, the Wars of the Roses broke out, not only in competition for the throne, but to demonstrate, as it seemed, the weakness of the King's government. In Europe, moreover, Christianity and western civilization were menaced by the military power of the Turks, who in 1453 captured Constantinople. The tribulations of Scotland were insignificant in comparison with that disaster, but on his own smaller stage it was James—when he was of an age to do so—who saved his country from the miseries and devastation of civil war, and in the story of Scotland he must be recognised as the worthy son of a worthy father, whose early death reiterated the calamity of James I's many-wounded murder in Perth.

The boy was a mere spectator—a bewildered spectator—of the long struggle for power between Crichton and Livingstone. Crichton had the initial advantage, because James was lodged in Edinburgh, where Crichton was Keeper of the Castle. But Livingstone showed himself the better tactician, and presently had both James and his mother under surveillance at Stirling. Douglas, the King's Lieutenant, died unmemorably in 1439. The Queen, perhaps to find a guardian for her son, married Sir John Stewart, known as the Black Knight of Lorne; but Livingstone remained master of the situation, and the Black Knight was added to his captives. The Queen—that indomitable English-woman—got sufficient liberty for herself and her new husband to bear him three sons; but in 1445 died in poverty, it is said, at Dunbar.

Livingstone and Crichton then established, for a murderous project, an unscrupulous alliance. The Douglases, the most powerful family in Scotland, were a manifest threat to their authority. The successor to the King's idle Lieutenant was William Douglas, a young man of lively habit and high temper. He and his brother, with their faithful adherent, Malcolm Fleming of Cumbernauld, were persuaded to accept a seemingly friendly invitation to Edinburgh Castle, where the young King was living; and there they were treacherously put to death. The manner of their death became one of the dark legends of Scotland, and Sir Walter Scott preserved the traditional tale.

"Of a sudden," he wrote, "the scene began to change. At an enter-tainment which was served up to the Earl and his brother, the head of a black bull was placed on the table. The Douglases knew this, accord-ing to a custom which prevailed in Scotland, to be the sign of death, and leaped from the table in great dismay. But they were seized by armed men who entered the apartment. They underwent a mock trial, in which all the insolences of their ancestors were charged against them, and were condemned to immediate execution. The young King wept, and implored Livingstone and Crichton to show mercy to the young noblemen, but in vain. These cruel men only reproved him for weeping at the death of those whom they called his enemies. The brothers were led out to the court of the castle, and beheaded without delay. Malcolm Fleming of Cumbernauld, a faithful adherent of their house, shared the same fate."

The legend may be true, for it was recorded, not only by Scott, but in verses retained by popular memory:

> "Edinburgh Castle, towne and toure,
> God grant thou sink for sinne!
> And that even for the black dinoir
> Erl Douglas gat therein."

A party to the murder may have been the successor to young Wil-liam Douglas, his great-uncle James, who was known as James the

Gross. He took no action to avenge the crime which had enriched him, but for three years lived in enjoyment—which may have been as rude as his by-name—of the estates he had acquired. Livingstone and Crichton ruled the land and ensured the acquiescence of James the Gross by giving to his second son the earldom of Moray. Then James died, and was succeeded by his elder son William, who soon revealed an ambition as inordinate as his estates, and allying himself with Livingstone, made war on Crichton and his associates. That private or family conflict was indecisive, and Crichton, though defeated, retained a measure of authority. But William Douglas was adding to his power with sinister rapidity.

The lordship and broad lands of Galloway had passed to his cousin Margaret, called the Fair Maid of Galloway. Her he married, and reunited her lands with his. A younger brother had been given the earldom of Ross, and for Hugh, another brother, he acquired more territory in the north, and the earldom of Ormond. He made alliance, moreover, with David, Earl of Crawford, the most formidable of landed potentates beyond the Forth.

The first person who seems to have recognised that William Douglas was seriously threatening the King's authority was James Kennedy, a nephew of James I and Bishop of St. Andrews. He made alliance with Crichton, and was promptly punished for it when Crawford and his adherents raided and looted his diocese. He retaliated with his own weapons, which were spiritual, and for a whole year regularly pronounced the excommunication of all who had attacked him. Exactly a year after his invasion of the diocese, Crawford was mortally wounded in a family encounter, at the gates of Arbroath, between the Earl of Huntly, with Ogilvies at his side, and the noble family of Lindsay. The hand of God was made manifest, and for long the impious Earl of Crawford lay unburied.

Bishop Kennedy's spiritual triumph was muted and shrouded, however, by the outbreak of a limited war with England on the ever-debatable Borders. There was turn and turnabout of raid and reprisal, but the Douglases were foremost in defence of the kingdom, and in the southwest, near Gretna, William's younger brother, Hugh, Earl of Ormond, convincingly defeated a large English army led by a young Percy who later became the third Earl of Northumberland.

That was in 1448, and a year later James, at the age of eighteen, married Mary of Gueldres, a niece of Philip the Good of Burgundy. The boy-King had reached manhood, and quickly made known the royal quality of his manhood. The Livingstones—Sir Alexander, his two sons, and many adherents—were arrested, and Sir Alexander and both his sons, found guilty of high treason, were executed. But the Douglases remained in open opposition to the authority of their king, and fortified their opposition by an obscure and tenuous claim to the throne. Their power was greater than the King's, for William Douglas was Earl of Douglas, Earl of Wigtown, Lord of Galloway and Bothwell, of the forests of Ettrick and Selkirk, possessor of great estates in the sheriffdoms of Edinburgh, Haddington, Lanark, Roxburgh, Linlithgow, Peebles, and Aberdeen. He was Sheriff of Lanark, Warden of the West and Middle Marches; and his brothers Archibald, Earl of Moray, Hugh, Earl of Ormond, and John of Balveny held vast areas in the north and northeast.

As if to expose and declare his purpose, moreover, William Douglas made an alliance with Alexander, Earl of Crawford—called the Tiger Earl, and son of him who died after excommunication by Bishop Kennedy—and with John, Lord of the Isles and Earl of Ross. Confronted with that major challenge, the young King took matters into his own hand, and sending a safe-conduct to Douglas, invited him to a meeting in Stirling castle. With arrogant assurance Douglas accepted the invitation, and what followed was stark melodrama. It may be helpful, and possibly illuminating, to fall back again on Sir Walter Scott and his description of the scene:

"The King received Douglas kindly, and after some amicable expostulation with him upon his late conduct, all seemed friendship and cordiality between James and his too-powerful subject. By invitation of James, Douglas dined with him on the day following. Supper was presented at seven o'clock, and after it was over, the King having led Douglas into another apartment, where only some of his privy council and of his bodyguard were in attendance, he introduced the subject of the Earl's bond with Ross and Crawford, and exhorted him to give up the engagement, as inconsistent with his allegiance and the quiet of the kingdom. Douglas declined to relinquish the treaty which he had formed. The King urged him more imperiously, and the Earl returned a haughty and positive refusal, upbraiding the King, at the same time, with maladministration of the public affairs. Then the King burst into a rage at his obstinacy, and exclaimed, 'By Heaven, my lord, if *you* will not break the league, *this* shall.' So saying, he stabbed the Earl with his dagger first in the throat, and instantly after in the lower part of the body. Sir Patrick Gray then struck the Earl on the head with a battle-axe; and others of the King's retinue showed their zeal by stabbing at the dying man with their knives and daggers. He expired without uttering a word, covered with twenty-six wounds. The corpse did not receive any Christian burial. . . . This was a wicked and cruel action on the King's part; bad if it were done in hasty passion, and yet worse if James meditated the possibility of this violence from the beginning."

Sir Walter's description of the fatal party may be as true as his tale of the Black Dinner at Edinburgh castle; but should one agree with his denunciation of the King's action as "wicked and cruel"? It was murder unquestionably; but in view of all the circumstances it seems to have been murder required by a public need, and justified by the fact that no other means existed to serve that need. It may even be regarded as a profoundly moral murder, instinct with mercy in that it saved Scotland from an internecine war that would have spread death and desolation over much of the kingdom.

Assassination is not a comely or commendable exercise of government, but if it is the only way—the only possible way—to remove a manifest threat to public safety and preserve peace under legitimate authority, it may be excused and probably should be pardoned. When James I declared his intention of instituting such a rule of law that the key would keep the castle and the bracken-bush the cow, he made it known that he would suffer neither the roadside malevolence of the footpad nor the lordly violence of an arrogant nobility; and when James II was faced with the naked intransigence of the most powerful of his nobles—and the realm had no safeguard but his own strength of hand and mind—then surely he was right to evoke the ancient authority of a king and use it to keep peace in the land and give peace to his people.

His parliament had no doubt that he was justified in striking down Douglas. It exonerated him from blame, it declared that Douglas, by treason and conspiracy, was guilty of his own death. But the Douglases were not yet defeated.

After William's death his brother James led six hundred horsemen into Stirling to loot and burn. The dishonoured safe-conduct was dragged through the streets at the tail of an old horse, and James Douglas, renouncing his homage to the King of Scots, offered allegiance to the King of England. The Scottish King's response was immediate. John Major—a chronicler born only twenty years after James's untimely death—said of him that he was a soldier's king: he lacked his father's grace and accomplishment, but had inherited his vigour, both of mind and body. And in the continuing crisis of 1452 he showed a soldier's capacity for decision, and, it may be thought, a soldierly but untimely habit of generosity towards a beaten enemy.

He led an army into Galloway, into the Douglas lands where Douglas rule was absolute, and forced submission from the rebel James, the ninth and last Earl of a great family. But then he was lenient, he let James marry his brother's widow, the Fair Maid of Galloway; he accepted his protestations of good faith and honesty, and sent him into England, as his commissioner, to negotiate a truce. And Douglas played him false.

In England there lived Malise Graham, Earl of Strathearn, one of the hostages for his unpaid ransom whom James I had deposited at the English court about twenty-five years before; and Graham, descended from Robert II and his later marriage, had that benefit of legitimacy in his descent to which the King had only a contested title. Douglas secured his release, and Graham renewed an old claim to the throne. Douglas, moreover, seems to have established some sort of relationship with the Lord of the Isles and his trouble-making cousin Donald Balloch: a relationship that could only be construed as a threat to the throne.

Now James was patient and waited a year or two before launching a final campaign. Then, when the time was ripe, he marched in strength to the southwest and methodically broke the power of the Black Douglases. On Douglasdale, Avondale, and Ettrick Forest he wreaked his anger. The strong castle of Abercorn was taken, and Douglas with a few companions found refuge in England. His brothers, the Earls of Ormond and Moray, and Douglas of Balveny, were defeated at Arkinholm, near the present town of Langholm, where Moray was killed, Balveny fled across the Border, and Ormond, made prisoner, suffered a traitor's death. The castles of Douglas, Strathavon, and the island fortress of Threave were captured. By parliament the fugitive Earl was attainted, and the forfeited estates of his family were attached to the crown or given in reward to the King's faithful servants.

James had saved his throne and kept his kingdom whole. That was his great achievement, but in the next few years he showed, not only a vigorous interest in many parts of his kingdom and the well-being of his people, but an ability to conciliate his nobles, and placate so unruly a subject as the Lord of the Isles, that promised much for the future; if, that is, a kinder fortune had allowed him to live.

He had good reason for complaint against England—or, to be precise, against the partisans of York, who had given their help and encouragement to the Earl of Douglas—and in 1455, when England was deeply embarrassed by civil war, James made an unsuccessful attempt to recapture Berwick. A little while later he tried to persuade Charles VII of France to co-ordinate an attack on Calais with his renewal of the assault on Berwick; but Charles was too cautious to agree. James harried the northern parts of Northumberland, and when the partisans of York invaded Annandale they were punctually intercepted and properly routed at Lochmaben.

In the summer months of 1460 the Yorkists—the White Roses who had been making war against the Red Roses of Lancaster—won a notable victory at Northampton, and got possession of Henry VI, the English King. James saw an opportunity to ruffle the enemy and improve his own position, and made massive preparation to assault and lay siege to that Border stronghold, the castle of Roxburgh, which for long had been held by England. As a soldier he was rightly interested in modern weapons, and the sort of cannon called bombards, which had been in existence for less than a hundred years, promised to be useful in the operation he planned. With great labour several bombards were carried to the Border town.

To make a bombard, iron rods were tied round a wooden cylinder and compressed by white-hot iron hoops which, as they cooled, shrank and tightened the rods; the wooden core was burnt out; a chamber, forged from a solid block, was shaped to fit the breech. Constructed in such a fashion, cannon endangered not only the enemy, but the gunners who served them. A bombard, pointed at the castle, exploded while the King and the Earl of Angus stood nearby. A splinter wounded the Earl, another killed the King.

He was in his thirtieth year, and the vigour of his youth was already growing into the strong maturity of the statesman. His fiery temper had been cooled by experience, but his fiery face—reddened by a birthmark—has been kept in memory by both paint and verse. The earliest authentic Scottish portrait is a drawing on vellum, heightened by colour, of James II. It was done, apparently, in 1458, and shows a young-looking man under a broad-brimmed hat. His face, daubed with red, is firm and lively, the eyes large and intelligent. He wears a tunic with exaggerated shoulders, and a heavy gold chain; his legs, in tightly fitting overalls, taper to long slippers.

The verse that records his blemished cheek is in François Villon's *Ballade des Seigneurs de Temps Jadis:*

> "le roy Scotiste
> Qui demy face ot, ce dit on,
> Vermeille commè une amatiste
> Depuis le front jusqu'au menton."

The portrait on vellum may be an accurate likeness, but his character and achievements are more firmly printed in history itself; and what Scotland lost by his untimely death is made lamentably clear in the story of his successor.

Irrelevance on the Throne

James II was six when he succeeded to the throne; his son, a delicate child, was two years older. Of him, as of his father, there is an authentic portrait. It owes its existence to the beneficence of his mother, Mary of Gueldres, and the generosity of a man, otherwise little known, called Sir Edward Boncle.

In 1462 Mary of Gueldres founded, in Edinburgh, the Church of the Holy Trinity, and Boncle, its first provost, presented it with an organ and a set of pictures now framed in what may be the doors of an organ case.

The artist is believed to have been the Flemish painter Hugo van der Goes, and the pictures, which probably date from the year 1470, can be seen in the National Gallery of Scotland in Edinburgh. One of them shows an organ, with an angel to play it, another to work the bellows, and in the foreground, devoutly kneeling, a finely painted portrait of Boncle. Beside him and the angels are God the Father, a sadly wounded Christ, and the Holy Spirit in the benign shape of a hovering dove. On the reverse of the panels are portraits, possibly made from contemporary drawings, of James III with his patron St. Andrew, and a smaller figure who, it seems likely, is his brother; on another is his Queen, Margaret of Denmark, Sweden and Norway, with her patron, the canonised King Cnut.

If the pictures were painted in 1470, King James was then eighteen, and Margaret five years younger: Margaret was only sixteen when, in 1473, she gave birth to the infant who became James IV. Her portrait shows a child of quite remarkable grace, beauty, and dignity. Her hands piously clasped, she kneels within the protection of King Cnut—

he in black armour looms above her—and her face is demurely exquisite: a tall smooth brow above eyebrows faintly arched, grave eyes, a
long nose over a prim little mouth and a round chin that still shows
the charming plumpness of her youth. Not much is known about her,
but it is pleasant to quote some lines from the unnamed scholar who
completed a *History of Scotland* by William Maitland that was published in 1757.

"Queen Margaret," he writes, "arrived at Leith in the month of July,
was received, married, crowned, and banquetted, with all the solem-
nity, magnificence, and affection that a young prince, deservedly
enamoured with the ripening graces of one of the greatest beauties of
that age, could shew, and an applauding, generous people testify; and
yet her beauty and youth were the least valuable of her qualifications.
Her piety was a pattern to the cloistered virgin, and her whole deportment commanded respect, and taught modesty; a virtue which, for
some time before, seemed to have been banished the court: for so
entirely was she devoted to her husband, that she may with justice
be ranked among those who have been most famous for conjugal affection."

It will be recognised, of course, that the continuator of Maitland's
History was a more generous and perhaps a more credulous writer than
the jealously accurate scholars of today; but in a general way he may
have been speaking the truth, and it is not unseemly to hope so.
More than most men, perhaps, James III needed a wife who would
prove to be a model of "conjugal affection"; and it is regrettable that
so little is known of a woman who may have been a paradigm of excellence, and whose portrait is still able to excite affection and esteem.

In the Lord Treasurer's accounts for 1474 there is an entry that
shows provision for the little Queen's comfort when she took a bath.
It reads—to anglify the original—"Item, from Andrew Mowbray, 8 ells
of broad cloth, to cover a bath-tub to the Queen. Item, from the same,
3 ells of broad cloth, for a sheet to put about the Queen in the bath-
tub."—And a year later, for the infant who was to become James IV,
"Item, from Isabel Williamson, two ells and a half of French brown,
to cover my Lord's cradle. Item, four ells and a half of tartan, for a
canopy above his cradle. Item, an ell and a half of blue tartan, to line
his gown of cloth of gold."

The Queen in her bath was decently protected, the infant Prince
was adequately covered. It is difficult to judge whether Margaret found

Scotland more comfortable or less comfortable, in a physical sense, than her native Denmark—more conducive or less conducive to peace of mind—for neither was at peace in the world about it. Her father, Christian I, King of Denmark, Sweden, and Norway, engaged in intermittent warfare to establish or preserve his title over Sweden—it had been asserted on paper in the great Kalmar Union, proposing Scandinavian unity, of 1397—and in 1470 he was preparing for a new offensive that was to be defeated, near Stockholm, a year later. Preparation for a military expedition necessarily diminished his ability to find a suitable dowry for his daughter.

In lieu of cash he pledged his sovereign rights and lands in Orkney and Shetland to the Scottish Crown. It was a straightforward pawnbroker's bargain, and the probable reason for it was that King Christian was more intent on reducing Sweden—on persuading Sweden to accept his rule—than he was on providing his pretty little daughter with his promised endowment of 60,000 florins of the Rhine. It is possible, however, that his lands in Orkney were worth less than that; and having agreed to give Margaret a handsome dowry, he was able to keep a reputation for generosity without it costing him very much.

To that supposition it should be added that in the affection of his Queen, James may have found a solace for misfortune that was of more lasting value than Rhenish florins, for after her death, and near the end of his own life, he hoped to create for her an everlasting memorial. But he was disappointed, as he had been in graver issues. Like all the royal Stewarts he was a man of character, but in the circumstances of the time his character was inopportune and irrelevant. He had been born in the wrong century. Today, however, with the liberalism that distance often bestows, it is not difficult to be sympathetic and condone some of his disabilities. It must be remembered that he enlarged the realm of Scotland, and it should be admitted that, while Scotland was enriched by acquisition of the two northern archipelagos, Orkney and Shetland got no benefit whatever from their subjugation to the Scottish Crown until some two and a half centuries after the Union of the Parliaments of England and Scotland.

The beginning of James's reign was as untimely as his temperament. His father died too soon, and a child on the throne was an invitation to anarchy. Scotland was burdened by a ruthless aristocracy that knew no cohesion other than a loosely professed adherence to the principle of monarchy, and which rarely furthered a national purpose except when some dominant faction acquired possession of the King's person, and could pretend to rule in his name. Like his father, however—whom Livingstone had snatched from Crichton—James fell into the hands, not of a great feudal noble, but of a momentarily brilliant, briefly successful family of little previous importance.

His mother, Mary of Gueldres, had died in 1463, when James was only eleven; his other guardian, Bishop Kennedy, died eighteen months later. Kennedy, whose mother was a daughter of Robert III, was a man of great influence and notable extravagance: he founded the college of St. Salvator at St. Andrews, and built a tomb for himself which was said to have cost as much as the college. After his death the boy James had no protector strong enough to ensure his safety, and at the age of fourteen he became, in effect, a prisoner in Edinburgh castle, whose Governor was Sir Alexander Boyd.

The Boyds were a landed family of Kilmarnock: historically respectable but relatively undistinguished until they got possession of the young King. Then their advancement was meteoric. Before the Estates of the Realm the King was persuaded to declare that what had been done was done with his consent, and the Estates approved a charter appointing Robert, Lord Boyd—head of the family—to be Governor of the King's person and Keeper of the fortresses of the kingdom. There is no evidence that the King was subjected to harsh treatment, and he may, indeed, have regarded Sir Alexander, his gaoler in Edinburgh, with affection and respect: Sir Alexander had previously been his instructor in military exercises. But the Boyds took full advantage of the power that audacity had given them. They won large estates, they added greatly to their wealth, and Thomas, a son of Lord Boyd, was created Earl of Arran and married the Lady Mary, the King's sister. She, it is true, may have been more than willing to marry him, for Thomas is said to have been a person of great charm, wisdom, and kindliness; and it has to be admitted that he and his relations had shown themselves to be alert, imaginative, and practical.

Nor can they be denied credit for extending the power and wealth of their King, for it was Lord Boyd who engineered the treaty of 1468 by which James acquired, with a delectable wife, King Christian's lands in the northern islands; and it was Thomas Boyd—that kind and courteous man—who went to Denmark to fetch the Princess to her new home, while his father led an embassy into England to secure the goodwill of an ever-suspicious neighbour.

It was then, while the Boyds were absent, that their enemies saw their opportunity, and filled the young King's mind with malicious gossip—or, perhaps, told him stories as dark but true—until James, as was said, "conceived great hatred of Arran." When the ship, with Margaret aboard, came back from Denmark, the Lady Mary, the King's sister, was waiting on the pier at Leith; and while Margaret and her attendants went ashore, Arran listened to the direful news his wife had brought, and prudently decided to re-embark. He must have been truly kind and courteous, for when he sailed again to Denmark, his wife went with him.

Though James had inherited little of his father's strength and authority, his reign, for a few years, was fortunate. His kingdom had been enlarged by the acquisition of Berwick and Roxburgh in the south, as well as by his father-in-law's estates in the islands; and then, by the shrewd advice of an unknown counsellor—or, perhaps, by the exercise of some obscure authority—James persuaded William Sinclair, Earl of Orkney, to exchange his earldom for the castle and lands of Ravenscraig in Fife. William Sinclair was the last of the Orkney earls who owed his title to a connexion of blood with the old Norse dynasty, and to investiture by the King of Norway. He came of a family that had lived in almost princely state, and it is difficult to understand why he consented to the bargain which the King proposed. It had the effect, however, that when the islands were annexed and united to Scotland in 1472, the ancient title that James had added to his throne was fortified by the incorporation, within his kingdom, of the earldom of Orkney.

The birth of a son in 1473—the prince who would become James IV —gave, almost immediately, pretext for negotiation with England and the preliminaries of a royal marriage. When the boy was little more than a year old, he was engaged to Cecilia, the youngest daughter of Edward IV of England, who, at the age of three, was slightly more mature. Distinguished proxies took the marriage vows on behalf of the royal infants, a dowry of 20,000 English marks was pledged, and the truce that hazardously existed between the two kingdoms was optimistically extended for forty-five years.

Diplomatic conversation, moreover, had revealed an old treasonable connexion, with England, of that recurrently troublesome, almost independent potentate in the west, the Lord of the Isles. There is little doubt that the Hebridean chiefs who fetched descent from Somarled of the Isles were convinced of their true title to independence; and there is no doubt at all that they were often on such friendly terms with England that they could, without loss of dignity, accept subsidies from its monarch. But now, with an English treaty in his pocket, James felt strong enough to attack and condemn the intransigent chief. Parliament declared the forfeiture of his life and lands, an army under the Earl of Atholl and a fleet commanded by the Earl of Crawford advanced against him, and John, Lord of the Isles, was forced to surrender to the Crown his earldom of Ross and his sheriffdoms of Nairn and Inverness.

Two or three years later James was relieved of another embarrassment, of a different sort, when Patrick Graham, the first Archbishop of St. Andrews, was removed from his see and imprisoned at Loch Leven. He was insane, and believed himself to be Pope of Rome as well as Archbishop of St. Andrews. He who replaced him was more amenable: he had previously served as court physician, the King's astrologer, and keeper of the royal wardrobe. He was a man of humble origin. James often showed his preference for people of the workaday sort, and those whom he distinguished by his favour may indeed have been more agreeable than many of his barons and territorial despots.

But by now his run of luck was nearing its end. Again there was a threat of rebellion in the Western Isles, and England revealed how shallow was its friendship by refusing to pay the agreed instalment on the infant Cecilia's dowry, and by plotting to regain the Border town of Berwick, which Henry VI had ceded to Scotland. At home, moreover, James was faced by the continuing hostility of his nobles, the increasing hostility of his parliaments.

His pretence to rule was, in fact, undermined by idleness and further weakened by a fatal habit of clemency. He paid less attention than he should have done to the enforcement of his laws, he forgave too often those who infringed them. His father and his grandfather had striven, with hard-headed determination, to assert the authority of the crown and make effective the administration of justice. But James III too often felt pity for unhappy creatures who found themselves on the wrong side of the law, and angered his proud, illiterate nobles by his preference for clever and gifted men who owed nothing to the fortune of their birth. He was fond of solitude, but enjoyed the company of those who could play and sing. He took no pleasure in talk of war, and much preferred the conversation of musicians to that of urgent men who would remind him of the unceasing need to defend the Borders, of his imperative duty to make law effective.

In the more lenient temper of our own age, his choice and preferences may well win approval. He was manifestly intelligent—though not in a kingly way—and he had the gift, it was said, of taking an interest in all manner of things, except those things that should have occupied his mind. But he was devoid of energy, and energy was essential to a monarch of the Fifteenth Century. He was, moreover, a greedy, grasping man, and superstitious. He resented criticism, and if ever he showed decision, he chose the wrong moment for it.

It was not his fault, however, that he suffered under the grievous disadvantage of having two brothers who enjoyed the temperament necessary for a brutal age, who were accomplished in those hearty exercises that James despised. There was Alexander, Duke of Albany, who loved brave men and good horses; there was the Earl of Mar, who spent his leisure time—which was most of his time—on hunting and hawking and archery. And James was superstitious. He thought it probable that his brothers were using witchcraft to destroy him. In self-protection, therefore—as he judged it—he ordered their arrest, and their agents, the suspect witches and warlocks, were burnt.

The Earl of Mar died in captivity. That was not an unusual end for a state prisoner: the first Duke of Rothesay, when imprisoned by a previous Duke of Albany, was thought to have died, not by open murder, but of starvation so painful that, before his death, he had eaten his own hands. It was inevitable that James should be suspected of contriving Mar's death, but there is no evidence of his guilt, and he may well have been innocent. Albany, the older brother, is said to have made a sensational escape from Edinburgh castle: if the story is true, he killed his guards, let himself down the Rock on a rope, and picking up a fellow prisoner who had fallen, carried him to Leith and found a ship that took them first to Dunbar, then to France.

Albany was well received by Louis XI, who found him a wife and sent an envoy to Scotland with a twofold purpose: he had to ask forgiveness for the exile, and persuade James to make war against England. James at first refused, but then consented, and an army of considerable size crossed the Tweed, and after burning Bamburgh castle came idly home again.

English retaliation was prompt, and rather more effective. Edward IV mobilised an army, mustered a fleet, and though James offered to expiate his breach of the truce the English ships came into the Firth of Forth, captured a few Scottish vessels, and burnt Blackness castle. Then James gathered an army which was stopped on its march, not by English arrows, but by an envoy who came out of England with letters, alleged to have been written by the Pope, which threatened James with excommunication for menacing a Christian power when his manifest duty was to hold his troops in readiness for an offensive, meditated by more fervent Christians, against the infidels of Turkey. The Scottish army was disbanded, the English fleet returned to plunder in the Firth of Forth, and English raiders burnt and harried on the Borders.

But the English were not the only enemies. Scotland has always been accustomed to seasons of hard weather, but if the meteorologists of the Fifteenth Century and their records can be trusted, it has never endured such fearful storms as beat upon it during the first three months of 1481. There was, it is said, a continuous tempest from New Year's Day till the end of March; and the wind and the rain aggravated the discomforts of a people who, always poor, now suffered the added poverty which a debased coinage had induced. Copper farthings had been put into circulation, and silver pennies which were copper with a silver complexion. They were easy to counterfeit, and as black money flooded the country, the price of food rose alarmingly. Now in popular opinion the creation of a worthless coinage had been inspired—for the benefit of the Exchequer—by Robert Cochrane, who was one of the King's favourites.

Illiterate nobles complained that the King's favourites were "masons and fiddlers"; and the simple people of the land—subject to English depredation, appalling weather, and the diminishing value of their few pennies—blamed their unhappy monarch for listening to the evil designs of a gifted man who, it is probable, had very little to do with monetary policy.

Cochrane, so far from being a mere mason, was in fact an accomplished and imaginative architect who built the Great Hall of Stirling castle. Another of the King's favourites—he who was called a fiddler —was William Roger, a musician who is thought to have founded an influential school of music. Others whom the King honoured with his friendship were William Torphichen, a fencing master; James Hommyl, a tailor; and Leonard, a shoemaker. Translate those terms into contemporary usage, and what monarch of today would be thought unwise if he associated, in a discreet and genial way, with someone who coached him to play golf or tennis, with others who designed and cut his clothes according to fashion, and built his Italian shoes?

There is no evidence whatever that James was influenced, in policy or strategy, by Cochrane and Rogers and the others; but when he was forced, by an event that none had foreseen, to gather an army for the defence of his realm, he was so unwise as to let his favourites go with him. A crisis had been precipitated by his brother, the Duke of Albany. With astonishing cynicism Albany had crossed the narrow sea to England, and pledged his allegiance to the English throne in return for English help in conquering a kingdom for which he promised to do homage, and whose southern fortresses he would surrender to Edward. An English army was mustered, and under the joint command of Albany and the Duke of Gloucester marched into Northumberland.

James found mobilisation more difficult. Many of his nobles would not march with him. The Earls of Angus, Huntly, Buchan, and Lennox called up their followers, and led their own army. James, with a smaller force—and his favourite friends—marched as far as Lauder in Berwickshire, and made camp there. The rebel earls took the town, without resistance, and decided that the King should be presented with an ultimatum; but, like the mice in the fable, who had reasoned that the only way to disable their enemy the cat was to hang a bell round its neck, none was eager to face their angry monarch. It was Angus who volunteered, and as "Bell-the-cat" he was known for the rest of his life.

He told the King that he must withdraw the black money from circulation, and surrender his favourites. The King was not intimidated, and refused the latter demand. But the nobles—infuriated, it seems, by the sudden appearance of Cochrane dressed in extravagant splendour—seized him and his unhappy companions, and without even the pretence of a trial hanged them, before the King himself, from the bridge at Lauder.

The rebels made no attempt to oppose the English invaders, who took the town of Berwick and advanced on Edinburgh, where James was a prisoner in the castle. By Albany's persuasion they did not, as was their custom, burn the town, but contented themselves with discreet blackmail of the richer merchants and returned to Berwick to reduce its stubbornly defended castle. Albany found himself in a position of unexpected difficulty, for, as so often happened, the nobles of Scotland disagreed with each other, and opposition to his claim to the throne was stiffened by rumour and suspicion of his secret compact with the King of England. He temporised, and accepted the return of his forfeited estates. He assured the Duke of Gloucester that he would keep his promise to Edward, and devised an elaborate plan by which he appeared as the saviour of his royal brother, and released him from imprisonment.

It was then, at the feverish height of crisis, that James showed, not only intelligence, but a self-control that must elicit admiration. He pretended to believe what Albany told him, he made a convincing show of reconciliation. He appointed Albany his Lieutenant-general in Scotland, he conferred on him Cochrane's briefly enjoyed earldom of Mar; he ate his meals with his treacherous brother, he shared a bed with him, he bribed the burgesses of Edinburgh with a gift of legal authority to their Provost.

Albany maintained his treasonable correspondence with England, but made no headway towards the throne he coveted. Suspicion, if not knowledge of his treason, was now general; and again, for a little while, the King seemed to be master in his own house. With parliament to support him he confronted Albany, and with a promise of pardon persuaded him to confess the shame of his bargain with Edward. Albany, humiliated, fled into England, but found no comfort there: his old friend, Edward IV, died in April 1483, and his successor, Richard III, was too insecure on his own throne to have much interest in any other. Albany made a last flourish of defiance in the following year, when, with the old Earl of Douglas—banished thirty years before—he led five hundred horsemen at a gallop to Lochmaben Fair, and fought for a long afternoon till the indignant Borderers drove off the remnant that survived. Albany fled again to France, where, by accident, he was killed at a tournament.

If James had been prudent—if he had been able to control his recurrent avarice—he might have lived out his life in reasonable comfort, in a measure of security, within that tolerance, if not respect, which is accorded to someone who, over the years, has shown a capacity for survival and become something like an institution. Good judgment perhaps, good fortune most certainly, brought into his service that learned churchman and sound statesman, William Elphinstone, whom James promoted to the bishopric of Aberdeen, and was rewarded by sermons that persuaded him to abandon his more profligate habits and take to the study of theology. It may have been by Elphinstone's advice that James made friendly approaches to England; it was by sheer good luck that Richard III, the monarch to whom his approach was made, was killed at the battle of Bosworth and succeeded by Henry VII; for the Welsh usurper was even more intent than his predecessor on avoiding unnecessary difficulty in his foreign relations.

A friendly or acquiescent England was always God's blessing to its leaner neighbour. It seemed, too, that James had established a good relationship with the Papacy. His wife, Margaret of Denmark, had lately died, and James expressed a hope of her canonisation: that must be accepted as evidence, not only of Margaret's virtue as a woman, but of her loyalty as a Queen, and—despite his occasional infidelities—of James's devotion to her.

But nothing he did commended him to the majority of his subjects. He was a man, it was said, who could inspire neither love nor fear. He showed, said his adversaries, too much eagerness for friendship with both England and the Pope of Rome; and when the Pope granted his plea that the Priory of Coldingham should be repressed, and its revenues annexed to the Chapel Royal at Stirling, the Pope, at James's request, signed the King's death warrant.

The rich Priory of Coldingham had long been a possession of the powerful Border family of Home. The Homes resented the proposed alienation of their property; their neighbours on the Border, the Hepburns, loudly offered their support; and the kingdom fell apart. The rebels, by force or guile, got possession of the Duke of Rothesay, heir to the throne, and when, after policy had aborted and argument found no conclusion, the army of the King faced the forces of rebellion, James again—and for the last time—showed his fatal lack of judgment. He had allies in the north, but would not wait for them. With a gesture both forlorn and infinitely pathetic, he sent a messenger to Edinburgh castle to bring him the sword that Robert the Bruce had carried at Bannockburn; and strapped it to his side.

The fond and foolish battle was fought at Sauchieburn, not far from Bannockburn; and when the tide turned against him, James was persuaded to seek his safety on the great grey charger that Lord Lindsay had given him. But the horse threw him, a miller and his wife carried him into the nearby shelter of their mill, and there, in fear of death, he called for a priest. A stranger appeared—who he was has never been discovered—and having administered the viaticum by stabbing the poor King four or five times in the chest, "syne gat him on his hack and hied him away."

It is easy to condemn King James III; not quite impossible to find excuses for him. The portrait of him by Hugo van der Goes shows a boy of brooding sensitivity: thin of face, a long nose, dark withdrawn eyes under arching brows, a delicate mouth and chin: his Queen is purely mediaeval, but James could be a deeply troubled and troublesome young man of today.

3

The Glittering and Tragic King

1

Erasmus, the great scholar who avoided extremes and firmly trod the middle road, was for some time the tutor of Alexander, a natural son of James IV. Of the King he wrote: "He had a wonderful intellectual power, an astonishing knowledge of everything, an unconquerable magnanimity, and the most abundant generosity."

To that encomium it is proper to add that a parent who employed Erasmus to tutor a clever son must have had sound judgment, and, in an age that was loud with controversy, he showed also independence of mind and intellectual courage. It is an accepted fact—in Scotland it is almost an article of faith—that James was the brilliant centre of a court which seemed, for a little while, to be lighting Scotland's politically grey climate with a comforting glow, caught by reflexion from the renaissance of learning that had illuminated more fortunate parts of Europe. It would, indeed, be imprudent, and darkly ungenerous, to belittle the King or doubt the achievements of his reign, but it cannot be denied that in James there existed, between his virtues and his grace, a defect of character, a curiously indeterminate flaw, which in the tragic conclusion to his reign pulled down upon himself, as if he were a Samson, the ruins of his kingdom. If it is true that a deeply traumatic experience can create a permanent moral weakness, that flaw might have been implanted at the battle of Sauchieburn; but it may be more realistic to suppose that his engagement in a battle which brought death to his father revived and enlarged some malady of conscience that was almost as old as himself.

When the Homes and the Hepburns came out in open rebellion, they got possession—probably by guile—of the young heir to the kingdom, the Duke of Rothesay; and at Sauchieburn James and his bodyguard, under the royal banner, rode immediately behind the vanguard of the insurgent army. James is said to have given orders that no one should lay hands on his father, but his father was murdered at the mill by Bannockburn, and James, crowned at Scone a fortnight later, cannot have acquitted himself of all responsibility.

He was only fifteen, however, and while the Homes and their allies did what they could to conciliate their opponents, and made strenuous efforts to maintain or restore the orderly administration of the country, James flew his falcons and enjoyed his new liberty. But he was not allowed to enjoy idleness. He was soon entered into the serious business of kingship. He sat with the Lords of Council, he attended the travelling courts called Justice Ayres, he worshipped at St. Giles and wrote impatiently to the Pope when Rome was tardy in replying to his demand that the see of Glasgow should be erected into an archbishopric. An official account of the fatality at Bannockburn was distributed for the information of foreign courts, and James may have been comforted by its bland assertion that on the unhappy day his father "happinnit to be slane." If chance ruled all men's lives, he was not to blame.

He was quickly made familiar with one of a monarch's recurrent duties when Lord Lyle, his own Justiciar, made a treasonable compact, and preparation for a war to avenge the late King, with the Earl of Lennox and others. The rebellion appeared to be serious, and the great cannon Mons Meg was included in the siege train that moved slowly, and with infinite labour, from Edinburgh to Glasgow, and thence to Lyle's castle of Duchal. The castle surrendered, and in Perthshire a threatened campaign was checked when the royal forces made a swift attack by night on the rebels' encampment near Dunblane.

Parliament continued its policy of conciliation, and busily passed laws for the suppression and punishment of domestic violence. It decided to seek alliance with France, Spain, and Denmark, but discovered it could not afford to furnish and equip the necessary diplomatic missions; so in pursuit of economy it found means to restrain the young King's cheerful inclination to bestow on his friends such valuable gifts as silver plate, jewels, and crown lands. Disapproval of popular enjoyment—so typical of parliaments in every age—may have prompted laws that forbade the playing of golf and football, and encouraged the practice of archery; but the problem of defence was ever present— Scotland had never developed a sufficient fire power—and to repair the lack of bowmen there was again resort to an old unhappy policy.

In 1491 a large embassy embarked for France to renew the "auld alliance" and find a bride for the King. The ambassadors, who included —as well as barons and a pair of earls—Bishop Elphinstone and the poet William Dunbar, came home without a bride but with confirmation that the alliance, then about a hundred and sixty years old, would be renewed in the expected terms: France and Scotland pledged themselves to make war on England should England make war on either of them.

Officially there was friendship between England and Scotland, but political visibility was poor at sea. The chronicler, Lindesay of Pitscottie, is not always reliable, but many of his stories are vivid and may be true. According to his account, Scottish shipping in the Firth of Forth, in 1489, was repeatedly attacked by five well-armed English ships, which, after taking much plunder, were defeated by the *Flower* and the *Yellow Carvel* whose commander, Sir Andrew Wood of Largo, shepherded his prizes into Leith. A year later, when Wood was on his way home from Flanders, he was intercepted by the Englishman Bull, whose three large, heavily gunned ships he fought for a long summer day, and when dawn broke again, on both sides the trumpets blew and battle was renewed. But the ships were drifting north, and when the English vessels ran aground near the mouth of the Tay, Bull surrendered and his little fleet was towed into Dundee.

English reprisals followed, and in 1491 Henry VII, the Welshman who had acquired the English throne, was involved in a very curious transaction. To the Earl of Buchan, James's great-uncle, and Sir Thomas Tod, the Master of the Mint, he offered the cheese-paring sum of £266 13s 4d to kidnap the King and his younger brother. It is not known whether Buchan and Tod took the offer seriously or regarded it as a Tudor aberration about which it was better to say nothing; but the plot, if there was a plot, was still-born.

Henry's next venture was to suborn the Earl of Angus, who commanded the great castle of Hermitage in Liddesdale on the western road into Scotland. Suspicion was aroused, and James relieved Angus of his command, which he gave to the Earl of Bothwell. But it was impolitic to offend so important a man as Angus, and after a period during which his resentment was obvious, he was compensated with the lands and castle of Kilmarnock. With England a truce was concluded for the cynically brief period of eight months.

It was increasingly evident, however, that Henry had no wish for war. He might deplore the perpetual insecurity of the Border, but he could not afford the cost and danger of a major campaign. He was already embroiled with France, and embarrassed by the emergence from obscurity of Perkin Warbeck, a youth who claimed to be the son of Edward IV and who, to Henry's consternation, had been recognised as her nephew by Margaret, a sister of Edward IV who was Duchess of Burgundy. To Henry it seemed advisable to negotiate a more lasting peace with Scotland, and attach its young King by a marriage alliance. But he was unsuccessful. Parsimonious by nature—always reluctant to pay for what he wanted—Henry offered as a bride, not a princess of the blood, but a distant cousin whose value, by social or political standards, was negligible. The Scots had no difficulty in deciding that the lady was not good enough, and they would only agree to another truce.

In 1493, when Henry's offer was declined, James was twenty, and had begun to show that he was King in fact as well as in name. His father's murder had not been forgotten, and parliament had lately offered a reward for discovery of the still unknown assassin. In James himself remorse for his share of the tragedy appears to have grown with the years, for he now resolved to wear round his waist an iron chain, a penance that he swore never to forgo. Though a symbol of the burden on his conscience, it did not overburden his mind or impair his vigour, and in the year when he condemned himself to life-long mortification he determined to essay an overdue campaign against the Lord of the Isles—or the latest claimant to the Lordship—whose large possessions parliament had declared forfeit to the Crown.

2

The Lordship of the Isles resided in Clan Donald, whose chiefs fetched descent from Somarled, regulus or petty king of Argyll and the south Isles, and Ragnhild, the sister of Godrey, king of Man. Somarled, of mingled Norse and Celtic blood, acknowledged Norwegian suzerainty as did his successors until the battle of Largs, in 1263, and the cession of the Hebrides to Scotland. It was from Donald of Islay, a grandson of Somarled, that the clan got its name, and its stubborn claim to independence was clearly an inheritance from history to which geographical isolation gave an apparent substance.

The Gaelic-speaking people who lived beyond the Forth and Clyde were generally regarded, by their Lowland neighbours and visiting foreigners, as savages. "They live in the forests and mountains of the north, and are called the Wild Scots," said the learned John Major, a contemporary of James IV. He wrote of them: "From the mid-thigh to the foot they have no covering, and they clothe themselves with a mantle as upper garment, and a shirt dyed with saffron. They carry a bow and arrows, a very broad sword, a small partisan, in the belt a large dagger with one edge only, but very sharp. In war they clothe their whole body with a shirt of mail with iron rings, and fight in that. The common people cover their bodies with a tunic of quilted linen, waxed or dressed with pitch, and also with deerskin."

Some had flocks and herds, says Major, others took no trouble to earn a good livelihood but lived upon their neighbours and found their pleasure in hunting and fighting. It was commonly accepted that the main difference between the Wild Scots of the mainland, and those in the Isles, was that the latter were wilder. But all the men of the Isles —MacLeods and Mackinnons, Macleans and Macneils—acknowledged as their chief the Son of Donald, Chief of Clan Donald. However wild it might seem to Lowland eyes, it was an hierarchical society, with the social stability which that implies, and John Major's account is interesting, not so much for what it says, as for what it does not say. Lowlanders and Highlanders wear different clothes, the Highland way of life is pastoral, unsupported by industry: Major was aware of superficial differences, but, like other Lowlanders, ignorant of the deeper realities which distance masked and an unknown language closely concealed. Two cultures existed in Scotland, separated from each other by frowning hills, stormy seas, and the Gaelic tongue.

In earlier times the descendants of Somarled had intermarried with the High Stewards of Scotland and their offspring: Alexander the Steward, a Regent of Scotland in 1255, married a great-granddaughter of Somarled, and Eoin, Lord of the Isles, married Margaret, daughter of Robert II. But between royal Stewarts and the chiefs of Clan Donald the distance had grown wider as the former became more closely involved with England and the continent, and the latter retired into the stubborn conservatism of their islands. There was no more marital association, nor any contact except on the field of battle, in foray and reprisal.

In 1411 Donald of the Isles, a grandson of Robert II, claimed in his wife's name the earldom of Ross and led a formidable Highland army to a battle of exceptional ferocity at Harlaw, near Aberdeen; and less than twenty years later his son Alexander embarked on that prolonged dispute with James I which came to an end when Alexander, in his shirt and drawers, made submission to the King before the high altar in the chapel of Holyrood. Then his cousin Donald Balloch rose in rebellion, won a battle at Inverlochy, but was forced to find refuge in Ireland. He returned to Scotland as an ally of the Earl of Douglas when Douglas was challenging the royal power of James II, and having destroyed the castle of Brodick in Arran—presumably for Douglas's advantage—took from the island heavy tribute for his own.

While England was divided by the Wars of the Roses and the antipathies they nurtured, and Scotland was in some confusion after the death of James II, Edward IV, newly crowned, found it politic to promote division in the northern kingdom and enlisted a willing ally in John, Lord of the Isles and Earl of Ross, who had submitted to the late King but was now showing signs of Celtic restlessness. The Earl of Douglas and his brother Balveny—who had fled to England after their crushing defeat by James II—returned to Scotland with a remarkable offer from the Yorkist King. He promised protection to those who would help Douglas to conquest of the country, over the southern half of which Douglas was to rule, with John of the Isles and Donald Balloch dividing the north and west, all three to recognise Edward as Lord Paramount, and draw, in the meantime, lavish pensions from him. That ambitious plan was ratified by the treaty of Westminster, 1462, and John of the Isles promptly assumed almost kingly powers, sent his own ambassadors to England, demanded rents and revenues from Inverness and Nairn, and appointed his son Angus as his lieutenant over the two burghs.

On the Western Marches Douglas was again defeated, Balveny killed, but for twelve years John of the Isles lived in princely state, menaced only by a feud with the Earl of Huntly. Repeatedly summoned to meet the Estates of the Realm, he always declined to attend but never failed to send his deputy. Under a King of such indifferent authority as James III he maintained a virtual independence until the treaty of Edinburgh, in 1475, proposed peace between England and Scotland and its assurance by the marriage of James's infant son to Cecilia, the youngest daughter of Edward IV. Then it became possible to deal with the intransigent chief, and a combined assault—the Earls of Crawford and Atholl were joined by Huntly and Argyll—quickly broke his strength. He asked for mercy, and was treated with remarkable leniency. The Queen is said to have interceded for him, and though he had to surrender the earldom of Ross, the castles of Inverness and Nairn, and his lands in Kintyre, he was allowed to keep his other possessions and sit in parliament as Lord of the Isles.

He maintained his correspondence with Edward IV, and caused occasional alarm, but refrained from hostile action. That, however, does not mean there was peace in the Isles. John's submission was greatly resented by those who had accepted his authority, and when they sought another leader they quickly found one in Angus Og, an illegitimate son of John, whose temper was fiercely energetic and who had shrewdly enhanced his power by marrying a daughter of the Earl of Argyll. For ten years or more he was *de facto* Lord of the Isles. He invaded the mainland in a vain attempt to recover the earldom of Ross, and when driven back defeated his father in a naval battle near the Point of Ardnamurchan, or between Ardnamurchan and Tobermory. Again he raided and harried in the mainland, and captured the Earl and Countess of Atholl in the chapel of St. Bride in Atholl. Then his galleys were wrecked in a storm, he was assailed by remorse for the sacrilege he had committed, and made reparation to the chapel he had pillaged, and released his captives. But those acts of contrition did not avert the violent death his life had invited, and soon afterwards he was murdered in Inverness by an Irish harper.

John, the vanquished Earl of Ross, was still alive, and as his lieutenant appointed his nephew, Alexander of Lochalsh; who quickly showed a temper as fiercely ambitious as Angus Og's. He renewed a claim to the forfeited earldom, and Inverness was burnt again. But when Alexander harried lands of the Mackenzies in Ross, they rose against him, and having wrought as much ruin as the invaders, took Alexander prisoner and expelled his followers. Then it was discovered that old John of the Isles was again in treasonable correspondence with England.

It cannot be denied that the Kings of Scotland inherited a throne beset with difficulties. Across the Border was a powerful and hostile neighbour; beyond the English Channel an exigent and cynical ally; within their frontiers an anarchic nobility; over the Highland Line and beyond the island seas were the clans that spoke another language and lived in a different habit of life; and the usual environment of their throne was a disabling poverty. James IV, however, was so fortunate as to escape that common humiliation, for his father, though inept in many ways, had enriched himself by the avarice that so disfigures his life, and the considerable fortune he acquired seems to have been recovered intact for the benefit of his heir. For the tasks that confronted him he had many natural advantages, and the invaluable inheritance of a well filled treasure chest.

But when he resolved to face in the west a persistent danger, and resolve a recurrent problem, he made a bold decision and undertook a major work. In his favour was the fact that he was the sort of man whom the islanders were inclined both to like and respect. He was a gallant figure—lively and strong and recklessly brave—and he spoke Gaelic: not very much, it is probable, but enough to impress the outlying clans who, since the days of Robert the Bruce, had seen no Scottish king in their stormy seas. But despite his gifts of learning and nature, James, in the next six years, had to make as many visits to the truculent subjects whom he flattered by his acquisition of a few words of Gaelic.

His first expedition was quickly and easily successful. His ships met no resistance, and at Dunstaffnage, near the small modern town of Oban, the island chiefs made submission and received from their King charters for the lands they had previously held by use and wont and the favour of the Chiefs of Clan Donald. Alexander of Lochalsh, released from captivity, and John of Islay were knighted. But the Isles were not pacified, and in 1494 James had to return again, and yet again. At Tarbert in Kintyre, where that long peninsula is almost cut in two by West Loch Tarbert, the chiefs were called to meet him, and having repaired the royal castle there he sailed down to the butt-end of the peninsula and captured the old castle of Dunaverty. It did not remain long in his possession. Almost as soon as he had set sail, it is said, John of Islay took it by storm and hanged its newly appointed governor from the ramparts while from the galleys of the King they could still see what he was doing. But John of Islay, knighted the year before, did not live to enjoy his triumph. Made prisoner with several of his sons, he was taken to Edinburgh, tried and hanged.

During that winter preparation was made for a naval demonstration in strength, and in the following summer the King in a many-oared galley, escorted by Andrew Wood of Largo in his *Flower*, led a fleet of small craft through the western firths into the Sound of Mull, and having exacted submission from the chiefs of the Macleans, Macdonalds of Sleat, Macneils and Camerons, was so gracious or so politic as to confirm their titles to the lands they had long possessed. Two potential trouble-makers, however, both of them related to the Lord of the Isles, were removed, in the interests of peace, to Edinburgh castle; and then, having done all that was immediately possible to establish the rule of law in a society reluctant to admit its necessity, James turned to other projects. He had several in mind.

3

With seeming approval, James contemplated the prospect of war against England, and at Stirling castle welcomed the adventurer Perkin Warbeck as if he were the prince he claimed to be.

It is possible, and seems probable, that he was deceived by Perkin—who had been in correspondence with him for two or three years—and believed him to be Richard, Duke of York, the younger of the two sons of Edward IV who had been murdered, or were thought to have been murdered, in the Tower. Also possible is the supposition that James was willing to be deceived, or pretend to a belief in Perkin's *bona fides*, in order to find a pretext for war. To read the mind of Perkin himself is equally difficult. All impostors are moved by vanity and hope of gain, but in Perkin's case—he was an agreeable youth—vanity may have been the larger motive, with the excitement of a great and dangerous gamble to stiffen it.

The son of a poor burgess of Tournai in Flanders, he went into domestic service, and among his employers were an English lady, wife of an exiled partisan of York, and a Breton silk merchant in Cork. Ireland was Yorkist in sentiment, and Perkin—perhaps in his master's clothes—seems to have excited attention and curiosity by his distinguished appearance. Two ingenious Irish earls, Desmond and Kildare, are thought to have recognised in him a likeness to the late King, and decided to exploit the resemblance to embarrass Henry VII and his detested government. Their plot was much advanced in 1492, when

Perkin was summoned to Flanders by Margaret, Duchess of Burgundy and sister of Edward IV; either deluded by the boy or becoming a party to the plot, she recognised him as her nephew, and the plot was enlarged by the accession to it of Charles VIII of France and the Emperor Maximilian.

With the help of the latter Perkin mustered a small army of indifferent quality, and landed in Kent. Unsuccessful there, he sailed to Ireland and laid siege to Waterford. That attempt also failed, but already he had been assured of Scottish support, and when he arrived, in November 1495, his entertainment was lavish. He was given a pension, maintenance for the remnant of his army, and within a few weeks James had found for him a noble wife, the Lady Katharine Gordon.

Over Berwick, that town of long debate, flew the English flag, and if war was to be ventured, Berwick would be the main objective. During the Wars of the Roses, when Henry VI found refuge in Scotland, he had paid for hospitality by ceding it, but England had recaptured it, and James and his Great Council were eager to win it yet again. There were those in the Council who had no faith in Perkin Warbeck, but his pretensions were an excuse for war, and a majority were in favour of war. If it were successful, Perkin would be grateful and pay them well for their trouble; and if it failed, Henry VII would pay them for Perkin.

War was prevented, however, by a political complication in which Spain, France, and England were all involved. James was looking for a wife, and hoped to find one at the court of Ferdinand and Isabella. They listened sympathetically to his ambassador, but were more intent on marrying their youngest daughter, Katharine of Aragon, to Henry VII's elder son, Arthur. Spain, the Emperor, and the Pope were members of a so-called Holy League directed against France, and they were anxious to persuade England to join them. But England would not go to war with France if she was in danger of attack from Scotland, and therefore Scotland must be dissuaded from warlike ambitions.

James consented to postpone the attack he meditated, but was angered by his ambassador's failure to find a bride. His ambassador went back to Spain with a promise that there would be no immediate action, and marriage to a Spanish princess would be rewarded by a treaty of perpetual peace with England. Parliament, instead of voting supplies for war, discussed domestic problems, and Ferdinand and

Isabella despatched, not a daughter, but that most gifted, amiable, and enthusiastic of envoys, Don Pedro de Ayala. James accepted the fact that there would be no Spanish marriage for him—paid no attention to Henry VII's offer of his daughter Margaret, a child of seven—and agreed to support Perkin Warbeck in his attempt on the English throne in return for the town and castle of Berwick and a sum of 50,000 marks, payable in two years' time.

From Edinburgh the long gun trains laboured slowly, with enormous effort, south to Ellemford under the Lammermuirs in Berwickshire, and in September James and his protégé crossed the Tweed near Coldstream. Perkin was doubly disappointed by what followed. None rallied to his standard, but frightened people fled from marauding Scots to what shelter they could find. Some little castles or towers in the valley of the Till were taken and burnt. Their garrisons were killed, sheep and cattle were driven north again to the Border. Perkin had no stomach for work of that sort, and quickly returned to Scotland. But James laid siege to Heton castle, and a visitor more distinguished than Perkin remained with him. Ayala, that impressionable man, had quickly conceived a warm and wondering admiration for the King, and now, with what seems to have been a horrified fascination, watched under the walls of Heton his reckless bravery. More courageous "than a king should be," he undertook "most dangerous things," and defended his rash behaviour with the ingenuous explanation that as his subjects were prepared to obey him regardless of consequences, he thought it only right that he should first expose himself to danger. Ayala rarely uttered adverse criticism of James, but after the affair at Heton he was compelled to say: "He is not a good captain, because he begins to fight before he has given his orders."

He had, apparently, crossed the Tweed before giving consideration to what should then be done; for when there came news or a rumour that an English army was marching from Newcastle, he retired hurriedly to his own country. Perkin was now out of favour—his failure to appreciate Border tactics may have given offence—and though James continued to pay his pension, he dismissed his followers. He was allowed to stay in Scotland till the summer of 1497, when James provided him with a ship, appropriately called *Cuckoo*, in which he sailed from Ayr to defeat at Exeter, imprisonment in the Tower, and death at Tyburn. He, in his own way, was as reckless as James, for nothing compelled him to carry his imposture to battle under the walls of Exeter.

Henry declared war on Scotland, and James laboured to improve his defensive positions on the Border. But the army which Henry mobilised did not march very far. Suddenly there was revolt in Cornwall, and several thousand Cornishmen—indignant at being taxed for a Scottish war—advanced on London, and the army mustered to punish his northern neighbour was recalled to defend his capital. Henry made peaceful overtures, and was mollified by Perkin Warbeck's expulsion. James, with what seems complete irresponsibility, then attacked the strong castle of Norham on the Tweed—Ayala was once more his companion—and again retreated when he heard that an English army, 20,000 strong under the Earl of Surrey, was within two days' march of him. He was not prepared for a major campaign, and it was quickly discovered that Surrey's army was equally unwilling to fight in Scotland. It was August, and August is usually a wet month. It rained for five days, and with great resolution the English retreated.

Before that happened James had sent his heralds to Surrey with a romantic proposal. Let their armies meet and fight for possession of Berwick, he said; or failing that, let their leaders meet and fight hand to hand for the same prize. Surrey tactfully replied that Berwick was not his to gamble with, and gradually, as tempers cooled and the colder light of winter counselled wisdom, the prospect of war dwindled and grew dim. Before the end of 1497 a treaty was signed and a truce pledged until the death of both the contending sovereigns, and a year beyond that. Both James and his country had good reason for gratitude to Ayala, who did much to make the treaty possible.

4

The truce acquired substance when Henry repeated an earlier proposal—ignored in Scotland—that James should engage to marry his daughter Margaret. The marriage would put him within three or four removes of the English throne, and a romantic temperament does not necessarily exclude worldly ambition. James, moreover, was now much influenced by Ayala. The Spaniard admired the King—perhaps excessively admired him—who was, he wrote, a linguist of uncommon skill, quick-witted, ever busy but with time to read, astonishingly temperate, punctual in his religious duties and truly devout. He might well have added: "he shows, moreover, great wisdom in listening to me." By his own wish or insistence, Ayala had become James's ambassador extraordinary in England, and he who had been sent to Scotland to nullify the Franco-Scottish alliance, and establish a lasting peace between England and Scotland, firmly believed that a royal marriage was the obvious approach to such a peace.

Though well pleased by James's acceptance of his proposal, Henry was unwilling to give a daughter, only nine years old, in marriage to a son-in-law of twenty-five, and was much relieved when James declared his willingness to wait until Margaret should be of riper years. He waited four years indeed, during which time there was interminable discussion, endless negotiation, recurrent jollification, and a ceaseless traffic of envoys and ambassadors. But James was in no hurry. Marriage might bring him political advantage, but would add nothing to his life. The burden of guilt that he bore for his father's death impelled him to wear a belt of iron and make annual pilgrimage to the shrine of St. Duthac in Tain; but it did not prevent him from enjoying the reciprocal admiration, and the warmth of their caresses, of some agreeable young women who also took pleasure in their youth.

The disappointment of his failure to acquire a Spanish princess for his bed must, indeed, have been sensibly reduced by the discovery, about that time, of his ardent love for Margaret Drummond. Before meeting her his affection had been engaged by Marion Boyd, whose son Alexander, tutored by Erasmus, became Archbishop of St. Andrews and died at Flodden, fighting beside his father. In later years there were Janet Kennedy; Isabel Stewart, a daughter of the Earl of Buchan; a Lady Fleming; some others, identified only by initials in the royal accounts that record payments to them; and all their known children were decently provided for.

But Margaret Drummond enjoys a more lasting distinction than his lesser loves, for she inspired a poem that celebrates not only her beauty and kindliness, but the excellence of her mind. Marriage might only be a political burden to which kings were subject, but James, who eventually made a political marriage of the greatest significance, took liberal advantage of a permissive climate in which the amours of a king were regarded as the proper revelation of royal virility. And Margaret, if the poem retains any reflexion of the truth, was worthy of devotion:

"The blossomis that wer blicht and bricht
 By hir were blak and blew.
Scho gladdit all the fowl of flicht
 That in the forest flew.
Scho micht haif comfort king or knicht
 That evir in cuntrie I knew,
As wale and weil of wardlie wicht,
 In womanlie vertu.

Hir colour cleir, hir contenance,
 Hir cumlie crystal een,
Hir portraiture of maist pleasance
 All pictouris did prevene.
Of everie vertu til avance
 Quhair ladyis praisit bene,
Richtest in my rememberance
 That rois is rutit grene."

For six years their love endured—with some interruption to its constancy—but when James was about to marry Margaret Tudor, Margaret Drummond and her two lovely sisters died suddenly, perhaps of poison. An old passion had found renewal, and Margaret Drummond may have threatened the consummation of a marriage that politics demanded. Priests, paid by the King, said masses in Dunblane cathedral for her soul's repose, but elsewhere, it may be, were men of more practical interest who thought of her timely death with quiet contentment.

James himself, though flamboyant and extravagant, had a simple kindliness, a natural care for others, of which the royal accountants have left abundant evidence—roadside gifts are recorded, presents to masons whose work pleased him, fourteen shillings to a poor man whose horse had died—but a ruthless temper still dominated the age, and though stories of poisoning are always suspect—because poisons in the Fifteenth and Sixteenth Centuries were so inefficient—it is not improbable that Margaret Drummond died to make way for Margaret Tudor. The recurrent violence and casual manslaughter that Highland tales preserve can easily be matched in comparable Lowland tales: they were not Highlanders who murdered James I and James III; they were Lowland lords who hanged Cochrane and Roger on the bridge at Lauder; and it was the brutality of Lowland troops that horrified Perkin Warbeck in the valley of the Till. But what gives the reign of James IV its distinctive quality—a quality unknown in previous reigns and not to be repeated in later ages until the latter part of the Eighteenth Century—is its gaiety and riches, its air of leisure and the fact that many people were enjoying life.

Ayala, it is true, saw most things in *couleur de rose,* and what he wrote—in cipher, for the information of Ferdinand and Isabella—must be discounted. But he cannot be dismissed. One reads with surprise his statement that "The towns and villages are populous. The houses are good, all built of hewn stone and provided with excellent doors, glass windows, and a great number of chimneys. All the furniture that is used in Italy, Spain, and France is to be found in their dwellings."— Of that one can say, with some assurance, that it is not an accurate picture of Scotland as a whole; but of those parts which Ayala had seen, and chose to remember, it may well be a true description.

What he said of Scots women is well known, extremely flattering, and one feels that Ayala must have been uncommonly fortunate in the friends he made: "The women are courteous in the extreme. I mention this because they are really honest, though very bold. They are absolute mistresses of their houses and even of their husbands, in all things concerning the administration of their property, income as well as expenditure. They are very graceful and handsome women. They dress much better than here"—in London, that is—"and especially as regards the headdress, which is, I think, the handsomest in the world."

He is critical of Scottish agriculture—"They do not produce as much as they might, because they do not cultivate the land"—and in the Lowlands he finds some disabilities of character that Lowlanders would have said were typical only of the Highlands: "The Scotch are not industrious, and the people are poor. They spend all their time in wars, and when there is no war they fight with one another. It must, however, be observed that since the present King succeeded to the throne, they do not dare to quarrel so much with one another as formerly, especially since he came of age. They have learnt by experience that he executes the law without respect to rich or poor."

Ayala, it seems clear, was popular in Scotland, and because people liked him, he was inclined to like them though he was not blind to their faults: "They like foreigners so much that they dispute with one another as to who shall have and treat a foreigner in his house. They are vain and ostentatious by nature. They spend all they have to keep up appearances. They are as well dressed as it is possible for such a country as that in which they live. They are courageous, strong, quick, and agile. They are envious to excess."

If indeed they were ostentatious by nature, they had been given a natural leader in King James IV. Expert in the use of weapons and all martial games, he was a patron of that most dangerous of equestrian exercises, the tournament, and often rode in the tiltyard. Lords and gentlemen desirous of honour were invited to assemble at Edinburgh or Stirling, prizes were handsome, and such was the fame of Scottish jousting that foreign knights came to compete in tourneys honoured by the King's presence and accompanied by lavish entertainment. Of more lasting value was the pleasure he took in architecture. He built a new palace at Holyrood, he added both strength and amenity to Stirling castle, Linlithgow palace was enlarged, and beside the old castle of Falkland a noble hunting lodge was built in a great deer park. From one to another of his palaces he rode with a household of about a hundred people—councillors, friends, attendants, servants—horses and grooms were uncounted—and if a life of almost constant movement was due in part to natural restlessness, it had the advantage of making him known to many of his subjects. An active king, whose activity made him visible throughout his kingdom, was an addition of great value to the structure of that kingdom. And wherever he went his hawks went with him, for he was a passionate falconer and a peregrine on his wrist was his favourite companion.

It was the King, more than any other, who encouraged his people to live in pride and fine feathers, but the high temper of the age most obviously retains its lustre in the poetry of William Dunbar, where it is almost coruscatingly evident. From this distance in time it is hardly possible to read Dunbar without being reminded of King James; or remember the King without thinking of *The Thrissil and the Rois*, and *London, thou art the flour of Cities all*, that was written when Dunbar went with ambassadors to treat for the hand of Margaret Tudor. Dunbar in his youth appears to have led a wandering life, a little coloured, perhaps, with such rascality as dominated the vagrancy of François Villon; and in later years he hungered greedily for clerical promotion and was mortified by James's refusal to present him with a rich benefice. His poetry shows a similar tendency to swing from one extreme to the other: from roaring invective to tender piety, from fiercely ebullient satire to richly enamelled panegyric.

His masterpiece is *The Twa Merrit Wemen and the Wedo,* a long satire—dextrously poised against a background of vernal beauty—in which the licentiousness of women, that dearly cherished clerical theme, is balanced, with boisterous acceptance, by a pitiless exposure of the insufficiencies, dishonesty, and lewdness of men. Quotation would not show its character, for its effect is cumulative—deceit is piled upon iniquity, avarice is overwhelmed by carnal greed—and the whole flagrant story concludes, as it began, amid the birdsong and gardened sweetness of a summer day. It is possible, however, to show something of the disequilibrium—which is curious in a major poet—of Dunbar's emotions by reproducing a stanza, of grave beauty, from his poem *Of the Passioun of Christ,* and a very different confection, here translated into English, called *Kind Kitty.*

Here is the first:

> "Betwix tuo theiffis the spreit he gaif
>> On to the Fader most of micht;
> The erde did trimmil, the stanis claif,
>> The sone obscurit of his licht;
>> The day wox dirk as ony nicht,
> Deid bodiis rais in the cite:
>> Goddis deir Sone all thus was dicht;
> O mankynd, for the luif of thee."

And here is the second, in which are evident, not only Dunbar's un-inhibited comedy and wild invention, but also a cheerful irreverence remarkable in an age when God the Father and the Blessed Virgin lived much closer to men's consciousness than they do now:

> "A good sort was my Grandmama, though a little weak in the head,
>> Who lived a long way out of France but quite near Falkland Fell.
> Kind Kitty—that's her only name, to which she was christened and bred—
>> Had the handsome, hump-backed contour of a cuttlefish's shell,
> And died a seemly death of thirst, or so it was widely said,
>> And having died she had no doubt that she in Heaven would dwell.
> So that long highway to the sky she started out to tread,
>> But lost her way, and wandered, till she found a goblin well,
>>> And there she saw a happy sight,
>>>> A Newt upon a Snail!
>>> She shouted "Halt!", it heard her hail,

And she rode on its convenient tail
Under the gathering night.

She rode in comfort all the way until she could espy
An alehouse under Heaven, and dismounted in a trice;
For after such a journey her old throat had grown so dry
She drank a hogshead and a half, and could have drunk it twice.
She slept the sleep of innocence until the sun was high,
Then ran to the Gate where the Newt was asking a tourist ticket's price,
And sidled through it while the Newt still held St. Peter's eye:
God laughed aloud—it shook the stars—to see her neat device!
And there she stayed, till years were seven,
And lived a useful life
Employed as Our Lady's own Hen-wife,
A trade she had learnt in the Kingdom of Fife,
And practised now in Heaven.

But there comes a day, and an evil day, when old, old memories sing
To see the sun on the alehouse sign, and that was a fatal hour!
For out from the Pearly Gate she slipped, with a lilt in her step and a
spring,
Athirst for good ale, for Heaven's ale was very small and sour.
But when she turned to go home again—she heard the supper-bell ring—
St. Peter beat her cruelly, his blows fell like a shower,
For she had despised his own table, an unforgivable thing.
So now in the alehouse she must abide, the sudsy pots to scour,
To scrub the floor, to brew and bake—
Friends, hear my heartfelt cry!
Should you be thirsty, should you feel dry,
Stop and drink with Grandma as you go by,
Just for my sake."

5

In the poetry of James IV's Scotland Dunbar fills the central and
largest place between Henryson and Gavin Douglas. Henryson, the
last heritor of the undivided faith and temper of mediaevalism—he
died before 1508—wrote gay, charming, wryly amusing fables, and a
climax of moving terror to the old tale of Troilus and Cressida. Douglas,
a son of the Earl of Angus, translated Virgil's *Aeneid*—no English or

Scottish writer had hitherto dared a modern rendering of any of the great classical authors—and having overloaded his version with ponderous, unnecessary decoration, added to it, as preludes to Books Seven and Thirteen, some vivid lines that describe, with marvellous felicity, the bitterness of a Scottish winter, the undarkening bliss of early summer.

There were other poets, a dozen or more, whose work has vanished but whose names are remembered in Dunbar's *Lament for the Makaris;* and in a land so loud, for a little while, with lyric and panegyric, with ballad and fable, it was not inappropriate for James's marriage to take on the likeness of a pageant.

The Border nobles were warned of their need to dress with appropriate finery. Armourers came from France to clothe, more sternly, the knights who would ride, so heavily and noisily, in the lists at Holyrood, where carpenters were busily raising stands for the spectators. From Flanders came merchants with velvets and tapestries and cloth of gold. In England Henry VII commanded great processions to escort his daughter: she rode under a tumult of church bells, and in York the Earl of Northumberland in crimson velvet greeted her with a stately music. A magnificently attired cavalcade, and music all the way, accompanied her to Berwick. Early in August—the year was 1503—she arrived at the castle of Dalkeith, where the King in velvet and cloth of gold greeted her with tender consideration for her youth: she was only fifteen, frightened of a strange land, and he comforted her with friendly care.

Pageantry and the King on a bay horse escorted her to Edinburgh, Dunbar and Gavin Douglas had poems for her, and in the abbey church of Holyrood, before a great company caparisoned in splendour, the daughter of England—a dull-looking girl, plumply discontented—was married to the red-haired, red-bearded King of Scots. For the better part of a week there was constant revelry. Minstrels sang, trumpets sounded, bonfires blazed. There were dancers and acrobats and tables prodigiously laden. But the young Queen disliked the King's beard, and he, with uncommon courtesy, permitted the Countess of Surrey and her daughter to crop it.

Though tournaments and pageantry give unusual colour to the reign of James IV they neither distort nor obscure the energy and purpose of his domestic policy. Perpetually busy, he found time to be interested in the education of his people, and in what was hopefully regarded as the growth of science. Enthusiasm sometimes led him astray—though nowadays it is easier than in his time to deride alchemy—but when, with the King's approval, Bishop Elphinstone got papal authority from the Borgia, Alexander VI, for the establishment of Scotland's third university at Aberdeen, it included, for the first time in Britain, a faculty of medicine. It was under James's personal supervision that a fleet was built and great guns forged. Habitually concerned with the business of administration, he was insistent that law must be respected and justice done; but, like his father, he sometimes shrank from the rigours of law, and issued pardons as he scattered his gratuities.

He failed to pacify the Western Highlands and the Outer Isles. In 1495 the more intransigent chiefs had seemingly recognised royal authority, and three years later, returning to the west, James tried again to conciliate dissidents and establish his rule. It is evident, however, that he grew discouraged and lost patience. He delegated authority and made the Earls of Argyll and Huntly responsible for the maintenance of law. Argyll was to be his lieutenant in the south, Huntly in the north; and both accepted their commissions in the happy realisation that their new power could lawfully be exploited for their own advantage. James, however, can hardly be blamed for adopting so injudicious a policy, for he had no means of pursuing a better one. Even a standing army—which no Scottish king could afford—would not have been able to subdue, and keep in subjection, the haughty wilderness of the west without adequate means of communication to support and replenish it; and for serviceable roads the West Highlands would have to wait a very long time.

At vast expense James built a navy, and made no use of it. Pope Julius II, that magnificent and turbulent pontiff, tried to involve him in a devious project to use the maritime power of Venice against the infidels of Turkey; and James was more than willing to brush aside the realities of European politics to emerge as the champion of Christendom. All the woods in Fife were felled to build his great *Michael*, that mounted sixteen guns on either side, and carried a complement of three hundred. He built the *James* and the *Margaret*, bought and hired others, armed and provisioned them. But his fleet won no victories. In the great conflict between France and Spain there was no room for a Scots crusader, though Pope Julius had again exhorted him to make war on Turkey. When James at last led an army into battle, it was not against the Turk, but England, an older enemy. To that disastrous expedition he was incited by France, but James needed little encouragement.

6

Henry VII, the cold and politic usurper, had died in 1509. His successor was the youthful Henry VIII, who was bellicose, ambitious, and more practical than his brother-in-law in Scotland. There were skirmishes on the Border, and at sea the English captured a couple of Scottish ships. England joined the Holy League that Pope Julius had formed against France, and in 1512 the Auld Alliance was renewed. When danger threatened France, the shadow of danger fell on Scotland too. Now, under penalty of excommunication, the Pope warned James against war with England, though Henry made war against France, defeated a French army in Artois, and insolently reasserted the old discredited claim of the English throne to paramountcy over Scotland.

Pope Julius died, his Holy League collapsed. But in Edinburgh castle smiths were forging cannon, a small fleet of ships lay at Leith, and James was writing to Louis XII of France to ask for soldiers and guns. Between James and Nicholas West, Henry's ambassador, there was long and acrimonious discussion, but no agreement. West retired, and a French ambassador arrived. He would promise no help till the Scottish ships had joined the French in French waters. He wanted particularly to get possession of the *Michael;* for which Henry VIII had also asked. In France Louis begged a Scottish ambassador to persuade his King to invade England with the biggest army he could muster.

Henry VIII crossed over into France, to lead his army in person. He appointed the Earl of Surrey his lieutenant in the north, who at once made preparation for war. In Edinburgh old Bishop Elphinstone still prayed and argued for peace, but the Scottish fleet—fully armed and properly provisioned after long delay—set sail for France, and rash young men clamoured for the arbitrament of battle.

In July 1513 James sent his defiance to Henry in France, and in August rode on pilgrimage to the shrine of St. Duthac. About the same time the unwieldy artillery train put out from Edinburgh castle on its laborious journey—oxen hauling the gun carriages over unmade roads—

to the Border. The King came south again, and before the end of the month he and his army had crossed the Tweed. It was made known that the sons of all who died fighting would be exempt from the fines or "casualties" to which those who inherited property were normally subject; and James laid siege to Norham castle. It was stubbornly defended, but on the 28th August surrendered after six days of fighting. About three miles southwest of Norham the slow-running Till flows into the Tweed, and James, marching up its right bank, took the castles of Etal and Ford. He remained at Ford till the 4th September.

The weather was bad, his army had already suffered loss from sickness and desertion, after the prolonged siege of Norham he was short of ammunition, and some of his gun carriages had cast their wheels. He had made no attempt on Berwick, and his projected advance into England was checked by news that Surrey was already in the field. Surrey, an old man of seventy, was showing immense energy and total resolution. Under drenching skies he had pushed on through Durham to Newcastle, and on the 3rd September reached Alnwick in a gale of wind, where he was reinforced by a thousand soldiers and sailors whom his son, Lord Thomas Howard, Admiral of England, had brought from France. Surrey's whole army numbered about 20,000, against which James could probably show a small superiority.

Surrey was short of provisions—his soldiers complained bitterly that they had nothing to drink but water—and he was, perhaps, exasperated by the weather. He was determined to force a battle, but if the Scots withdrew behind the Tweed he might not be able to keep his army in being. He took advantage, therefore, of James's romantic temper and sent a herald to say he would be ready to fight by Friday, the 9th September; to that message the Admiral added his own contemptuous challenge. James imprudently replied that he would wait until noon on the 9th. He had, by then, crossed the Till from Ford and taken up a position on an easterly slope of Flodden Hill. It was a position of great natural strength, the only approach to which was covered by his guns. It was, in fact, so strong a position that Surrey refused to attack him there. He sent, instead, a further challenge, inviting James to come down to level ground and fight on a plain southeast of the hill.

James sensibly refused to move in obedience to Surrey's dictation, and Surrey, who had been advancing down the left bank of the Till, crossed over to the right with the intention of forcing him to do so. He intended to put his army between Flodden and the Border, and so cut

James's line of retreat. He marched as far as Barmoor Wood, northeast of Flodden, and made camp there. On the following morning his army crossed the Till again, the vanguard under the Admiral by Twizel Bridge not far from its junction with the Tweed, the remainder by a ford at Heton Mill, a mile or two upstream. The whole army swung left and began a four-mile march, facing south and the rain, over moors that rose to a height of 500 feet.

There has been argument about what happened when the armies came into contact—and how they made contact—and there is no Scottish account of the fighting. But about ten years ago there was published a life of James IV, a most scholarly and evocative work by R. L. Mackie, in which the author, drawing judiciously on several English sources, described the battle with such a knowledge of the ground on which it was fought, and with explanation so clear and reasonable, that his narrative seems wholly convincing.

Surrey's approach march was directed towards Branxton Hill, a mile and a half to the west of Flodden Hill. The approach was difficult, for under Branxton the Pallins Burn ran through a marsh which the rain had flooded, and only by Branx Bridge could his army cross to the high ridge beyond it. But if he reached the ridge while the Scots were still on Flodden Hill, James would find himself cut off from Scotland by an army established in a position as strong as his own. He was warned in time, however, and moving quickly beat Surrey in the race. There was dead ground between Flodden and Branxton, and the movement of the Scots was further concealed by the clouds of smoke that rose from the bonfires they made of the abandoned rubbish in their camp.

In five divisions they took position on the forward slope of Branxton Hill: Home of the Border and Huntly on the left; Crawford, Montrose, and Errol beside them; the King's division in the centre; Highlanders and men of the Isles on the right; and Bothwell in reserve. Advancing towards them, the English vanguard under the Admiral crossed the Pallins Burn, and as the smoke of the rubbish heaps cleared saw on the hillside the Scottish army disposed in close-ranked formations that bristled with their spears. The Scots were armed with swords and long, unwieldy, fourteen-foot spears; but the English carried bills, axe-bladed, of a shorter, handier length.

Hurriedly the Admiral sent back word to the main army, bidding his father make all possible haste, for he was heavily outnumbered; but

James II

James III and his son, afterwards James IV   Margaret of Denmark, Queen of Sco

Alexander,
Archbishop of St Andrews,
and bastard son of James IV

James IV

began his raign
1514 He maryed first
Magdelena dothier
of francis ye first
k of france

James V and his first Queen, Magdalene of France

he stood his ground and waited for the Scottish guns to fire. They fired indeed, but with no effect. It seems likely that the gunners could not depress their pieces far enough to hit an enemy two or three hundred feet below them, for their shot, flying overhead, did no hurt to the English. It was different, however, when Surrey, quickly arriving with the main army, brought up his artillery. His guns were lighter and more easily handled—perhaps more expertly handled—and their shot fell with fearful effect on the closely ranked squares of Scottish spearmen.

Rather than stand and be hammered, James gave the order to charge, and with that order no fault can be found. His fatal mistake was that he, in the midst of his soldiers, charged too, and left no one to order his battle. There was the failure that Ayala had seen in him: "He is not a good captain, because he begins to fight before he gives his orders."

To begin with, the Scots had the better of it. The English right quailed and fled. But the squares of spearmen, weakened by gunfire, lost cohesion as they charged downhill. The English bill proved a better weapon than the long-hafted spear. Both sides fought with implacable fury, and when the squares were broken the English bills—their broad axe-blades falling on spear and sword—made a fearful slaughter.

The battle began about four o'clock in the afternoon, and lasted till nightfall. Then, under cover of darkness, what remained of the Scottish army took to flight. Only on the left had the Earl of Home's division kept coherence and held its ground. He had beaten off a charge by English cavalry, and refused to attack again. "He does well that does for himself," he replied when asked for help. He has been blamed for his inaction, but he may have been justified in refusing to commit his men to a battle already lost.

Many Scots escaped pursuit because the English chose rather to plunder the riches they found on those who lay dead in what had been the King's division; and the English Borderers broke off to pillage the tents of their own army in Barmoor Wood. That night the victorious English lay without comfort in the wood, and in the morning the King's body was found under a heap of the slain. It was carried to Berwick and there identified. Fighting gallantly, he had died in the midst of battle, and the verdict on his bravery is that he had no right to be there.

In listening to Surrey's challenge, and accepting it, he behaved with lamentable irresponsibility. For the sake of a romantic gesture he threw away a strategic advantage, for when Surrey, in dreadful weather, was dangerously stretching his lines of communication, a strategic retreat would have served him well. He failed to take advantage of a tactical advantage when he surprised the Admiral's vanguard and by immediate attack might have overwhelmed it. And by adventuring his own body in the front of battle, he left his army without a commanding mind. *Dulce et decorum est pro patria mori*—but a King has other duties.

. Surrey's victory was complete. He had earned it by clever appreciation of James's personal weakness, by the marvellous energy of his advance, by daring and admirable generalship, and by the fortitude of his much-enduring soldiers. His army was in no condition to invade Scotland and occupy Edinburgh, but for that there was no need. In France Henry VIII had won another victory, and, on Branxton Hill, Surrey had crushed the menace of Scotland.

4

Foreign Interference

1

James IV, killed in battle, left as Scotland's King an infant barely eighteen months old. James V survived his childhood, but also died untimely. His heir was a girl born six days before her father's death. The consequence of such mortality was that for almost half a century—from Flodden in 1513 to the return from France of Mary, Queen of Scots, in 1561—Scotland was governed by regents except for the few years during which James V was able to impose his authority, and for most of that time the country was at the mercy of foreign influence. The periods of regency cannot be ignored, for they explain much, or nearly all, that happened when the throne was occupied again; but of what occurred during them only a skeleton will be shown here.

The English claimed to have slaughtered 12,000 Scots at Flodden, and though that estimate was probably exaggerated, the casualties were appalling. The King's son Alexander, Archbishop of St. Andrews, was killed, and with him two bishops, two abbots. Eleven earls and fifteen lords were killed, and among simpler folk there was so great a loss that to Selkirk, out of the many who had gone to join their King, only one returned; and other places suffered almost as sorely. But though Scotland was dismayed, it was not defeated. In Edinburgh the Burgh Council immediately put out orders that forbade wailing and mourning in the streets, and commanded all to look to their weapons and go about their work.

Margaret, the young Queen Mother, assumed the regency, assisted by Archbishop Beaton and the Earls of Huntly, Angus, and Arran.

Alexander Gordon, Earl of Huntly, was the most powerful of northern magnates; Angus was head of the "Red Douglases," and James Hamilton, Earl of Arran, was a grandson of James II. Angus and Arran were bitter enemies, and it was, perhaps, in the hope of preventing their open disagreement that an appeal for help was sent to John, Duke of Albany, a son of Alexander, James III's dishonoured and exiled brother. Albany, who had been brought up as a Frenchman, became heir presumptive after the death of the posthumous child to whom Margaret gave birth in April 1514. Margaret, who was only twenty-four, introduced a new complication when she married Angus, the Red Douglas, and thereby forfeited her authority as regent or "tutrix" of the infant King. The Council repeated its invitation to Albany, and he, who spoke no English, "came home" as Governor of the realm. He, a near-royal Stewart, was to show himself the most altruistic, the least self-seeking of men. Though intermittently involved in Scottish affairs for the next ten years he took no advantage of his nearness to the throne to promote his own interests.

His return to Scotland exasperated Henry VIII, who saw in him a potential hindrance to England's hope of establishing a balance of authority between the great powers of France and Spain. France, having grown vastly in strength, was faced—or circumscribed—by the phenomenal growth of Spain. Both sought England's friendship, or neutrality, and Spain won favour first: Henry, at that time, was married to Katharine of Aragon, his brother's widow. But France, in 1515, accepted a treaty, of policy rather than intention, that promised protection to England, none to Scotland, against Border forays; and two years later, when Albany returned to France, he signed the treaty of Rouen by which France and Scotland pledged mutual aid should England attack either party. But Albany, who had meant to stay in France for a few months only, had to remain for four years, and there can be no doubt that Henry insisted on his detention as a preliminary condition for the Anglo-French agreement of 1518.

Henry's interference was unfortunate for Scotland. Albany, as Governor, had shown himself to be strong, shrewd, and tolerant. He had suppressed a dangerous threat of rebellion by executing its leader, Lord Home, and in his absence there was no one to check the lordly dissidence of the Douglases and the Hamiltons. It erupted, at last, in Edinburgh itself, where in headlong conflict the Douglases and their Border allies met the Hamiltons and their episcopal friend Archbishop

Beaton, who wore armour for the occasion. From that shameful battle, long remembered as "Cleanse the Causeway," the Douglases emerged victorious.

Albany returned to Scotland in 1521, and was quickly drawn into one of the eddies of European politics. After brief friendship with Francis I, King of France—a friendship ostentatiously proclaimed at that scene of pompous folly, the Field of the Cloth of Gold—Henry VIII had engaged in conversation with France's rival, Charles V of Spain and the Empire, and formally decided on alliance with him. Thereupon France made new offers of friendship and assistance to Scotland, and Albany twice attempted, with no success, to invade and punish the north of England. On the second occasion he had behind him a considerable French army—as many, perhaps, as 4000 infantry, with cavalry, guns, money, and supplies—but in Scotland there was no enthusiasm for war. Flodden was too recent a memory, and enthusiasm for the Auld Alliance had waned. It was, quite obviously, a luxury which Scotland could ill afford, and there were those who had begun to think that friendship with England might be more rewarding.

The French troops went home again, and in 1524 Albany went too. A year later Francis I, badly beaten by the Imperial forces, was made prisoner at the great battle of Pavia, and such was France's discomfiture that England, to maintain an approximate balance of power, must go to its aid. An Anglo-French treaty was signed, and as the French lost interest in Scotland a pro-English party began to emerge.

Its leaders were Arran and the Queen Mother. She had divorced the Earl of Angus who, after "Cleanse the Causeway," had fled to France.—Arran had stayed in Scotland and retained his power.—A ceremony was devised for the "erection" of the King, now aged twelve, and he was invested with crown, sword, and sceptre. His uncle of England gave him a bodyguard of two hundred men, and parliament, agreeable to this new policy, restored Angus to his lands and dignities. He too was of the English party, and did it no good. The Queen Mother, perhaps tired of politics, married the inconspicuous Henry Stewart, sometime Lord Methven.

Parliament decided that custody of the King should be the responsibility, in turn, of the principal nobles and prelates; but when it came to Angus's turn he would not let the boy go again. Parliament admitted its impotence. Authority, said parliament, resided in the royal hand; which Angus, the Red Douglas, firmly held. He gave great offices to his own kinsmen, he grew in strength and arrogance. His enemies, however, grew in numbers, and several attempts were made to release the King. But all were defeated, and the power of Douglas seemed unassailable until the King himself broke it. He escaped from durance and rode to Stirling castle, where his mother lived.

Many great nobles came at once to his support. The Earls of Argyll, Rothes, and Eglinton declared their loyalty. From the Border came Home, Bothwell, and Maxwell; Moray and Keith rode down from the north. Arran, again humiliated by Angus, had lately pretended friendship with his old enemy, but he too joined the King's party. Angus, summoned for treason, was put to the horn but shut himself up in his strong castle of Tantallon, and for three weeks defied the royalists. Then a bargain was made. The Douglases surrendered their castles and were allowed to retire to England. At the age of sixteen James V was King in his own realm.

2

History preserves contradictory views of James's character. The popular, more agreeable portrait hangs, as if on a nail, from his nickname, the Goodman of Ballengiech: the tenant, that is, of Ballengiech, a steep pass leading down from the Castle Rock of Stirling. Walter Scott says that he "had a custom of going about the country disguised as a private person, in order that he might hear complaints which might not otherwise reach his ears"; and then discreetly adds, "and, perhaps, that he might enjoy amusements which he could not have partaken of in his avowed royal character." Scott relates several anecdotes in which James appears to be a kindly, genial man, capable of humour and easy in his manner. Some may be apocryphal and yet reflect general opinion.

John Hill Burton, a much respected historian of the Nineteenth Century, says "he was affectionately remembered by his people as 'the King of the Commons,' and tradition mixed him up with many tales of adventure among the peasantry, who not less enjoyed their memory that they were not always creditable to him." To poor people, it seems, he could be kind and openhanded when his sympathy was roused; in a record of royal expenditure Burton found many instances of his easy though limited generosity.

On the other hand, a modern historian* and scrupulous scholar draws attention to the greed which increasingly discoloured his reign—though he died young—and writes, without apparent scepticism, that "his personal fortune was reputed to be 300,000 *livres.*" Professor Donaldson, indeed, cannot regard James without revulsion, and declares: "The vindictiveness which made his later years something of a reign of terror went so far beyond what was politic that it suggests a streak of sadistic cruelty in his nature." He quotes, however, John Lesley, a near-contemporary, whose opinion was that James earned popular goodwill because his people "lived quietly and in rest, out of all oppressioun and molestacioun of the nobility and rich persones."—Did James, then, oppress and molest his nobility, not merely for his own enrichment, but to prevent them from oppressing and molesting the common people? He was no ordinary man, for he died in the robustness of his early manhood of no discernible cause, without any symptom of bodily disease; and his life may have had motives as deeply hidden as the vital failure which ended it.

There is, however, another explanation or excuse for his rapacity, which—if acceptable—has the advantage of simplicity. When James, at the age of sixteen, became King in reality, it must have seemed to him that the very foundation of sovereignty reposed on possession of wealth: on possession of money in such quantities as would enable a sovereign to purchase the power necessary to him. He and his councillors had to face, as their first and major problem, the lack of money. There was no general and effective system of taxation, the value of money was falling—crown rents had fallen steeply—and both Albany and the Queen Mother had been extravagant. There was, however, a source of revenue—almost comparable with the discovery of oil wells in the modern world—which a revolution in thought—no less productive than the revolutions of modern technology—had lately uncovered.

The Church was immensely rich, and throughout Europe the Church had suddenly become vulnerable. In 1520 Martin Luther had published three treatises which contained the thesis and proclaimed the case for reformation, and as Luther's teaching quickly spread, the old order was threatened and Rome began to feel the need of allies. Rome, moreover, was prepared to subsidise its allies, and when Pope Clement VII and his Church in Scotland gave timely help to James, he may have been fortified in the juvenile certainty of his belief that all prob-

* Gordon Donaldson: *Scotland, James V to James VII.*

lems could be solved by money. Then he saw the prospect of marriage to a wife who would bring him a handsome dowry, and that was not only a further comfort, but additional proof of his belief. In the meantime, however, the young King was compelled to deal with other matters, almost as troublesome as poverty, and to Scotland as native as poverty.

The people of the Border were as unruly as the Highlanders, but could justify their way of life as offering some defence against English aggression. To provide themselves with necessities they raided, without prejudice, on either side of the Border, but though unable to withstand an attack in force from the south, they created a picket line which could give warning of aggression, and which cost the Crown nothing. Their high temper, however, might provoke English retaliation when the King and his Council wanted peace, and they were sometimes guilty of intrigue with their southern neighbours. In 1529 and 1530 James—a robust, precocious young man, resolute beyond his years—found some occasion for displeasure, and rode south to assert his authority over the debatable lands, and over loyalties that may have been open to question.

With singular audacity he seized and temporarily imprisoned the greatest of the Border lords—the Earl of Bothwell, Lords Home and Maxwell, a Johnston, a Scott of Buccleugh—and then, in implacable pursuit of justice as he saw it, sent his summons to Johnie Armstrong of Gilnockie. Armstrong was not a man of noble rank, but in his own neighbourhood may well have enjoyed a greater popular fame than Bothwell or Home. He was a freebooter, a Border reiver of proved ability. The Red Douglas had tried again and again to take him captive, and had always been defeated or eluded. Men greater than he were his friends, and he was suspected of having given shelter to fugitives from English justice. He had enjoyed his power, and boasted of it. He was, in all probability, a public nuisance, but he had a quality, an individuality, which won him the immortality of a ballad in which he is the hero, and James his false friend.

> "The King he wrytes a luving letter,
> With his ain hand sae tenderly,
> And he hath sent it to Johnie Armstrang,
> To cum and speik with him speedily"—

so says the ballad, and continues:

> "When Johnie cam' before the King,
>   Wi' a' his men sae brave to see,
> The King he movit his bonnet to him,
>   He ween'd he was King as weel as he.
>
> 'May I find grace, my sovereign liege,
>   Grace for my loyal men and me?
> For my name it is Johnie Armstrang,
>   And a subject of yours, my liege,' said he."

But to Johnie the King replies:

> "Away, away, thou traitor strang!
>   Out o' my sight soon mayst thou be!
> I grantit never a traitor's life,
>   And now I'll not begin wi' thee."

Johnie argues, tries to melt the King's heart with gifts, but James is obdurate; and Johnie, still bitterly resenting the charge of treachery, makes a spirited declaration of the Borderers' creed:

> "'Ye lied, ye lied, now, King,' he says,
>   'Altho' a King and Prince ye be!
> For I've luved naething in my life,
>   I weel dare say it, but honesty:
>
> 'Save a fat horse, and a fair woman,
>   Twa bonny dogs to kill a deir;
> But England suld have found me meal and mault,
>   Gif I had lived this hundred yeir!
>
> 'She suld have found me meal and mault,
>   And beef and mutton in a' plentie;
> But never a Scots wyfe could have said
>   That e'er I skaith'd her a puir flee.
>
> 'To seik het water beneith cauld ice,
>   Surely it is a greit folie—
> I have asked grace at a graceless face,
>   But there is nane for my men and me.'"

He had come in state, apparently unaware of the King's anger, and possibly believing, not in his own innocence, but his own virtue. The young King, however, knew more about Johnie than history has preserved, and insisted that justice be done. So Johnie, and the twenty-four bold moss-troopers who had ridden with him, were seized and hanged from the nearest trees. It was ruthless punishment for unrecorded offences, but there is no evidence that James had written "a luving letter," and the brutality of his justice was effective. The Borderers, shocked and stunned, acknowledged their master.

In the Highlands and the Western Isles there was disorder after the death of the 3rd Earl of Argyll, who had dominated his own and nearby lands, and the southern Isles. The excessive power of the Campbells had antagonised the lesser clans, and Lachlan of Duart, chief of the MacLeans, who had married a daughter of the 2nd Earl, created an unusual scandal by depositing her on a half-tide rock when he grew tired of her. She was rescued, and her brother, who had married a northern heiress, avenged her disgrace by murdering Lachlan in his bed. The 4th Earl of Argyll claimed to have experience in "daunting" the Isles, but the lieutenancy for which he asked was given to Macdonald of Islay, and James himself showed such energy in displaying his own authority that the daunted Hebrideans lived quietly for several years.

Not until 1539 was there any trouble of a serious kind. Then there was revolt in Skye. Its leader, Donald Gorm of Sleat, was killed under the walls of Eilean Donan, a castle rising from a finger of land thrust into the waters of dark Loch Duich; but the menace of rebellion seemingly persisted, for James decided to circumnavigate his kingdom and visit all its island parts.

Twelve ships were armed and provisioned for the voyage, on which Cardinal Beaton, Archbishop of St. Andrews, and the Earls of Huntly and Arran accompanied their King. The fleet put out from Leith, and sailed to Orkney where James's new favourite, Oliver Sinclair, was installed as sheriff and tacksman. Kirkwall, the little capital of Orkney, presented an appearance of dignity, strength, and opulence that gave it a distinction unique in the north. The great Romanesque cathedral of St. Magnus dominated the town, beside it rose the tower of the Bishop's palace, and a castle of exceptional strength protected shipping in the bay and the well-built houses of church dignitaries. By a lady called Euphemia Elphinstone James had an illegitimate son, Robert, who in the course of time would enrich himself with the wealth that his father now saw, and ruin the islands which produced it; but as yet Robert was only three years old.

James left a garrison in Kirkwall, and his fleet sailed westward round Cape Wrath to the Hebrides: to the Outer Isles, to Skye and nearby parts of the mainland, to Mull, Coll, and Tiree, to Arran and Bute in the Firth of Clyde—and where he found disaffection he took into custody the chiefs who were thought to have fomented it. Into the royal bag went Donald Mackay of Strathnaver, Roderick MacLeod of Lewis and some of his kinsmen, Alexander MacLeod of Dunvegan, the Captain of Clanranald, Alexander MacDonald of Glengarry and others of his clan, John Mackenzie of Kintail—the mountainous land above Loch Duich—Hector MacLean of Duart, James MacConnel of Islay; and after their removal it was said that the Isles were so marvellously peaceful that the King was able to collect his rents.

That memorable voyage was undertaken in 1540: nine years after Pope Clement VII—and more materially the Church in Scotland—had rescued James from the poverty he inherited. A profitable marriage had then seemed his likeliest remedy, and in the early 1530s he was earnestly in quest of a rich wife. Albany, Scotland's faithful agent on the continent, suggested that his niece Catherine de Medici might be available, but the Pope was unwilling to countenance the marriage, and Henry VIII objected to it. Francis I had given initial approval, but Henry persuaded him that Catherine and her dowry were better suited for a French prince, and a disappointed Scottish emissary sought an alternative bride among the dependents of Charles V. He failed to find one. But the Emperor seemed well disposed to James, and the Pope, who was subject to imperial influence, was unwilling to alienate a Scottish King who might be helpful in a contest for power between Rome and the Reformation.

Out of this network of diplomatic purpose and personal ambition there emerged a welcome surprise, of which Albany was the progenitor. To the Scottish prelates Pope Clement sent his recommendation for an annual tax on Church property of £10,000, for defence of the realm, and in addition to that he imposed, for a period of three years, a levy of one tenth of their income for the protection of Scottish interests. To justify the tax it was proposed that a College of Justice should be established, and in 1531 a papal bull authorised both the College—half of its members were to be churchmen—and its endowment. The prelates offered a compromise, but were slow to pay the agreed composition of £72,000 in four instalments; and not until 1541 did parliament ratify the agreement and dignify members of the College as "senators." The judges were underpaid, and the College, when it came into being, was not a very conspicuous addition to the legal apparatus of the country. It inaugurated, however, the usage of today, by which judges of the Supreme Court are called Senators of the College of Justice.

There remained, as an economic and national necessity, the provision of a suitable wife for James, and it is curious to find him, a minor figure on the European stage, at the centre of political matchmaking. As if to advertise his eligibility, James was given the Order of the Garter by Henry VIII; the Order of the Golden Fleece by Charles V; and by Francis I the Order of St. Michael. In his infancy he had been promised a daughter of Francis, but that promise was forgotten. Henry's daughter Mary was considered, and princesses of Denmark and Portugal were offered, on approval, by the Emperor. Henry advised his nephew to break with Rome, but James wanted a French bride, and appeared to have found one when the Duke of Vendome offered his daughter with a dowry of 100,000 crowns. James, having seen her portrait, asked for a pension as well, and the privilege of free trade for Scottish merchants in certain French ports. His conditions were accepted, James put to sea, and after a stormy voyage landed in Dieppe. But when he saw his intended bride he broke off the match.

He preferred Madeleine, the King's daughter. She, more than once, had been talked of as a possible consort, but she was delicate and her father was unwilling to let her go abroad. John Hill Burton, in the massive history he wrote a hundred years ago, abandoned Victorian sobriety to write: "She was brilliant to behold, in the hectic beauty of fatal consumption"—and it seems undeniable that James fell suddenly in love with her, for he married her with a dowry of 100,000 *livres* and the rent on 125,000: which was less than half of the Duke of Vendome's proffered *dot*.

They were married on New Year's Day, and sailed for Scotland in mid-May. But Madeleine died in early July, leaving as a fatal gift to her widower a love of France, or French women, that her consumptive beauty may have bequeathed. In search of a second wife, he remembered Mary of Guise-Lorraine, whose first husband, the Duke of Longueville, had providentially died a month before Madeleine. Henry.

VIII was a rival for her hand—he, having divorced Katharine of Aragon, beheaded Anne Boleyn, and survived the death of Jane Seymour, was again a widower—but James was preferred, and in June 1538, Mary of Guise-Lorraine came to Crail in Fife with a dowry of 150,000 *livres*. She was, moreover, a great beauty, with eyes lifted by arched and lofty brows to a gaze of marvellous candour—perceptive and perhaps incredulous eyes—and her chin pointed in most delicate aggression under a reticent and pretty mouth. After her husband's death she would show that her character, not always agreeable to her Scottish neighbours, was as firmly chiselled as her beauty, and more stubborn than her chin.

The dowries that his French wives brought him did not satisfy James's cupidity, and interlined with the record of his assiduous respect for justice, of his stern repression of the criminous, there are reports of unrelenting animosity to some of his nobles that seem evidence, not so much of a regard for law, as of rapacity and a black insistence on revenge. It was natural enough for him to cherish hatred of the Earl of Angus and his Douglas kin, who had held him captive when he was a boy; but it was perversely unnatural to pursue with his hatred some whose crimes appear to have been little more than some association with Angus. The Master of Forbes was the Red Douglas's brother-in-law, and he was charged with "a design to shoot the King with a culverin as he passed through Aberdeen." No evidence remains of any plot to murder the King, but the Master was found guilty and executed. The Lady Glamis was a sister of Angus, and she, after surviving an accusation of having poisoned her husband, was condemned, and burnt to death, for conspiring to poison the King. Was she more guilty than James Douglas of Parkhead, accused of treason? Was either guilty of anything more serious than incurring the King's dislike?

Others than Douglases suffered, and he acted with insensate greed in despoiling the Earls of Buchan and Morton, the young Earl of Crawford, a Scott of Branxholm, a Colquhoun of Luss, a Colville of East Wemyss, and others. The lands he took and the fines he exacted added to his wealth—and gratified, perhaps, an acquisitive temper he may have inherited from his Tudor mother—but his avarice made enemies when he needed friends.

For support, the King depended on his clergy, and the clergy packed his Council. Threatened by heretics and Reformers, the Church could be relied on to succour a monarch who had shown his loyalty to Rome

—but who, if succour failed, might be tempted to follow the malignant example of his royal uncle in England. Cardinal Beaton was his faithful friend, and those among his nobles who were strongly attached to the old faith were thereby attached to him. The Church, indeed, extended its beneficence beyond James himself, for in its rich abbeys and priories he found a welcome source of revenue for the clutch of bastards he had fathered. A son by Elizabeth Shaw of Sauchie became Abbot of Kelso and Melrose; Robert, the son of Euphemia Elphinstone, was the Prior of Holyrood before he became Earl of Orkney; John, Prior of Coldingham, was the son of Elizabeth Carmichael; and Adam, Prior of the Carthusians at Perth, was the son of Elizabeth Stewart, a daughter of the Earl of Lennox.

Others of his illegitimate flock were comfortably provided for, but tragedy darkened his married life. Mary of Lorraine had borne him two sons, and within a few days of each other, both died in 1541. The kingdom was left without an heir. But James had not oppressed and impoverished it by his exactions—he had oppressed his nobility, he had wrung a handsome income from the Church—and many of his subjects had still a warm affection for him: to a majority, perhaps, he remained "the Goodman of Ballengiech." In 1541, when he and his Queen made a progress to the north, they were given enthusiastic welcome in Perth and Aberdeen and Dundee. In Aberdeen they stayed for fifteen days, and the university that Bishop Elphinstone had founded paraded its learning for their benefit. They were entertained with plays and rhetoric and loyal addresses "in Greek and Latin and other languages."

Nor should it be forgotten that James encouraged and applauded Sir David Lindsay of the Mount, a poet remarkable for the freedom of his language. At Linlithgow in 1540 James and his Queen attended a performance of Lindsay's ribald and abusive satire on *The Three Estates.* The Church was ridiculed, and James himself rebuked for sensuality; but he did not take offence. Perversely biassed he often was; but also he could be tolerant. Like some of his predecessors he found pleasure in good architecture, and it was said that he cared little about the character of his architects if their work was aesthetically pleasing. The royal palaces of Holyrood, Stirling, Falkland, and Linlithgow were all decorated and improved by his appreciation of the new fashions of the Renaissance.

In lack of judgment—of politic good sense—he exceeded his father.

By his marriage to Mary of Lorraine he had angered Henry VIII, but Henry, alarmed by Catholic menace and the growing friendship—or so it seemed—of Charles V and Francis I, made friendly overtures to James; and James, persuaded by the foolish advice of his clergy and his own incapacity, rejected them.

Cardinal Beaton was in France, and James was without his counsel when Henry proposed a meeting at York in September 1541. James accepted his uncle's invitation, and Henry, for the first time in his life, paid a visit to the northern part of his kingdom. But James was not there to welcome him. Perhaps he was afraid of being kidnapped. His clergy, undoubtedly, feared the possibility that Henry might persuade him to share England's rejection of Roman authority. So James was persuaded or constrained to remain in Scotland, and his uncle, that portly and choleric man, was infuriated by the insult to his dignity and the tedium of a long journey that had brought no profit.

He took his revenge, or tried to, in the late summer of 1542. Without the usual civility of declaring a state of war, his troops crossed the Border and were resoundingly defeated at Hadden Rig, near Berwick. Among the several hundred prisoners taken was Sir Robert Bowes, who commanded the foray, but in spite of such abundant evidence of the origin of assault, Henry denounced the Scots as the aggressors, and reinforcing his offensive by new attack, burnt Roxburgh and Kelso. The Border towns had suffered such reprisal in the past, and England gained nothing by its depredations.

But when Scotland retaliated, Scotland gained less. Scotland, indeed, was utterly humiliated. James mustered an army that refused to do his bidding because his nobles would not take part in a war that, as they thought, was being waged on behalf of France. He gathered another force, with Cardinal Beaton's help, and promoted to its command his much favoured Oliver Sinclair—of an old and highly respected family in the north—whom he had previously made his sheriff and tacksman in Orkney. They marched on the western route to England, and were broken, as it seems, by failure of three sorts. The army marched in two divisions, and there was no communication between them; Sinclair's division refused to accept his command; and among the Liddesdale men there was active disaffection.

The King advanced to Lochmaben, at the innermost end of the Solway Firth, and waited till the tide should ebb and let him cross. Sinclair, moving south from Langholm, was halted at Solway Moss, not far away, by Sir Thomas Wharton, the English Warden of the Western March; and Sinclair's division declined the offered battle. Who led the rout is not known, but the Liddesdale men seem to have given active help to the English, who took 1200 prisoners as if they had been rounding-up cattle. Having alienated his nobility, the Goodman of Ballengiech had also lost the trust and affection of his people.

He retired to Linlithgow, where on the 8th December his Queen gave birth to a daughter. But James again retreated, to his favourite palace of Falkland, and died there six days later. He was a young man, not yet thirty-one, sturdily built and capable of great exertion. But he died of no apparent cause except despair. The birth of a daughter gave him no comfort. He remembered the lamentable death of Marjorie Bruce in 1316, who fell from a horse and gave premature birth to the infant who became the first of the Stewart kings. "It cam' wi' a lass, it will pass wi' a lass," he said; and turning his face to the wall, died.

Defeat at Solway Moss was unalleviated humiliation, but nowhere near so great a calamity as Flodden. Yet Solway Moss, apparently, was the cause of James's death. According to John Knox, whose history is not always to be trusted, he was stricken with "suddane fear and astonishment." Pitscottie says he was put "in despair that he could nevir recover his honour agane." Sir George Douglas was of the opinion that "the Scotis Kyng ys richt feryd for losying of his hale realme. He is so abbayshid that he can not perfytly determine what he should do."

There was no evidence of disease, no rumour of poison. Was it, then, a psychosomatic collapse that precipitated death? If that were so, the compulsive sense of failure in James's psyche had an influence on his somatic parts of a sort rarely suspected since the heyday of Victorian romanticism; when, in popular novels, it was the common fate of young women, crossed in love, to die of a broken heart.

3

Foreign interference at once intruded upon the affairs of the stricken kingdom, and for almost a score of years Scotland was a battlefield on which France and England engaged in a bitter and destructive conflict that was aggravated by the new demands and new emotions which Luther's Reformation had created or released. Misfortune was no stranger in Scotland, but the misfortunes it suffered in the middle years of the Sixteenth Century must have been exacerbated by a sense of total impotence. Scotland could neither win nor lose nor declare its neutrality. Its grim and bloody fate was to be a field on which others fought for their own purpose.

To begin with, England appeared helpful and magnanimous. Henry VIII was the nearest male kinsman of the week-old child who was the heir to James V and his disordered realm, and Henry had a son, Edward, aged five. What Henry proposed was a treaty of peace and the eventual marriage of Prince Edward and the infant, called Mary, who lay in her cradle at Linlithgow. It was an admirable idea, but Henry ruined any hope of its realisation by an insensate display of arrogance and cupidity. He demanded custody of the infant Queen, proclaimed himself as her successor, and behaved as if Scotland were already a subject land. The natural, the inevitable consequence was that Scotland renewed its alliance with France.

There was, however, no unity in Scotland. The Queen Mother and David Beaton, Cardinal Archbishop of St. Andrews, were consistent Francophiles, but the nobility was divided and there were those who had a habit of changing sides in response to seeming advantage. Henry of England had his friends in Scotland, but they were not strong enough to impose his will. Only by invasion and conquest could he achieve his purpose, and the instructions that his Privy Council sent to the Earl of Hertford—commander of the army of invasion—were explicit and ferocious. Hertford's mission was not merely to conquer, but to destroy.

The Scots were taken by surprise, Hertford landed in the Firth of Forth and burnt Leith, Holyrood, and Edinburgh. Another army burnt Jedburgh and its great abbey. French intervention was ineffective, and in renewed assault on the Border Hertford burnt the abbeys of Kelso, Dryburgh, Roxburgh, and Coldingham, as well as the year's harvest. "Henry's rough wooing"—so its victims called it—was abetted by some Highland clans who had accepted an English subsidy, and in the following year the scene was complicated by the execution, at St. Andrews, of George Wishart. He was a popular preacher, probably an English agent, and his crime was heresy. A few weeks later a band of men broke into the castle of St. Andrews, advised the Cardinal Archbishop to repent of Wishart's death, and murdered him.

Joined by numerous sympathisers, among whom was a priest called John Knox, Beaton's murderers held the castle against an ineffective siege. Henry VIII died in January 1547, but England's policy did not change, and the besieged were promised help. France moved first however, and a French fleet battered the castle into submission. English retaliation followed.

Edward VI was a boy of ten, and the Protector of his realm was the ruthless Hertford, now advanced to the dukedom of Somerset. Again he invaded, and defeated the Scots at the battle of Pinkie, near Edinburgh. The Scots appealed to France for help, and the French price for an army of 6000 men was the child Queen: Mary must be sent to France and married to the Dauphin. Francis I had been succeeded by Henri II, who was as exigent as Henry VIII of England. The English withdrew from Scotland, but the French garrisons were reinforced, and Henri II declared that "France and Scotland are one country."

Now the Reformers emerged as the patriotic party. Against English aggression the Auld Alliance and the Church of Rome had been the bulwarks, but bulwarks were now needed against French ambition, and the Reformers, opportunely discovering divine sanction for their cause, called themselves the Army of the Congregation of Christ.

In a land seething with discontent, Mary of Lorraine maintained an unpopular cause and her position as regent with varying authority. She was materially assisted by the early death of Edward VI, for he was succeeded by his half sister Mary, a devout Catholic who married Philip II of Spain. Her succession deprived the Congregation of Christ of their Protestant ally, and when the English began to burn heretics at Smithfield, English Protestants fled into Scotland to find refuge under its Catholic regent and her French advisers. Mary of Lorraine could afford to be tolerant, and won favour by her liberality.

The Reformers grew in strength, however, and were determined to establish a Protestant church. Mary Tudor died childless in 1558 and was succeeded by her half-sister Elizabeth, unmarried at the age of twenty-five, and illegitimate in the eyes of Rome and the great continental powers, which had never admitted the validity of Henry VIII's divorce from Katharine of Aragon. According to Catholic opinion the rightful Queen of England was Mary, Queen of Scots, the granddaughter of James IV and Margaret Tudor, sister to Henry VIII; and a few weeks after Elizabeth's succession Mary and her husband the Dauphin assumed the arms of sovereigns of England. Again a Protestant country, England stood defiantly isolated from Catholic Europe, and for her security Elizabeth could depend only on her Englishmen and the Protestant groups in Scotland. The Reformation was essential to the safety of England and its Queen, and its success was thereby assured.

France and Spain made peace, and showed a common front against heresy. In Scotland Mary of Lorraine grew tired of politic toleration, and Protestant preachers were threatened with expulsion. But John Knox was now a force in the land, and his rabble-rousing sermons brought the Reformation to life as rebellion. Scotland again became a battlefield where French and English fought against each other. But now the English were successful, and by the treaty of Edinburgh Elizabeth and the Congregation of Christ were proclaimed the victors.

Both armies withdrew from Scotland, and the Reformers' Confession of Faith became the law of the land. The authority and jurisdiction of the Pope were abolished; the sacraments were reduced to baptism and the eucharist; the celebration of mass was forbidden; and whatever the Confession of Faith did not approve, was condemned. The new Kirk of Scotland, indeed, arrogated to itself an authority independent of, and superior to the conventional authority of the state.

Mary of Lorraine had died, in Edinburgh castle, just in time to escape the humiliation of so resounding a defeat.

5

The French Widow

1

Too much, and much too much, has been written about Mary, Queen of Scots, and the only excuse for writing more is that mischievous propaganda, painstakingly confected by her political enemies, has been, and still is, widely accepted as a true account of her deeds and character.

Her enemies were rebel subjects whose reputation and defence in law depended on their ability to exculpate themselves by inculpating their Queen. In their own time they had the advantage of being able to pose as champions of the Reformation, leaders of the Congregation of Christ against the impious Church of Rome, to which Mary belonged; and posterity has been inclined to accept as true their case against Mary because it became the official case—or "history"—when Presbyterianism was finally established as the ruling faith and practice in Scotland. Its acceptance was facilitated, moreover, by a human tendency to prefer a good story—a dramatic, strongly emotional story—to a narrative dominated by dynastic purpose of a sort unknown to the majority of people, and unrelated to their lives.

To repair a popular error and alter cherished opinions may be impossible, but the following account is written in an attempt to show such an approximation to truth as the available evidence can furnish, and to expose some obvious falsities in the propaganda designed to blacken Mary's character.

She was a young woman so attractive that in her life she enlisted the devotion of many who knew her. By the tragedy of her life she has retained the interest of a multitude of people who have found a pleasure—that may be thought perverse—in their ability to condemn a woman of such manifest distinction. That she was a reigning queen has exalted her tragedy, aggravated her supposed guilt, and enhanced the luxury of blaming her.

Suspected of complicity in the murder of her husband, she committed the unforgiven error of marrying the man who, among several suspects, most certainly played an active part in that murder. The great majority of human beings have known fear as one of the commonest emotions, but few have been willing to believe that Mary married Bothwell in fear of her life, because fear is a shabby motive and cannot compete, for a reader's interest, with guilty love, a preposterous and overwhelming passion. As the subject of a story, a young and gracious, guilty and submissive queen—her pride cast out by lust—is clearly a more popular attraction than a woman, playing at politics for high stakes, whose purpose, at a critical moment, is defeated because she succumbs to the shabbiness of fear. Yet all the evidence points to the fact that she did succumb to fear, and none of the evidence can substantiate the pretence that her life was ever shaped or dominated by sexual passion.

The story of Mary's life, from the time when she was sent into France to satisfy a political demand, till that later time when she fled to a delusive refuge in England, will be briefly told: with no more detail, that is, than is necessary to make the story clear. But of the documents by which her supposed guilt was propagated, the most important will be examined with a little more care than is customary in a short and general narrative of her reign.

2

Born at Linlithgow in early December 1542, Mary's childhood was harassed by English aggression, or the fear of it, and when it became necessary to appeal to France for help, she was the price that had to be paid. Politics, and the admitted supremacy of politics, dominated her life from infancy: she was only six years old when the Three Estates of the realm agreed to the French proposal for her marriage, at a proper age, to the Dauphin, son of Henri II and Catherine de Medici, and in July 1548, she put to sea with a suitable complement and four companions of her own age—Mary Fleming, Mary Livingstone, Mary Beaton, and Mary Seton—who were to become, and remain, her loving and devoted friends until tragedy invaded and scattered their friendship. They landed near Brest after a ten days' voyage, and by her new neighbours the charm of the little Queen was immediately recognised: "She has only to smile to turn all French heads," said her prospective mother-in-law.

She was educated in a manner becoming to the designated Queen of France, and carefully trained to virtuous habits, fear of God, and devotion to the Church of Rome. She was married to the Dauphin at the age of sixteen, and after marriage she was much influenced by her austere and pious grandmother, Antoinette de Bourbon, and her uncle —the dominating spirit in the house of Guise—the Cardinal of Lorraine. It was he, presumably, who persuaded her to sign a secret document by which, should she die childless, she bequeathed to France her kingdom of Scotland and the title to England which she claimed. It seems likely that the health of her husband precluded the possibility of children, and by her uncle—a prince of the Church to which she was devoted—Mary was again made aware of the fact that politics ruled the lives of all who were born to bear the burden of a crown. But the crown of France was no burden: she wore it too short a time. Her puny little husband—a sickly boy, a year younger than she—succeeded to the throne in 1559 and died, apparently of a mastoid abscess, before the end of 1560.

For a year and a half Mary was Queen of France, courted, flattered, her poetry praised by scholars, her wit extolled by courtiers, and the grace of her dancing acclaimed by all. It was poor preparation for the harshness and hostility that awaited her in her own kingdom of Scotland.

During her absence abroad the new doctrines which assailed the authority of Rome had been widely accepted, and the Reformation of 1560 had demolished the Church which for centuries had assumed the spiritual direction of Scotland and lived richly as its largest landowner. Cupidity as well as Protestant zeal had persuaded many of the nobles to accept a new order which assumed the right to redistribute the Church's property, and their leader was the Lord James, the Queen's half-brother. He, a son of James V and Margaret Erskine, was about ten years older than Mary, a man of considerable ability who was endowed with sufficient patience to let his ability be quietly used until he should see opportunity to use it for his own advantage. Second to him, in political importance, was William Maitland of Lethington, a more interesting man, who could, perhaps, be called an intellectual. He was set apart from the enthusiastic Reformers by his lack of zeal, by his dislike of ecclesiastical interference in affairs of state, and by his manifest belief that moral considerations must always be subject to pragmatism.

More conspicuous than they, however, was the remarkable figure of John Knox. Iconoclast-in-chief, demagogue, God-intoxicated, it was Knox who was mainly responsible for the Reformers' sudden, dramatic achievement. The Calvinism he had learnt in Switzerland was fortified by the temper of an Old Testament prophet, an instant faculty for turning argument into drama, and a political sense which could always mute a histrionic instinct and allow expediency to moderate fanaticism. Noisily he had asserted that the celebration of Mass could not be permitted in Protestant Scotland; but sensibly he ignored a public statement, designed to win popular approval, and more discreetly accepted the fact that a Catholic Queen must be allowed to admit her belief and follow the practice of her own religion.

Popular hostility to it was brutally apparent on Mary's arrival in Edinburgh, and the natural difficulties of a young woman who was so manifestly a French widow—but less obviously a Scottish Queen—were aggravated by her relations with England and her cousin Elizabeth. In Paris, after the death of Mary Tudor, Mary Stuart had been proclaimed Queen of England and Ireland, and though in 1560 the treaty of Edinburgh pledged her renunciation of that claim, she had refused to ratify the treaty. Mary was debarred from succession to the English throne by the will of her great-uncle, Henry VIII; but in Catholic opinion Elizabeth was debarred by bastardy.

Elizabeth, whose strength was rooted in the Protestantism established by her father, had no interest in ecclesiastical debate, and refused to recognise Mary as her heir. Mary, on the other hand, never renounced her claim to the succession. Elizabeth retained her predecessors' stubborn belief that England had a natural right to shape or restrict Scotland's foreign policy; and she had a personal as well as a political interest in the matter of Mary's remarriage. That she would marry again was regarded as inevitable, and England, uneasily aware that her most powerful neighbours were Catholic and potentially hostile, could not afford to let one of them instal its nominee as Mary's King-Consort in Edinburgh.

To Elizabeth, unmarried on her Protestant throne, it seemed obvious that some quite innocuous pillow partner must be found for Mary; and Cecil—Elizabeth's most able, energetic Secretary—saw clearly the necessity of maintaining in Scotland the authority of the Reformed church and its leaders, the Lords of the Congregation of Christ. That necessity dominated Anglo-Scottish relations, and eventually determined the fate of Scotland's Queen.

In spite of domestic enemies and English suspicion, the first four years of Mary's reign were comparatively peaceful, and in the material state of Scotland there was considerable improvement. For that the Queen was indebted to Lord James, her half-brother, and to Maitland of Lethington, who served her well. She herself is also entitled to credit, for she behaved with conspicuous restraint when faced with outrageous provocation, and in circumstances totally different from the country where she had grown up—in conditions lamentably less happy than those to which she had been accustomed—she showed judgment remarkable in one so young. She retained her faith but abated its fervour and made no attempt to foist it on her people; she recognised good advice and acted on it; she bridled ambition and added to the number of her friends by gentleness, grace, and discretion.

With John Knox she had some remarkable conversations, complacently reported by Knox himself. On one occasion he defended the right of subjects to resist their rulers by analogy with a domestic crisis in which the father of a family, stricken with a frenzy, has to be disarmed and imprisoned to save his children from harm.

"It is even so, Madam," said Knox, "with princes that would murder the children of God that are subject unto them. Their blind zeal is nothing but a very mad frenzy: and therefore, to take the sword from them, to bind their hands, and to cast them into prison until they be brought to a more sober mind, is no disobedience against princes, but just obedience, because it agreeth with the will of God."

The Queen, says Knox, was silent for a long time, standing "as it were amazed." Then she replied: "Well, then, I perceive that my subjects shall obey you, and not me; and shall do what they like, and not what I command; and so must I be subject to them and not they to me."

Knox answered that his task was to persuade both princes and people to obey God, who would like his kings to be foster fathers to his church, and queens to be nurses to his people.

"Yea," said Mary, "but ye are not the Kirk that I will nurse. I will defend the Kirk of Rome, for I think it is the true Kirk of God."

Knox lost his temper. "Your will, Madam, is no reason!" he shouted. "Neither doth your thought make of that Roman harlot the true and immaculate spouse of Jesus Christ. Wonder not, Madam, that I call Rome a harlot; for that Church is altogether polluted with all kinds of spiritual fornication, as well in doctrine as in manners."

The Queen answered, "My conscience is not so."

"Conscience, Madam, requires knowledge: and I fear that right knowledge ye have none."

"But I have both heard and read."

"So, Madam, did the Jews that crucified Christ Jesus read both the Law and the Prophets, and heard the same interpreted after their manner. Have ye heard any teach, but such as the Pope and his Cardinals have allowed? Ye may be assured that such will speak nothing to offend their own estate."

"Ye interpret the Scriptures in one manner," said the Queen, "and they interpret in another; whom shall I believe? And who shall be judge?"

But there she gave Knox his opportunity, and promptly he took it: "Ye shall believe God, that plainly speaketh in his word; and farther than the Word teaches you, ye shall believe neither the one nor the other."—Knox and his Kirk had taken possession of the Word of God, and claimed all rights in it, including the right of interpretation.

Few people could hope to hold their own in argument with John Knox, but more than once, in debate with him, Mary showed her hardy spirit. In a different way and in very different circumstances—in the wildness of a Highland landscape—she showed it again when the Earl of Huntly, in rebellious mood, had to be disciplined by military action. Huntly was the most powerful of the northern magnates, and had offered to seat Mary on the Catholic throne of a country Catholicised by himself, his friends, and his redoubtable clan. Mary, with politic good sense, had refused his offer. Only the wild Gordon temper had prompted the rebellion, only a brief campaign was needed to subdue it. Mary rode with her troops and enjoyed the experience. Randolph, an English agent, wrote to Cecil: "In all these broils I assure you I never saw her merrier, never dismayed, nor never thought that so much stomach to be in her that I find. She repented nothing but (when the lords and others at Inverness came in the morning from the watch,) that she was not a man, to know what life it was to lie all night in the fields, or to walk on the causeway with a jack and knapsack, a Glasgow buckler, and a broad sword."

The four years of sound and constructive rule came to an end in 1565, when Mary, with lamentable folly, married her cousin Henry Stewart, Lord Darnley. His father, the Earl of Lennox—who had long been an exile in England—had married a granddaughter of Henry VII, and was himself a great-great-grandson of James II of Scotland: Darnley had therefore a claim, after Mary, to the English throne, and was a possible heir to that of Scotland.

There had been suitors and marriage proposals before him, all of which had come to nothing. Elizabeth had offered her own favourite, Robert Dudley—suspected of having murdered his wife, Amy Robsart —whom she created Earl of Leicester, apparently to enhance his prospects; but Elizabeth's purposes were commonly less than crystal-clear, and her attempt to provide a throne for Dudley is as open to question as her attitude to Darnley's marriage. She let him go to Scotland, and then seemed angrily opposed to the match. Her disapproval stiffened Mary's determination to marry her weak-willed, nominally Catholic, tall and pretty cousin; and it is not impossible that Elizabeth had foreseen its effect.

By marriage to Darnley Mary would reinforce her claim to the English throne, and Darnley, three years younger than she—Mary was not yet twenty-three—may have seemed likely to be a submissive, undemanding husband. He was yellow-haired and good-looking in a rather effeminate way—he had a graceful carriage and amiable manners—and soon after his arrival in Scotland he had the good fortune to fall ill with measles. Mary nursed him—she had had much experience of a sickroom during her marriage to the little French king—and in a familiar atmosphere she fell in love with her cousin: her emotion, one may suppose, was a feminine, protective affection rather than a clamant sensuality. Whatever its nature, she soon had cause to regret it.

She had made Lord James, her half-brother, Earl of Moray; and Moray objected to a marriage which would deprive him of power, and in which he may have seen a threat to re-establish Catholicism in Scotland. He led his Protestant supporters in a rebellion against his sister which was subsidised, though less generously than he had hoped, by

England. Mary had another opportunity to show her pleasure in military exercise, and enthusiastically rode with her army in what was known as the Chase-about Raid; for there was no fighting. Moray escaped over the Border to Carlisle, and Mary was able to enjoy her little triumph and her first experience of seeming independence. But among those who supported her newly won freedom were some friends of ill omen.

Darnley, her husband, was vicious as well as weak, and on him neither she nor anyone else could depend for honesty, fidelity, or help at need. To counter the menace of Moray's rebellion she had recalled from exile a stalwart, aggressive, and ambitious Border noble, James Hepburn, Earl of Bothwell—whom Moray detested—and made him Lieutenant of the East, West, and Middle Marches. And she had raised to favour, as her French secretary, an Italian called David Rizzio who had come to Scotland among the followers of an ambassador from Savoy.

Holyroodhouse was coldly devoid of entertainment; in a social sense it was almost unfurnished. It lacked good company, and hardly ever can there have been good conversation. Since the death of James V Scotland had been sorely hurt, and repeatedly hurt. Manners had deteriorated, and the Reformation had not helped them: religious zeal had fortified the surly temper engendered by misfortune. And so, in a palace open to grim Calvinists and titled ruffians, it is not surprising that Mary found pleasure in the company of a man who could speak of foreign courts, who had a good singing voice and some scholarship in music, who reminded her of the courtesies common to her younger days in France. Rizzio was black-avised and ill-favoured—both friends and enemies agreed on that—and though some thought he was only twenty-eight, others put his age at fifty. But though his appearance did little to recommend him, he aroused the jealousy and hostility of Scottish noblemen who resented the promotion of a low-born, foreign fiddler. They pretended to believe that he was a papal agent, an enemy to the Congregation of Christ, and the Queen's lover.

Never until now had Mary's behaviour attracted slander. At the French court, where the pursuit of love was not unknown, her name was untouched by gossip, and in her first four years in Scotland, when hostile eyes watched all she did, she had stirred no thought or whisper of impropriety. But now the kindliness she showed to an Italian of swarthy aspect prompted tales of her misconduct; and her misconduct was said to be the true cause of her breach with Moray. Before her marriage Rizzio and Darnley had been friends, but now Darnley, who had no more stability than a weathercock, was persuaded of his wife's infidelity, and news of it—or news of the slander that imagined it—was sent hurriedly to England.

Thomas Randolph, the English agent who had reported Mary's gallant demeanour on the little Highland campaign against Huntly, wrote to the Earl of Leicester to say that Darnley and his father were plotting to secure the crown, that Rizzio was to have his throat cut, and Mary's own life might be in danger. About the end of February 1566, he wrote again, to Cecil, and his later news was that old Lennox was about to meet the Earl of Argyll and promise him that if he and Moray would support Darnley's claim to the crown-matrimonial, then Darnley would assure their pardon and bring them home again.

There were those who had good reason for cutting Rizzio's throat: better reason than their pretended belief that he had stained the Queen's honour. The Chancellor of Scotland was the Earl of Morton, and there was a rumour that Rizzio was to replace him in that high office. It was said, too, that Rizzio had opposed Darnley's request for the crown-matrimonial. Rizzio was a Catholic, a foreigner, and his influence with the Queen cannot have failed to antagonise all who thought themselves entitled, by birth if not ability, to that privilege. And Moray, about to return from exile, had many friends in Scotland.

A parliament was summoned to meet on the 12th March, its purpose to declare Moray and his rebellious companions guilty of lèse majesté and to be forfeit in life, lands, and goods. But the plotters anticipated parliament, and on the 9th, after darkness fell, the palace of Holyroodhouse was occupied by troops under the command of the Earls of Morton and Lindsay. The Queen was supping quietly, for it was Lent and she in the sixth or seventh month of her pregnancy. With her and a few friends was Rizzio, who sang to her for the last time. Then the rebel Lords broke in, led by Lord Ruthven, thought to be a warlock, who had risen from a sickbed and put on armour above his nightgown. Rizzio, crying loudly for mercy, was stabbed and murdered, either under the Queen's arm or in the doorway of her room.

It was a cold-blooded and atrocious crime, and he who had made it possible—he who must bear the heavier guilt for Rizzio's betrayal and death, and for the danger that threatened the Queen—was Darnley. It cannot be supposed, however, that either Darnley or his father were principals in the plot, or instigators of it. For so large a demonstration of opposition to the Queen—Rizzio's murder was incidental, Rizzio was the sacrifice that brought Darnley into the plot—there was only one man who could be responsible; and that was Moray. In the eye of history, unclouded by emotion, the interest of that bloody occasion lies chiefly in the fact that it was an open declaration of hostility to Mary's sovereignty uttered by the Lords of the Congregation of Christ whose leader—on earth, shall one say—was the Queen's half-brother. Latent until her marriage to Darnley, that hostility became visible when Moray and Lethington lost the authority they had enjoyed, and though it was concealed as circumstances required, it remained as the disruptive force which finally achieved its purpose when Mary was imprisoned at Loch Leven and forced to abdicate.

After Rizzio's assassination, however, it was she who took the next round, and that she did by as daring, as coolly calculated, as high-spirited an evasion as ever decorated the better pages of a romantic fiction. She lay in Holyroodhouse surrounded by her enemies. Some attempt at rescue was made by the Provost and people of Edinburgh —always alert for trouble and its excitement—but Darnley went out to assure them that the Queen was safe, though she herself was forbidden to speak under pain of being cut "in collops" and thrown over the wall. Bothwell and the Catholic Earls of Huntly and Atholl lay in or near Holyrood, but they, taken by surprise, had been unable to resist the conspirators; though Bothwell had made his escape from them. In the conspiracy, however, there was an inherent weakness, and that was Darnley.

He came to speak with Mary, and was passionately reproached. But then she persuaded him to let her women attend her. Lady Huntly knew where to find Bothwell, and while a message was sent to him, Moray had some conversation with the Queen. She may have been glad to see him, for he was more reasonable, more moderate in temper, than some who followed him. When Darnley returned her manner was mild, she pretended to accept what had happened, and agreed to pardon those who had plotted against her. Either Lethington or Darnley was persuaded that the soldiers who guarded her could safely be withdrawn, and she frightened Darnley by warning him of the danger he would invite by relying on the friendship of such men as Morton and Ruthven. Later she wrote, most demurely, to the Archbishop of

Glasgow: "he was induced to condescend to the purpose taken by us, and to retire in our company to Dunbar, which we did under night."

It was a wild and desperate escape. A secret stairway, a silent retreat through deserted kitchens and a cemetery, took her to a gate where horses waited. The Queen mounted behind her esquire of the stables, an attendant woman rode pillion with another horseman. Darnley was mounted, and for ten miles they rode hard till at Seton, on the coast, they saw soldiers waiting. Darnley called for faster flight, and when the Queen spoke of the child she carried, exclaimed coarsely that they could make another if he were lost.

But the soldiers were a picket of Bothwell's Borderers, and he, with Huntly and some of their friends, was waiting for them. They rode on to Dunbar, another fifteen miles, and there, at dawn, the Queen cooked eggs for the soldiers' breakfast.

Bothwell raised three or four thousand spearmen from the Borders, and at the head of a convincing force Mary returned to Edinburgh. There, most reasonably, she sought, not revenge, but the pacification of her kingdom. Many of the late rebels submitted, and Moray, while righteously declaring that he had no association with Rizzio's murderers, took pains to secure a kindly welcome in England for those who could make no such denial. Knox, still commending the murderers, fled into Ayrshire, and Lethington discreetly retired to the Highlands.

Edinburgh, ever volatile, welcomed the Queen, and the Queen with a true politician's suavity publicly accepted Darnley's assertion of his innocence. He had signed one document which authorised the murder of Rizzio, another which declared his purpose of accepting, from his fellow conspirators, the crown-matrimonial; and Mary had seen both of them. But Darnley was the father of her child, and to banish him would have involved her in a sentimental difficulty as well as a constitutional problem. There was evidence that England had sent 3000 crowns to support the rebels, but Mary politely accepted Elizabeth's indignant denial that she had given any help at all. Elizabeth, moreover, threatened to make Moray welcome in England should Mary refuse to pardon him; and Mary, who had already forgiven him, replied softly that she had done so to oblige her cousin.

In the peace she had patched up her son was born in Edinburgh castle, after a long and difficult labour, on the morning of the 16th June 1566; and in the afternoon, when she was still feverish, Darnley came to see her and the child.

"My lord," she said, "God has given you and me a son, begotten by none but you."

The truth of that assertion—which no reasonable person will doubt—is visibly established by a pair of portraits, the one in the Duke of Devonshire's possession, the other in the National Portrait Gallery in London. The former shows Lord Darnley, the latter King James at the age of eight; and James's head, eyes, and mouth are quite obviously the bequest of his unworthy father.

More significant, as a confession of her ruling ambition, is Mary's recorded statement: "This is the son who (I hope) shall first unite the two kingdoms of Scotland and England." There, in that small and stuffy room above the Rock of the Castle, can be heard a Queen's true voice and motive.

Popular applause, the resounding echoes of rejoicing gunfire, and innumerable bonfires greeted the birth of Prince James, and du Croc, the French ambassador, wrote: "I never saw Her Majesty so much beloved, esteemed, and honoured; nor so great a harmony amongst all her subjects, as at present is by her wise conduct, for I cannot perceive the smallest difference or division." But Darnley was a disintegrating element in that apparent harmony. Against all reason the Queen still held him in affection—she had lately made her will, and among the bequests to Darnley was a diamond ring with the note: "It was with this that I was married"—and by her grace and toleration both Moray and Lethington had been restored to favour: that, perhaps, was why Darnley now chose to regard Moray as his enemy. There was a rumour, however, that Mary had begun to show undue cordiality to the Earl of Bothwell; to whom, indeed, she had much cause for gratitude.

As Warden of the Marches he lived at some risk, and in October, badly wounded in a Border scuffle, he lay dangerously ill in the tall, gaunt castle of Hermitage in Liddesdale. Mary was attending a justice ayre at Jedburgh, thirty miles away, and with Moray and some others rode to Hermitage, and back to Jedburgh on the same day. The exertion was too much for her and she fell ill, possibly of an intestinal haemorrhage. The appalling treatment she endured at her doctors' hands was worse than the injury she had suffered, and for nine days her life was in danger. The long ride to Hermitage had been a cheerful escapade—a boyish escapade, comparable with her delight in the hard riding of the Chase-about Raid—but she paid heavily for it in suffering. And a little while later she had to pay again, when it was represented as a love-sick gallop to Bothwell's bed.

George Buchanan was a great scholar, but unscrupulous in the use of his talents. When Moray and his associates found it necessary to accuse Mary of complicity in the murder of her husband, Buchanan composed his *Detection* of her iniquities for the information of Queen Elizabeth's commissioners. It is a remarkable tale—more sensational than plausible, but never dull—and his account of the ride to Hermitage will give a fair impression of its veracity. "When (Bothwell's injury) was reported to the queen at Borthwick," he wrote, "she flew madly by forced journeys, though it was bitter winter, first to Melrose, then to Jedburgh. Though she learned there on good authority that his life was safe, her affection could brook no delay, and she betrayed her infamous lust by setting out at a bad time of the year, heedless of the difficulties of the journey and the danger of highwaymen, with a company such as no decent gentleman would entrust with his life and goods."

The truth is that Mary was already at Jedburgh when she heard that Bothwell had been wounded; that so far from "flying madly" to see him, it was not until five or six days after the news had reached her that she set out on her ride; and the company "such as no decent gentleman would entrust with his life and goods" included her half-brother, the Earl of Moray.

Mary's convalescence was slow and seemingly unwilling. She spoke of the unhappiness that Darnley had brought her, she talked of suicide. But she recovered spirit enough to make arrangements for her son's baptism, and with Moray and Lethington she discussed the possibility of obtaining a divorce. They, perhaps, were the first to suggest it. They wanted to secure a pardon for Morton and many others who were implicated in the murder of Rizzio, and the Queen, consenting to a pardon, appears to have agreed, with reservations, to their proposal. She wanted assurance that the divorce could be legally obtained, and that it would not prejudice the status of her son. But early in the New Year Darnley, in Glasgow, postponed all legal proceedings by falling seriously ill.

The nature of his disease was variously reported. Buchanan said he had been poisoned, others preferred scabies, smallpox, or syphilis. Buchanan may be ignored; sufferers from scabies are seldom bedridden; and the evidence of syphilis depends on a lesion said to be visible on a skull not positively identified as Darnley's. His illness was small-pox, and Mary was qualified to nurse him by her acquired immunity: as a child in France she had had the disease, and escaped pocking by the skill of her doctor.

Darnley's behaviour had lately been so curious as to rouse a good deal of anxious speculation. When Philip II of Spain was planning a campaign in the Netherlands, Darnley had spoken of joining him. Then he was said to be provisioning a ship to go to France. He was writing to the Pope as well as to Philip of Spain, and a rumour that he and his father were plotting to crown the infant Prince, and make Darnley Regent, was heard in France and echoed back again. When Moray and Lethington spoke to the Queen about the advisability of divorce, Lethington is alleged to have said, "We shall find the means that your Majesty shall be quit of him."

There is circumstantial evidence of a Catholic plot to re-establish the Roman Church in Scotland, and Darnley and his father seem to have been involved in it. The Reformation had excited the animus of counter-reformation, and at the heart of that movement were Pope Pius V and Philip of Spain. Mary had disappointed them by her re-fusal to lead a Catholic restoration in Scotland—her good sense and dynastic purpose were both opposed to that—and it may have been thought advisable to eliminate her as well as the Protestant Lords who, in alliance with English interests and Elizabeth's good Secretary, Wil-liam Cecil, defended the Reformed Church which was England's bas-tion as well as the ark of Scotland's faith. But no plot could succeed if Darnley was a participant. He had no need to betray his fellow con-spirators, he merely talked about them. Whatever was being hatched for the discomfiture of Moray and the Protestant Lords was probably as well known to them as it was to Darnley's associates.

Mary was afraid that her child might be kidnapped. On the 14th January she brought him from Stirling to Holyrood, and a week later rode to Glasgow, where Darnley lay on his sickbed. Her intention was to take him to Craigmillar castle, near Edinburgh. It was obviously advisable to keep him under surveillance, and Mary, who had nursed him before, as she had nursed her little French husband, may well have been moved by a womanly belief that she alone was qualified to care for him and supervise his convalescence.

It was on Tuesday the 21st January that she began her journey; she reached Glasgow on Wednesday; and about five days later returned, carrying Darnley in a litter. They did not go to Craigmillar, but to the Provost's House at Kirk o' Field on the south side of Edinburgh. It was, it seems, by Darnley's own wish that he was lodged there. Some of his friends had told him that Kirk o' Field enjoyed a superior climate, and the house had been made ready for him by Sir James Balfour.

Some twenty years before, Balfour had been implicated in the murder of Cardinal Beaton and condemned, with John Knox, to eighteen months' servitude in a galley of the French fleet. That enforced association had not promoted friendship. Balfour and his brothers, said Knox, were "men without God." They had "neither fear of God nor love of virtue, further than their present commodity persuaded them." James was known as Blasphemous Balfour, and flatteringly described as one of the two worst men in Scotland. With his brother Gilbert he was soon accused of complicity in Darnley's murder, and du Croc, the French ambassador, was convinced of his guilt. His brother Gilbert had been Master of the Queen's Household, and later in the year became Sheriff of Orkney and Keeper of Kirkwall castle: appointments of some significance to James Hepburn, Earl of Bothwell, when he fell out with fortune.

The third brother was Robert, Canon of Holyrood, to whom the Provost's House belonged.

3

What happened at Kirk o' Field is known to all, but precisely how it happened is one of those mysteries which survive the erosion of time with no better purpose—or so it seems—than to tease enquiring minds.

Early in the morning of Monday, the 10th February, a tremendous explosion demolished the Provost's House and woke all Edinburgh. Nothing remained of the building but a great heap of rubble, and in the garden, near a pear tree, lay the dead bodies of Darnley and Taylor his valet. There was snow on the ground, they wore nothing but their nightshirts, and neither body was marked in any way.

On Sunday morning there had been a wedding at Holyroodhouse: Bastien, a good servant of the Queen, was married to one of her women. Later in the day there was a banquet in honour of Moretta, the ambassador from Savoy: it was in Moretta's train that David Rizzio had come to Scotland, and now, when Moretta returned, he brought with him David's brother Joseph. At the banquet, held in James Balfour's house in the Canongate, the Bishop of Argyll was the host, the Queen a guest. But strangely absent were Moray and Lethington—the former's wife was pregnant, the latter newly married: they had no better excuse for absence—and Morton, though pardoned, was not yet welcome at court.

From the banquet Mary rode to Kirk o' Field, where she had promised to spend the last night of Darnley's quarantine, sleeping in a small room below his. In a high chair, upholstered in purple to match the bed, she sat for a couple of hours while Darnley and the Earls of Bothwell, Huntly, Argyll, and Cassilis played a game with dice. Then she remembered—or perhaps was reminded—that she had promised to dance at Bastien's wedding party. Darnley objected to her leaving, but she insisted on keeping her promise. As if to pacify a fretful child, she gave Darnley a ring, and as she was going out encountered a servant of Bothwell's called French Paris, and exclaimed "Jesu, Paris, how begrimed you are!" Then, accompanied by Bothwell, and lighted by torches, she went back to Holyrood.

The house was blown up, and Darnley killed, a few hours later—about two o'clock in the morning—and according to the rumour which first, and quickly, reached London and Paris, Darnley's father, the Earl of Lennox, had also been killed.—He was, in fact, at Linlithgow, not far away.—The Venetian ambassador in Paris wrote that the double murder was the work of heretics "who designed the same for the Queen"; and Mary herself, on Monday, the day of the crime, told the Archbishop of Glasgow that she believed the explosion had been intended to kill her as well as her husband. The Archbishop had already written to warn her of a plot against her life.

Mary, with the approval of her Council, offered a reward of £2000 for information and a free pardon to the informer. Within a week a placard nailed to the door of the Tolbooth named Bothwell, James Balfour and some others as the murderers, adding "and if this be not true, speir at* Gilbert Balfour." Elsewhere in the town bills were posted, denouncing Bothwell, and in the darkness of the streets voices cried that Bothwell had murdered the King. Bastien, the loyal servant, and Joseph Rizzio were also accused.

It seems improbable that denunciation of Bothwell and the two

* ask.

Balfours was a spontaneous expression of popular fear and indignation. It is more likely to have been inspired by some who, having knowledge of what was intended, made haste to find culprits, and identify them, before they themselves were named. The very curious absence of Moray and Lethington from the banquet in Balfour's house suggests the possibility that they had instigated it; and English interest in what was purposed is indicated by the fact that Cecil had an agent in Edinburgh who, in the early daylight of Monday, made a detailed and informative drawing of the scene of devastation—the ruined house, the bodies of Darnley and his valet under the pear tree—and sent it to his master in London.

Bothwell, with fifty Borderers behind him, walked defiantly in the Canongate, and stood high in the Queen's favour: she had little choice, for few remained whom she could trust. But in March she promised that he and several others should stand their trial, and Bothwell himself consented to it. A rumour was now current that he was making arrangements to divorce Jean Gordon, his wife—a sister of the Earl of Huntly—to win freedom for marriage to the Queen; and before his trial he brought an army of his supporters into Edinburgh. The jury included several of his known enemies, but no one could be found to swear to the truth of the indictment, and after several hours' debate the Earl of Caithness, foreman of the jury, announced a unanimous acquittal. A few days later, when the Queen rode to her parliament, Bothwell carried the sceptre, and not long after asserted his authority by inviting, or summoning, twenty-eight peers and prelates to sup with him. He offered, for their signature, a document that recorded his acquittal, and requested those present to help and further his plan to marry the Queen. That insolent suggestion was approved, and the extraordinary document received the signatures of eight bishops, nine earls, and seven barons; whether drunk or sober, no one knows.

Moray was in London at the time, but Morton and Argyll are said to have been among the nine earls who signed. It is unlikely that they —and, indeed, the other signatories—were frightened into obedience; they may not have been men of exemplary character, but the barons of Scotland were not poltroons. Their predicament may have been similar to that which the Queen had faced: she had shown favour to Bothwell, given him her trust, because there was no one else whom she could even pretend to trust; and at Bothwell's supper party his guests may have thought, and drunkenly decided, that he alone had the strength to rule and govern a distracted kingdom. It was observed, however, that his guests made haste to leave Edinburgh for the greater safety of their own estates, and a year or two later they produced various excuses for their curious behaviour.

The judicial enquiry into Darnley's murder proceeded slowly, and not until midsummer—when the state of affairs in Scotland had suffered radical change—was the official account of what had happened made public; and that account was quite incredible. Two of Bothwell's kinsmen and two of his servants had been captured and put to the torture of boot and rack, screws, hooks, and pincers in the Tolbooth of Edinburgh; and what agony induced them to say was shaped and distorted to suit their persecutors' purpose.

Bothwell, declared the Justice Clerk in his report, had brought gunpowder from Dunbar and stored it in his quarters at Holyroodhouse.—That, for a start, was improbable.—At ten o'clock on Sunday evening, said the Justice Clerk, two of Bothwell's men took the powder to Blackfriars Gate, a couple of hundred yards from Kirk o' Field. It was packed in bags, in a leather portmanteau and a trunk, carried on a grey horse, and two trips were necessary.—Now on that Sunday evening, with a wedding party at Holyroodhouse and a banquet in the Canongate, the street must still have been full of inquisitive, gossiping people, and it was hardly possible for so strange a convoy to pass unobserved. But according to the report the powder was carried, by other conspirators, from the Blackfriars Gate to the Provost's House, where the bags were emptied in a heap on the floor of the room where the Queen was supposed to be sleeping, or would have slept had she not chosen to dance instead at Bastien's wedding. But Darnley and his valet slept upstairs, there was another servant in the house, and it seems improbable that they could have slept undisturbed by conspirators busy on the floor below.

Let that pass, however, and consider the explosion and what caused it. It has been calculated[*] that the maximum load of powder, carried in portmanteau and trunk on a horse—the horse made two journeys—would be about 250 pounds. Now that quantity of powder, as made in the Sixteenth Century, was ludicrously insufficient to blow up such a solid building as the Provost's House. But there is uncontested evidence that the house was totally demolished, and the implication—impossible to avoid—is that it had been prepared for demolition be-

[*] Major-General R. H. Mahon: *The Tragedy of Kirk o' Field.*

fore that busy Sunday, and perhaps well before it. There were cellars under the whole length of the house and they must have been filled with such a weight of powder that when a fuse was lighted the explosion had the violence of a landmine.

Who prepared the landmine? Almost certainly, James and Gilbert Balfour. What was their purpose, for whom were they working, and who was their intended victim? Du Croc, the French ambassador, felt sure that James Balfour was *le vrai traître*, and the plot in which he was involved was aimed against the Queen. If she were removed the way would be open for a Catholic restoration under the leadership of Darnley and his father; who, on that Sunday night, waited at Linlithgow only twenty miles away.

But Darnley was a babbler, Darnley could never keep a secret, and through his indiscretion Moray and Lethington learnt what was intended. They, deliberately, did not attend the reception for Moretta. If Mary were murdered by Catholic plotters it was they, not Darnley, who were likely to profit by her death. But Bothwell grew suspicious and made, perhaps, a timely discovery. As Mary was leaving the Provost's House she saw French Paris and exclaimed, "Jesu, Paris, how begrimed you are!"—Had he, by accident or obeying Bothwell's instruction, discovered what lay in the cellars beneath them?

Bothwell and the Queen, with torches to light them, went back to Holyroodhouse, and Bothwell returned to Kirk o' Field to investigate. Did he there meet James Balfour?—A little while later there emerged evidence of a very curious understanding, if not complicity, between them.—And when Bothwell found the Provost's House prepared for demolition, did he realise his opportunity to rid the Queen of her husband—himself of an obstacle to his ambition—and light the fuse which Balfour was about to remove?

There was plot and counterplot—that seems certain—and if it was James Balfour who persuaded Darnley to complete his convalescence at Kirk o' Field, then the explosion there killed a victim unintended by the original plotters. It is, however, not impossible that Moray and Lethington found means to suborn Balfour—one of "the two worst men in Scotland"—and by menace or bribery made him their agent in a different task: the elimination, that is, of Darnley as well as the Queen.

The mystery is insoluble, but out of the darkness emerges the belief that Bothwell, the quick-minded, daring leader of Border forays, saw sudden advantage and promptly took it. Then he outfaced his enemies, and the Queen, as she had done after Rizzio's death, accepted the brutal reality of the world she lived in. She played coldly at politics, and by so doing invited a growing cloud of slander. She had, it was said, fallen intemperately in love with Bothwell, and was already his mistress.

He, fortified by the promised help of eight bishops and sixteen peers of the realm, declared his suit, and decisively she refused him. She had friends and he had enemies, said the Queen, and in her opinion neither side was likely to encourage or permit a marriage for which she herself had no inclination. Her final answer was "nothing correspondent to his desire."

Towards the end of April 1567, she rode to Stirling to see the infant Prince, now ten months old. She was escorted by Huntly, Lethington, Melville—sometime her ambassador in England—and thirty troopers. She spent a day with the child, and slept at Linlithgow. Cecil heard a rumour that Bothwell arrived there at midnight, talked to Huntly, and made some proposal to him that Huntly angrily rejected. Bothwell, with eight hundred horsemen, lay at the House of Calder, ten miles away, pretending that some Border crisis had necessitated his mobilising so large a number of men. But on the following day he surprised and halted Mary and her escort. He had come, he said, to save her from a grave danger and take her to Dunbar. There were those in her company who were prepared to fight, but Mary, with a prudent acceptance of the odds against her, would not let them. She was more willing, she said, to go with Bothwell than to provoke useless bloodshed.

That was the mistake for which her enemies—enemies in her own time, enemies as virulent in later ages—never forgave her. She was unnerved by fear. She had spent some hours with her infant son, and feared for him. She was confronted by eight hundred horsemen, and her spirit failed her. No English or Scottish historians of the Nineteenth Century had had any such experience, and they, lapped in comfort and security, were almost unanimous in condemning her for yielding to physical fear of a sort that they had never known. But we, in this century, have all known fear, and can be sympathetic. Fear is a humiliating experience, and Mary was humbled by it, as we have been.

She submitted to Bothwell and his eight hundred troopers. She went with him to Dunbar, and there he raped her. Of that there is no reasonable doubt. There were violent scenes at Dunbar. Huntly tried to kill Lethington, and Lethington was saved by Mary's own fierce display of temper. Melville said plainly that Bothwell had ravished the Queen, others found explanation for her submission in witchcraft, at which Bothwell was thought to be adept. Mary herself, in a letter to the Bishop of Dunblane, wrote pathetically: "As by a bravado in the beginning he had won his first point, so ceased he never till by persuasions and importunate suit, accompanied not the less with force, he had finally driven us to end the work begun at such time and in such form as he thought might best serve his turn."

Bothwell had obtained his divorce, and he and Mary were married in mid-May. The nonsensicality of the stories propagated about her infatuation with him was immediately exposed by what, with lamentable promptitude, became miserably obvious. A woman obsessed by guilty love may be expected, when love is not only consummated but legalised, to show some pleasure: to show, indeed, a glowing delight in happiness made licit. But nothing of that sort comforted Mary in her *mésalliance*. Melville heard her ask for a knife to stab herself, and du Croc, astonished by her sadness, was told, "If you see me melancholy it is because I do not choose to be cheerful; because I never will be so, and wish for nothing but death." Lethington wrote: "From her wedding day she was ever in tears and lamentations, for he would not let her look at anybody, or anybody look at her, though he knew that she liked her pleasure and pastime, as well as anybody." And Bothwell, it is said, returned for comfort to his divorced wife Jean, with whom he spent several days a week.

When married to her young cousin Darnley—a weak, pliable, good-looking boy—Mary had failed to hold his affection for even a year. Married to Bothwell—though married by force, she might, if she had had the aptitude, have secured his goodwill and obedience—she showed, without attempt at concealment, the unhappiness that the physical relationship of marriage imposed upon her. Here, too, it is relevant to observe that when, a year or so later, she fled for safety into her cousin's realm of England, she became a prisoner, not closely warded, for nineteen years, and never had a lover. She was a comely and attractive young woman, twenty-six years old, when she became an English captive, and England was full of doughty and adventurous young men. But Mary's long imprisonment was never enlivened by love, and that omission, added to the almost immediate collapse of her two adult marriages, surely proves that she was by nature indifferent to the familiarities of love, and probably averse from them. That inference—which seems inescapable—precludes, of course, all possibility of believing that Bothwell had been her lover. She was raped by him, and tried to cover the insult to her pride by marriage; but found marriage unendurable.

· Bothwell, it must be admitted, showed for a little while some aptitude in government, but the forces of opposition were too strong for him—Lethington was already asking Cecil for money to mount a new rebellion—and Bothwell hastened his own defeat by removing a loyal commander of Edinburgh castle and replacing him with James Balfour. It is inconceivable that he did so except under compulsion: the compulsion, that is, of blackmail. Balfour threatened him with exposure, and demanded the castle as the price of his silence. But what sort of exposure could Balfour have threatened that warranted so extravagant a payment? Something that had happened on the night of Darnley's murder? Did Balfour see him light the fuse?

(It may be remembered that his brother Gilbert—sometime Master of the Queen's Household, and obliquely accused of complicity in Darnley's murder in the placard nailed to the Tolbooth door—became Sheriff of Orkney and Keeper of Kirkwall castle. When Bothwell fled from Scotland he put to sea and sought refuge in Orkney; but Gilbert, refusing to receive him, fired on his ships, and Bothwell retreated to Shetland. There, by Gilbert's help, his pursuers surprised him, and he was forced to fight. Defeated off the island of Unst, he fled finally to Norway.).

The Balfours had no sense of loyalty, no knowledge of fidelity. Within a little while of his receiving the castle, Sir James surrendered it to Lethington; or, more accurately, sold it for a large sum of money and other rewards. It was Gilbert Balfour who completed Bothwell's discomfiture, but it was James who made it inevitable. When Bothwell lost Edinburgh castle he lost control of the capital; and when he and Mary mustered an army at Carberry Hill, near Musselburgh, there was no fighting, but only bluster. Bothwell's army melted away, and he, with the Queen's consent, who hated bloodshed, mounted and rode off, unpursued. But Mary, a captive, was taken to Edinburgh where an excited crowd shouted "Burn her! Burn the hoor!" The Edinburgh mob was almost as volatile as the Roman crowds that Shakespeare so warmly disliked.

No one can measure the misery of the Queen, nor fathom the depths of her defeat. She had lived in Scotland as in the midst of a quicksand, seldom knowing where she could set her foot in safety, and now she was faced with the seeming hatred of the people for whom she had compromised her faith and won, by patience and sagacity, a little season of peace in the internecine savagery to which they had long been subject. She was defeated—utterly defeated—but her spirit was not broken.

She was imprisoned within the dank and meagre walls of the island castle on Loch Leven, and there, by the *force majeure* of the Confederate Lords, her rebel subjects, she was compelled to abdicate. There, too, she suffered the pain and humiliation of a miscarriage of twins, the consequence of Bothwell's unmannerly assault. But her spirit and ambition both revived. She recovered from physical weakness and the collapse of hope, she made her escape from that grim islet, and gathering a little force again, offered battle to her enemies.

But resistance was in vain, she was again defeated, and fleeing to the Solway crossed over to the safety and shame of surrender to England.

Of her long imprisonment nothing need be said here. There were plots on her behalf, and some of them she encouraged. She endured much discomfort, and finally, at Fotheringay, she faced death with queenly dignity and marvellous composure.

The manner of her death, the courage with which she faced those who accused her of complicity in a plot against Elizabeth's life—these are well known. But less well known is the falsity of the evidence by which, nineteen years before, her enemies in Scotland had tried to prove her guilty of complicity in the plot that culminated in the death of Darnley.

4

On the 19th June, 1567, Lethington and the Earl of Morton dined together in Edinburgh. They were told, by an unnamed informant, that three of Bothwell's servants were in town, and had been seen going into the castle. Morton, on a sudden impulse—this is his story—sent out sixteen of his own men to search for them, and discovered one called George Dalgleish. He, being threatened with torture at the Tolbooth, led his captors to his lodging in the Potterow, and from under a bed produced a locked silver box which, he said, he had taken from the castle on the previous day. The castle was commanded by Sir James Balfour, but there is no suggestion that he knew of the casket's existence; nor is there any explanation of how it came to be in the castle.

On the 21st, said Morton, the contents of the casket were inspected by several nobles and gentlemen. In it were eight letters in French, and some French "sonnets," alleged to have been written by Mary. Morton declared on oath that he had not tampered with the papers; but few critics have been impressed by the value of Morton's word. If, however, the letters were genuine, they were proof of Mary's adultery with Bothwell, and of her complicity in Darnley's murder. There has been much controversy about the authenticity of the letters, which no one has seen—neither letters nor casket—since the Earl of Gowrie's death in 1600; and there is a possibility that none, except those who accused Mary of guilt and guilty knowledge, even saw them before that. Many copies circulated, but the "originals" seem never to have been subject to impartial examination, though they may have been briefly exhibited when English commissioners assembled in York to hear evidence against both Moray and the Queen.

Moray and his associates—the Confederate Lords who opposed Mary and Bothwell at Carberry—were in trouble because, after confining her in the small castle on Loch Leven, they had compelled her abdication and crowned the infant James. Moray had returned from France to assume the regency, and thereby accepted responsibility for rebellion. But Moray's cause was England's policy, and when Mary fled south across the Border Elizabeth wrote and offered her help on condition that Moray be given liberty to defend himself, while Mary must answer such accusations as he might bring against her. Mary agreed, and Moray, who depended on English recognition, acquiesced.

In June 1568, Moray told Elizabeth that his secretary, John Wood, then in London, had been sent "that which we trust shall sufficiently resolve her Majesty of anything she stands doubtful unto." The parcel which Wood had received contained translations of the Casket Letters, and also, perhaps, Buchanan's *Detection*. Wood was told to inquire "if the French originals are found to tally with the Scots translations, will that be reckoned good evidence?"

The "originals" could be altered if necessary: that, surely, is the manifest inference. And other translations existed, or were being made: there are still extant Scots, English, and Latin translations, and French translations from the Latin. Only the "originals" defy examination and disappoint curiosity. They may have been seen by Elizabeth's commissioners, or court of inquiry, which met at York, removed to Westminster, and then to Hampton Court; but of that there is no certainty: they saw letters which, they were told, were in Mary's writing. Mary herself was not permitted to see the evidence offered in proof of her guilt, and the Scottish commissioners abetted their English colleagues in the sort of discussion which so often prolongs, to little purpose, government inquiry today. The court of inquiry solved nothing, but avoided trouble. It acquitted Moray and his adherents of rebellion, and affirmed that nothing had been proved against Mary. But the Casket Letters had usefully blackened her reputation.

The behaviour of the Duke of Norfolk, however, may be thought interesting. He, the senior English commissioner, is said to have been a man of timorous disposition. He must have seen the original letters—if they were produced in evidence—and formed his own opinion of Mary's alleged guilt. There was long debate about her proper disposal—she was the sovereign head of a friendly power who had abdicated under duress—and he proposed to meet the difficulty by marrying her. His offer was serious—of that there is no doubt—and to some it may seem improbable that a Catholic nobleman, timid by nature, would be eager to wed a woman proved guilty of adultery and the murder of her husband. The Duke may have had an opportunity, not given to others, to form his own opinion about the validity of the evidence.

The authenticity of the "sonnets" is easily disproved. They are written in a doggerel French of which Mary could not have been guilty, and in an illuminating study of Bothwell by Robert Gore-Browne[*] there is the ingenious suggestion that their author was, in fact, Anna Throndsen, a Norwegian girl to whom Bothwell had, at one time, promised marriage.

Letter One is incriminating only because it appears to have been written from Glasgow, and the assumption was that it had been written when Mary went there to take Darnley to Craigmillar. But "from Glasgow this Saturday morning" is an addition that could easily have been made to a genuine letter previously written and in a previous context quite inoffensive. Letter Eight is wholly unlike the others: its style is laboured and overblown, and Anna Throndsen may have writ-

[*] Robert Gore-Browne: *Lord Bothwell.*

ten it as well as the "sonnets." Its inclusion was a mistake which the Confederate Lords—or those of them responsible for sending that parcel to John Wood—must have regretted if there was a literary critic among the commissioners at York.

Letter Two is a remarkable document which has claimed the startled attention of all who have read it—the alleged translation, that is—and exercised endless inquiry. Its length is the first surprise, and surprise may turn to incredulity when consideration is given to the circumstances in which it is supposed to have been written. Mary had gone to Glasgow to make arrangements for Darnley's return to Edinburgh. She stayed there for about five days, and during that time is supposed to have written twice to Bothwell. Letter One is short, but Letter Two contains over three thousand words. Now Bothwell had ridden with her on the journey to Glasgow; he returned to Edinburgh, and promptly rode again to lead a raid through Liddesdale. Bothwell, in command of his Border constabulary, was on duty, and it may seem unlikely that a messenger, bearing a letter, could easily reach him. It may also appear probable that the Queen knew what he was doing, and appreciated the difficulty of finding the Warden of the Marches when he himself was in search of Border thieves.

In Letter One Mary writes of Darnley, "He is the meryest that ever you sawe," but in Letter Two she speaks of his grief; tells of his self-pity and pretended remorse, says "he hath no desyre to be seen" but "has allwais the tears in his eye." That is a strange contradiction, but stranger still are the differences in tone so apparent in the letter.

Its opening paragraph is frankly sentimental, and then, abruptly, it proceeds to a matter-of-fact recital of what happened during the last stages of the journey to Glasgow. Then comes a description of the meeting with Darnley, and of his attempts to discover, from the Queen and some of her servants, the real purpose of her visit. Much of the letter reads like an *aide-mémoire*, and that, most probably, is what much of it was. It contained matter, perhaps, for further discussion with Lethington on the topic of divorce. Parts of the letter must be accepted as Mary's own writing, or a translation of it; but for whom she wrote—for herself, for Moray or Lethington—is less apparent. In one place she records a cry of great pathos that seems to anticipate one of the most dramatic utterances of the Elizabethan stage. Darnley, she writes, complains that "when I offend you sometime, you are cause thereof"—as though he were Othello murmuring above Desdemona's beauty in the taper-light, "It is the cause, it is the cause, my soul."

But then occur little passages that speak of guilt, or her dissembling, of her love for him to whom the letter purports to be addressed, and the change of tone suggests that these are additions or interpolations, the purpose of which is obvious. There is, moreover, a passage, quite incoherent, that consists only of notes, of things to be remembered, that cannot be accepted as part of a letter but could well be paragraph-headings for pages of the *aide-mémoire* that she had no time to write.

The writer speaks twice of a bracelet that she is making, and mysteriously adds "send me word whether you will have it and more monney." If, of course, Mary was truly in the habit of making keepsakes for Bothwell, and sending him money, suspicion of her relations with him would be wakened in the most innocent of minds. But she had no intention of spending more than a few days in Glasgow, she would take Darnley to Edinburgh, and she would presumably see Bothwell as soon as he had finished his business in Liddesdale. Is it likely, then, that she would ask him if he wanted the bracelet—and more money—when she was well aware that she would meet him before there was any prospect of receiving a reply to her letter?

There had been a stimulating variety in Bothwell's life, and rough adventure had left room for love. It is unlikely that he never received letters from the ladies he loved, and some that he received he may have kept; as many men do. The offer of money and a bracelet was, perhaps, found in a genuine letter—genuine, but not written by Mary—and added to Letter Two with other insertions that had the same purpose. The final paragraph of the letter may also have been written by the lady who made the bracelet. It reads, in part, "Excuse my evill wryting, and read it over twise. . . . Pray remember your friend, and wryte unto her and often. Love me allwais as I shall love you."

Mary, Queen of Scots, was a proud woman, accustomed to flattery, very conscious of her queenliness. That she would apologise for her handwriting is improbable—she wrote in a large, Italianate hand—and in "Pray remember your friend" there is a suburban note that never sounded in her voice. Nor can one discern any reason why she should plead with Bothwell to write often to her, when Bothwell had his own quarters in Holyroodhouse.

From the Scottish version of Letter Two there hangs a tail omitted from the English. "Lufe me as I sall do zow," writes the unknown lady; but then comes:

> "Remember zow of the purpose of the Lady Reres.
> Of the Inglishmen.
> Of his mother.
> Of the Erle of Argyle.
> Of the Erle of Bothwell.
> Of the ludgeing in Edinburgh."

But if Letter Two was written by Mary to Bothwell, why was she impelled to remind him of his own existence?—It is difficult to find an explanation unless it be admitted that Letter Two was a compilation too hurriedly put together to be plausible. It was a patchwork quilt designed to smother Mary's good name, and cover, in one capacious bed of lies, the guilt of the Confederate Lords who had been her rebellious subjects.

To that conclusion must be added one more fact. There is, in Letter Two, a passage that reports at some length Mary's conversation with Darnley while he lay abed in Glasgow. She questioned him about his sickness and unhappiness, and he replied—according to the English translation—"I am young. You will say that you have also pardoned me in my time and that I returne to my fault. May not a man of my age for want of counsel, faylle twise or thrise and mysse of promis and at the last repent and rebuke himself by his experience? If I may obtayn this pardon I protest I will not make fault agayn. And I ask nothing but that we may be at bed and table together as husband and wife; and if you will not I will never rise from this bed."

Now when the Commissioners met at York there was brought to them, to give evidence, a man called Thomas Craufurd, who had been in Glasgow at the time of the Queen's visit. Craufurd told the Commissioners that he had set down in writing what he saw and heard, and that Darnley had been very communicative about occasions when he and the Queen were alone together. He read to the Commissioners the document he had so thoughtfully prepared, and part of what he read was this: "I am but yonge, and ye will saye ye have forgivne me diverse tymes. Maye not a man of mye age, for lacke of counselle, of which I am verye destitute, falle twise or thrise, and yet repent, and be chastised bye experience? Gif I have made anye faile that ye but think a faile, howe soever it be, I crave your pardone, and proteste that I shall never faile againe. I desire no other thinge but that we maye be together as husband and wife. And if ye will not consent hereto, I desire never to rise forthe of this bed."

The looking-glass resemblance to the passage quoted from Letter Two is immediately apparent, and that startling resemblance continues for about four hundred words of Craufurd's testimony. Was he a witness who had been coached too well? Had he zealously committed parts of Letter Two to heart? If so, those who sent him—he was a blood-relation of the Lennox family—may have intended to offer an apparently independent witness who would substantiate a letter that might not of itself carry conviction. But the looking-glass quality of Craufurd's memory destroys any belief in the independence of his evidence.

It is possible, however, that he did write out what Darnley had told him, and those who composed Letter Two incorporated his notes. In that case the letter was not a letter, but—as already suggested—a compilation, the authors of which had much to gain by it.

Arrogant Byblows, an Interlude

If one had a large and generous knowledge of history it might be possible to show, as an interesting and curious fact, that those ages most
clearly distinguished and extensively decorated by architecture of the
greatest merit were, in temper, anti-social or indifferent to the needs
and welfare of common humanity.

The Egyptian pyramids—most hideous but technically impressive
of ancient buildings—were raised by the servile labour of men to whose
minds no thought of human dignity had been allowed to penetrate.
In ancient Greece the Parthenon and the Erechtheum were built by a
nameless population that existed beneath the lowest levels of democracy. The cathedral at Chartres and King's College Chapel in Cambridge were the work of men who lived in an age when it was proper
to worship God in the highest, but few condescended to think of the
plight of those left destitute by his Creation. When Palladio built palaces in Vicenza, or Vanbrugh created the great mansion of Blenheim,
there was little regard for the common needs of poor people in Italy
and England who had rarely enough for their bellies and never much
comfort against the brutalities of winter.

Other examples come readily to mind—Asia abounds in such dis-
crepancies, from Fatehpur Sikri to Angkor Wat—but one could hardly
anticipate discovery of the anti-social effects of an enthusiasm for
building—of an aesthetic delight in architecture for its own sake—in the
remote archipelago of Orkney. In the second half of the Sixteenth
Century, however, the inhabitants of those islands suffered grievously
under two arrogant byblows of the royal house of Scotland; men whose

temper was cruel, their ambition excessive, and who built castles or palaces with the greatest ardour.

By Euphemia Elphinstone James V fathered a son called Robert, born in 1537, who as a boy had been made Commendator of the abbey of Holyrood, and thus assured of a comfortable income. At the time of his half-sister's marriage to Darnley he seems to have been friendly with that disastrous youth, and it may have been by Darnley's influence that in 1564 Robert Stewart received, as a gift, the crown estates in Orkney and Shetland. Gilbert Balfour, sometime master of the Queen's household, was Sheriff Principal in the islands, and the Bishop of Orkney was Adam Bothwell, son of a provost of Edinburgh. In 1567, however, Robert Stewart—by means unknown—became Sheriff Principal in Balfour's place, and a year later he persuaded or compelled Adam Bothwell to exchange the estates of the Orkney bishopric for the abbey of Holyrood and its revenues. Established in both castle and palace, he thus acquired almost absolute power in the islands, and in 1581 his authority was reaffirmed and underlined when he was created Earl of Orkney.

He had married a daughter of the Earl of Cassilis, by whom he had a son, Patrick. Robert died in 1591, and Patrick, succeeding to title and estates, showed a temper even more grasping, arrogant, and overbearing than his father's. That they were both men of considerable ability can hardly be disputed; that their ability wore a criminal complexion must be frankly admitted. They were unscrupulous enough to use to the full their natural gifts and unusual opportunities, and in their lordly buildings they exposed their pride and took their pleasure. Father and son, they ruled the islands for some forty-five years, and ruined their economy to enhance their appearance.

The strong castle of Kirkwall was theirs, and the Bishop's palace. They also built a fortified palace at Birsay, on the north shore of the mainland of Orkney; another, of great beauty, in Kirkwall; a castle at Scalloway in Shetland; and they may have had a hand—a hand discreetly concealed—in the building of a sombre and most formidable castle on the island of Westray. It is improbable that the population of Orkney numbered more than 20,000, and Shetland's would be rather less; it was a small population to be burdened with so many great buildings. But the Stewart earls financed their work by tyrannous exaction, bland illegality, and forced labour. They reduced the islands to poverty, but left as memorials of misrule some very imposing masonry.

Orkney and Shetland had been left in pawn by Christian I of Denmark, in lieu of his daughter's promised dowry when she married James III. They were still subject to Norse or odal law, and their status had not been clarified by formal cession, though Scotland had formally annexed them. Earl Robert took advantage of these anomalies to raise rents and taxes: rents were paid in kind, not cash, and he found it simple to increase them by enlarging statutory weights and measures. He took possession of common lands, and compelled the free burgesses of Kirkwall to pay for a license to trade. The natives were not allowed to leave their islands without permission, but Robert asserted his right to banish those who displeased him. To courts of law he dictated their verdicts, and ingeniously devised a procedure for charging dead men with old crimes, and punishing them for their misdeeds by confiscating the properties they had left behind. Many proprietors who held their land by odal law were either ejected or threatened with eviction but permitted to remain "as true servants and vassals." The old Norse families were systematically despoiled.

Earl Robert was guilty of a grave indiscretion in 1576 or 1577. He embarked on negotiations with the King of Denmark, and whatever his purpose may have been, it wore a treasonable look. He accepted, for Shetland, a lawman appointed by the Danish King, and by that sovereign was confirmed in his possession of Orkney and Shetland. To the government in Edinburgh—the Earl of Morton was Regent—such behaviour seemed darkly suspect, and for the safety of the realm Earl Robert was imprisoned at Linlithgow. There he remained for a couple of years, but then found friends whose influence obtained his release, and by 1579 he was again in Orkney.

The ruins of the palace he built at Birsay stand on the Atlantic shore, red walls of crumbling sandstone that have been robbed for later and much smaller buildings. Its three sides enclosed a large, oblong courtyard, and were dignified by rectangular towers. It had a frontage of a hundred and twenty feet, and its length was more than that. It was supplied with barns and stables, cornfields and vegetable gardens, a bowling green and archery butts; and in its walls were many gunloops. Its upper rooms had painted ceilings, adorned with pictures of Noah's Flood, Christ riding to Jerusalem, and other Biblical subjects; and at the entrance, above the arms of Robert Stewart, was the arrogant motto *Sic fuit, est, et erit.*

On the island of Westray the castle of Noltland has walls about seven feet thick, ponderous towers at its northeast and southwest corners, and a general appearance so aggressive, so pugnacious, that to many it resembles an old-fashioned man-of-war with gunports opening along its sides. It stands in a commanding position above the only safe harbour in the island, and obviously it was built, not for pleasure, but defence.—Defence against whom?

Now in 1560 Adam, Bishop of Orkney, conveyed the lands of Noltland to Gilbert Balfour, who was his brother-in-law. Gilbert was Sheriff Principal of Orkney in 1564, but by 1567 had surrendered that office to Robert Stewart; and experts agree that the castle was most probably built in the 1560s. From what is known of Gilbert it seems unlikely that he had the resources to build so largely, or any reason to defend himself behind such formidable walls. But if he was acting as Earl Robert's lieutenant, and Robert's negotiations with the King of Denmark were indeed treasonable, it is possible that Noltland and the strong castle of Kirkwall were intended to be fortresses within which the ruler of Orkney could proclaim his independence or declare his allegiance to Denmark.

That Balfour and his brothers were deeply involved in the murder of Darnley became fairly evident in the previous chapter; and in 1576, when he was in Swedish service, he joined another set of conspirators in a plot against the King, and was executed. It seems clear that Gilbert was the sort of man who might have been employed on a treasonable enterprise by Robert Stewart, and that Robert would not have hesitated to make use of him. Robert was a king's son, though born on the wrong side of the blanket, and he must have known the temptation to emulate his sister and make a throne for himself.

Patrick, Robert's son and successor, behaved more outrageously than his father, and by his zeal for architecture left a memorial of marvellous and unexpected beauty. Patrick was a ruthless despot who ruled his islands with unflinching tyranny, and was long remembered for his oppression of the "gentlemen tenants" of the country. He set them to work both by sea and land, especially in the quarries that grew ever deeper as he excavated more and more stone for his building.

He built a castle at Scalloway on the west side of Shetland—turreted, four storeys high, but not very attractive—and a few years later, in 1606, began his masterpiece. Neighbourly with the cathedral of St Magnus, in Kirkwall, rose the walls of a palace that has been described, with all the authority of a Royal Commission, as "possibly the most mature and accomplished piece of Renaissance architecture left in Scotland." The great hall, with its soaring windows and vast fireplace, is indeed magnificent; from a wing emerge turrets exquisitely poised on discreet corbelling; and the kitchen is noble testimony to enormous though forgotten hospitality. The masons who built the Earl's palace were Scots, but their inspiration was French, and in the northern isles they domesticated a fragment of French elegance. Though a wicked and destructive man, Earl Patrick was an artist—or knew enough to employ artists.

But he lacked his father's ability to keep out of trouble, or extricate himself when overtaken by trouble. By making his own laws, and intolerably enforcing them, he had defied crown and parliament. Worse than that—for the consequences were more grievous—his extravagance had brought him to the very edge of bankruptcy. But when he was arrested, in 1609, his defence was so arrogantly simple that it is difficult to deny it admiration: he had had the power and authority, he said, to do what he pleased.

Nor was he willing to admit defeat. He had an illegitimate son, Robert, a gallant, attractive, irresponsible youth whom Patrick sent to Orkney to collect his rents and recover the fortresses he had been compelled to surrender. Against all probability Robert mustered a following of about two hundred men, recaptured the palace at Birsay and then Kirkwall castle, where he prepared for defence and sent a ship to Bergen to buy ammunition.

But rebellion was short-lived. In two ships, armed with cannon from Edinburgh castle and carrying an army of five hundred, the Earl of Caithness sailed to Orkney and laid siege to the rebel stronghold. But for five weeks the castle held out—its strength was notorious—though at the end young Robert's companions numbered only fifteen. Eventually the castle was reduced to ruin, its defenders hanged, and Robert was taken prisoner to Edinburgh.

Death was the only sentence to be expected, and on the 1st January, 1615, he was hanged at the Market Cross. Some weeks later his father was about to start on the same journey when the ministers attending him found him "so ignorant that he could scarce rehearse the Lord's Prayer," and requested that his execution be delayed for a few days until he "were better informed." Then, enlightened if not repentant, he was taken to the Cross and beheaded.

The islands he had impoverished retreated into obscurity, but near the cathedral of St. Magnus the walls of his palace—it suffered badly under Lord Caithness's siege guns—still remain for evidence of his good taste and evil rule. Whether legitimate or otherwise, the royal Stewarts were seldom commonplace.

Success Unhonoured

1

King James VI of Scotland realised his mother's ambition and became James I of England. He was most warmly welcomed by a majority of his subjects in the south, but gradually he lost favour, and for that his growing self-indulgence was largely to blame. By historians, and their readers, he has seldom been given much respect, and for that mishap a man called Weldon, and the mischievous tales he wrote, must bear almost as much blame as the King himself; for mischief and malice have an ageless and universal appeal. It may, then, be useful to look at Weldon's portrait of King James before essaying, from a suitable point in time, a more sober and objective view.

Sir Anthony Weldon, bred to court service—his father may have been a clerk of the kitchen in Queen Elizabeth's household—was a man of malignant mind, jealous of his betters, and resentful of his failure to win preferment. He had, unfortunately, some literary ability, and when he found solace in slandering his successful contemporaries his gossip bit deeply, and like a graving tool his pen scratched on popular opinion—and popular memory—the arabesques of his own malice. He wrote a commentary that he called "The Court of King James, or A General Discourse of some Secret Passages in State"; which, when advised not to publish it, he inscribed to Lady Elizabeth Sedley, mother of the minor poet Sir Charles Sedley. To her he wrote, "You shall find in it the most perfect form of undeniable truths," but added, as if in self-defence, "it was written in a melancholy humour, therefore fittest for your melancholy temper."

Of Robert Cecil, Earl of Salisbury—Secretary of State and devoted servant to both Elizabeth and James—he wrote, quite untruthfully, that he died in the most miserable circumstances, having lost all favour. English courtiers he denounced, *en bloc,* as potential traitors: when a new Spanish ambassador came to London there was none of note "that tasted not of Spain's bounty, either in gold or jewels." The Earl of Northampton was a man whose character defies admiration, but Weldon probably exaggerated when he wrote of him that he was "of so venomous and cankered a disposition that he hated all of noble parts."

Many people disliked and derided the Scots who followed James VI when he rode south to his richer kingdom; and his northern subjects complained that their new neighbours had the unfriendly habit of referring to them as "beggarly Scots." King James, says Weldon, "had a very ready wit," and happily replied to the complainants: "Content yourselves! I will shortly make the English as beggarly as you, and so end that controversy."

In England the noble, rich, and influential Howards excited, in those who knew them, as much dislike as the Scots; and Weldon was pleased to tell Lady Elizabeth that among those who hated them was the young and gallant Prince Henry, who would often say that "if ever he were king he would not leave one of that family to piss against a wall." Of Henry's untimely death, probably of typhoid fever, he wrote that he "died not without vehement suspicion of poison; and I wish I could say *but suspicion only.*"

Weldon wrote about the favour that James showed to the handsome young man called Robert Kerr, later Earl of Somerset, and as if he had been a witness of the scene pretended to describe the King's last farewell, when he had determined to part with Somerset: "The earl, when he kissed his hand, the king hung about his neck, slabbering his cheeks, saying 'For God's sake, when shall I see thee again? On my soul, I shall neither eat nor sleep until you come again.'"—It was a Friday, Somerset promised to return on Monday, and the King, says Weldon, kissed him "at the stairs' head, at the middle of the stairs, and at the stairs' foot"; but before Somerset had stepped into his coach James, "in the hearing of nine servants," declared "I shall never see his face more!"—But for that spirited anecdote Weldon needed more than the testimony of nine servants; he could hardly have written it without the instinct or impulse of a frustrated playwright whose dramas had never reached the stage.

The King's new favourite was George Villiers, subsequently Duke of Buckingham, and Weldon tells an hilarious tale of Buckingham's assiduity—after high rank had given him authority—in providing for his relations. A multitude of impoverished cousins were married off—even kitchen wenches got the eldest sons of knights—and the consequence was that Whitehall swarmed with unknown women and their young, the King's own apartments were as full as a rabbit burrow with strange children, and "old Sir Anthony Ashley, who never loved any but boys, was snatched up for a kinswoman."

A later paragraph is less agreeable. Buckingham and Charles, Prince of Wales, went off on a foolish journey into Spain to find a royal bride for Charles, and Weldon suggests that James, by then, was so tired of Buckingham that he would have welcomed news of some misadventure, in which Charles lost his life, if the same accident carried off Buckingham. That, of course, is the most nonsensical and gross of libels, for James was not only devoted to Buckingham, but loved Charles, his surviving son, with an excess of sentiment. Weldon's description of the King, his person and his character, is well known, and has been widely accepted as a true portrait. But to read, as a preliminary, his description of Scotland may offer a caution against too ready a faith in the veracity of an ingenious author.

Scotland, he wrote, "is too good for those that possess it, and too bad for others to be at the charge to conquer it. The air might be wholesome, but for the stinking people that inhabit it. The ground might be fruitful, had they the wit to manure it.

"They think it impossible to lose the way to heaven, if they can but leave Rome behind them.

"Their beasts be generally small, women only excepted, of which sort there are none greater in the world.

"As for fruit, for their grandsire Adam's sake, they never planted any; and for other trees, had Christ been betrayed in this country (as doubtless he should, had he come as a stranger) Judas had sooner found the grace of repentance than a tree to hang himself on."

Parts of that description are merely offensive, but parts are witty too. His portrait of James is not witty, and may be a lampoon rather than a likeness. He was more corpulent through his clothes than in his body, says Weldon. His doublets were quilted to make them stiletto-proof, his breeches folded in great pleats. He was naturally of a timorous disposition. His eyes were large and ever rolling, so that many left the room in embarrassment. His tongue was too large for his mouth, and made his drinking uncomely. His skin was soft because he never washed. His legs were weak, at the age of seven he had not been able to stand. His manner of walking was circular, his fingers always fiddling with his codpiece. He was constantly drinking, but not to excess, and he never changed his clothes until they were worn to rags. He was, however, very witty, and despite the impediment of too large a tongue, delivered his witticisms in a grave and serious manner.

It is possible that some historians and many of their readers have been too willing to accept as fact what Weldon wrote for the release of spleen and Lady Elizabeth's melancholy entertainment. The samples of his gossip, given here, do not persuade one to accept him as a reliable and unprejudiced witness. He can be witty, he can be amusing, but malevolence intrudes too nakedly to let much credence be given him. It is instructive, indeed, to compare Weldon's portrait of the King with a description, written when James was eighteen, by a man called Fontenay whose brother was employed by Mary, the imprisoned Queen Mother, as her French secretary.

Fontenay wrote of him:* "Three qualities of the mind he possesses in perfection: he understands clearly, judges wisely, and has a retentive memory. His questions are keen and penetrating and his replies are sound. In any argument, whatever it is about, he maintains the view that appears to him most just, and I have heard him support Catholic against Protestant opinions. He is well instructed in languages, science, and affairs of state, better, I dare say, than anyone else in his kingdom. In short, he has a remarkable intelligence, as well as lofty and virtuous ideals and a high opinion of himself.

"I have remarked in him three defects that may prove injurious to his estate and government: he does not estimate correctly his poverty and insignificance but is over-confident of his strength and scornful of other princes; his love for favourites is indiscreet and wilful and takes no account of the wishes of his people; he is too lazy and indifferent about affairs, too given to pleasure, allowing all business to be conducted by others.

"He dislikes dancing and music, and the little affectations of courtly life such as amorous discourse or curiosities of dress, and has a special

* Quoted by D. H. Willson: *King James VI and I.*

aversion for ear-rings. In speaking and eating, in his dress and in his sports, in his conversation in the presence of women, his manners are crude and uncivil and display a lack of proper instruction. He is never still in one place but walks constantly up and down, though his gait is erratic and wandering, and he tramps about even in his own chamber. His voice is loud and his words grave and sententious. He loves the chase above all other pleasures and will hunt for six hours without interruption, galloping over hill and dale with a loosened bridle. His body is feeble and yet he is not delicate. In a word, he is an old young man."

Though Fontenay was critical of the young King's deportment, his admiration of James's intelligence was explicit and devoid of the extravagance into which courtiers and royal servants were so often tempted. That James's manners lacked grace and polish is no matter for surprise when one recalls the deprivations of his childhood and the narrow discipline of his youth.

2

Separated from his mother when he was barely a year old, James was brought up by guardians who, before his fourth birthday, committed him for education to that malignant and sadistic scholar, George Buchanan; a gentler tutor called Peter Young; and Alexander Erskine, a good-tempered young noble who taught him to ride. By Buchanan, who had been paid to traduce his mother, James was instructed, in the classical tradition, with ferocious intensity; by Peter Young, as it appears, he was persuaded to enjoy the learning forced upon him; and Erskine instilled that passion for horsemanship and the chase which, almost certainly, gave him a robustitude that preserved his health against Buchanan's tyranny, but induced so extravagant a love of hunting that he could ride with untroubled delight in pursuit of deer when he should have been studying—with Robert Cecil at his elbow—the urgent problems of England's economy and her foreign policy.

A reigning King before he could talk, James VI lived and eventually ruled in Scotland for thirty-seven years before Elizabeth of England died in the decrepitude of her magnificence, and he was translated to a richer kingdom whose larger throne he occupied as James I. In the imperfect light of present judgment those thirty-seven years now look like a calendar of fearful insecurity punctuated by violence that recurrently challenged James's capacity for survival. In his nonage, though he was allowed some escape from Buchanan's teaching, he was, by modern standards, intolerably burdened. A library of six hundred volumes was assembled for his edification, and from his nursery he was pushed into a world dominated by the Greek and Latin classics. He learnt Latin very thoroughly, and in later years was grateful to Buchanan despite his memories of being thrashed for an occasional levity. There were many theological works in his library, there was history, and natural history, and mathematics. There were books written in French and Spanish and Italian. He was given a scholar's education while beyond the dark bookshelves his kingdom was seething with lordly riot, unscrupulous ambition, and the pugnacious dogmas of a lately reformed church.

After Mary's flight into England the Earl of Moray ruled as Regent for three years, and then was murdered by one of the Hamiltons, who were now demanding the restoration of the Queen. An English army crossed the Border, captured the town and castle of Hamilton, and the Earl of Lennox was elected Regent with English approval. By bold assault the strong castle of Dunbarton was captured for the King's party, and Archbishop Hamilton, an unexpected prize, was found within. He, the head of his powerful family, was tried on the dubious charge of having been party to the murder of both Darnley and Moray; and on the very day of his trial, being conveniently found guilty, was hanged at the Market Cross of Stirling. Civil war, of a somewhat inchoate sort, then ensued. Edinburgh castle, held by the Queen's party, was hotly besieged; in a confused affair at Stirling the Regent Lennox was killed; and the Earl of Mar, who succeeded him, died within a year. He was followed by James Douglas, Earl of Morton, who had been closely implicated in the murder of Rizzio. Morton was ruthless, competent, and assisted by England. He broke the strength of the Queen's party, restored order, and lived till 1581. He, in his turn, was then overthrown, and against him also convenient evidence was discovered: he was found guilty of complicity in the murder of Darnley, and executed.

Morton's downfall was largely due to the arrival from France of Esmé Stewart, Seigneur d'Aubigny, a cousin of James's father, who quickly won the young King's affection, and was generously rewarded.

He was made Earl of Lennox, Keeper of Dunbarton castle, and a privy councillor. He used French gold to enlist support, and roused the united opposition of England and the Protestant reformers. Against Esmé Stewart, Earl of Lennox, the inconstant tide was turning, and in the summer of 1582 the King, who was then sixteen, was captured by Lennox's enemies while hunting near Perth, and taken to Ruthven castle, a seat of the Earl of Gowrie. Lennox retired to France, and died a few months later. The ministers of the Reformed kirk were triumphant, but Elizabeth of England, who had promised them help, sent none. James, by his own wit, escaped his captors, and found support in the north. The Earls of Huntly, Argyll, and Crawford rallied to his side; again the tables were turned; and Gowrie was executed.

James was of a timorous disposition—so say Fontenay and Weldon —and this brief account of the people and events which filled the background of his youth can leave no occasion for surprise at his disability. If there is cause for wonder, it is that he did not succumb to the neurosis of total despair. Fontenay, however, says that he wanted to be thought courageous, and the fact that he outlived all dangers—those of his boyhood and adolescence, those that still awaited him—may be proof that he possessed a determination not unrelated to courage. Of intellectual contest—of the savage cut-and-thrust of theological argument—he had no fear whatever, and that was fortunate indeed. There was a new cloud on the horizon, dark with anger, and at the heart of it was a minister of the Kirk.

In the years that followed Mary's flight into England, Scotland shows on the surface of its history the anarchy of a jungle overcrowded by predators; but it must be insisted that beneath the violence—moving with purpose under self-destroying rivalries—there was a gathering together of the faith and forces that were to shape or perturb the story of Britain for a century and a half. The security of England depended on a Protestant Scotland, and in Scotland the Congregation of Christ depended, not only on a continuing and absolute faith in the teaching of John Calvin, but on the pugnacity of those who expounded it. Calvinism was a fighting creed, and rejoiced in its enemies. France and Spain were always suspect; and while the Pope of Rome was anti-Christ in living flesh, all temporal power was hostile in essence.

In 1574 the Reformation had been stiffened by the return to Scotland, from Geneva, of Andrew Melville, a scholar and a stronger man than John Knox. Melville, who became principal of the university of

St. Andrews, greatly enhanced the prestige and influence of the General Assembly of the Kirk. The Kirk, he declared, possessed an authority which, derived directly and exclusively from God, was superior to the authority of civil magistrates. He told James that there were two kings and two kingdoms in Scotland, and one of the kings was Christ Jesus, whose kingdom was the Kirk, of which James was "not a king, nor a lord, nor a head, but a member." The anarchic power of the great nobles was waning, but waxing in opposition to the throne was the power of the Kirk; and to Melville and the menace of presbyterianism was due King James's liking for episcopacy. He needed a screen of bishops to stand between him and the hostility of Calvinist pastors.

After the execution of Gowrie, James relied for some years on an educated adventurer, of splendid presence and great independence of mind, called James Stewart; whom he created Earl of Arran. Andrew Melville's growing power was checked, the presbyterians were shocked by a reaffirmation of the authority of bishops, and there was an exodus of pastors to England. Elizabeth was still unwilling to admit that James must be her successor, but the need for agreement between the two countries was increasingly evident, and in 1586 a league of friendship was established that gave Scotland an annual subsidy of £4000. The Protestant lords who had been Gowrie's associates, when he kidnapped the King, had found refuge in England after his execution; they now returned, and the adventurous Arran retired from the scene. A few months later James was confronted with a major crisis, of the most serious implications, and was much blamed for his behaviour.

3

For nineteen years Mary, his mother, had been a prisoner in England and recurrently a menace to the security of the southern kingdom. The Catholic Duke of Norfolk, who had proposed to marry her, was sent to the Tower and in 1572 executed for his share in a plot which required the invasion of England by Spanish troops. Parliament demanded Mary's death, but Elizabeth refused to approve the demand. A northern rising, in her favour, by the Earls of Northumberland and Westmorland did no more than rescue Mary from a vile, insanitary prison at Tutbury in Staffordshire: the rebels approached so closely that she was removed to Sheffield, where, cared for by the Earl of

Shrewsbury and his redoubtable wife, she remained for some fourteen years.

News of the massacre of St. Bartholomew excited the English Protestants against her, but Elizabeth still shrank from signing her cousin's death warrant. There was a scandalously ingenious plan to let her return to Scotland if the Regent, Mar, and his Chancellor, Morton, would promise to execute her immediately; but Morton's price was too high, and the plan came to nothing. For some years plotters and politicians lost interest in her, and Mary filled idle days by writing endless letters, playing with her lapdogs, and embroidering small gifts for her royal cousin. There was a romantic dream of marriage to Don John of Austria, but the Dutchmen killed him and Mary took to her needlework again.

She was removed to another prison, and briskly engaged in a dangerous correspondence with foreign agents who again suggested the feasibility of Spanish invasion. That correspondence was intercepted, and then came the Babington plot, which brought her to her death. There is reason to believe that Elizabeth's very able minister, Walsingham, was aware, from its inception, of the details and purpose of the plot, if he did not contrive it. Mary was to be liberated, and after a Roman Catholic rising Elizabeth would be murdered. Babington was an enthusiastic but impractical young man, his associates no better. With some ingenuity he established communication with Mary, but the conspirators were arrested and on the 25th September, 1586, she was taken to Fotheringay castle in Northamptonshire, where she was tried for complicity.

At the preliminary enquiry a letter from Elizabeth was read, which, by foretelling the verdict, somewhat invalidated the pending trial. With acumen and great dignity Mary conducted her own defence. She protested against the injustice and illegality of the proceedings, and denied the jurisdiction of an English tribunal. She offered to answer the charges against her before parliament, or the Queen in Council, on condition that her protest was recorded and she declared next in succession to Elizabeth. That was refused, but though she was in no position to bargain, it was finally agreed that she would answer the commissioners on one point only: her alleged concurrence in that part of the plot which threatened Elizabeth's life.

The trial resembled bear-baiting rather than a court of law, and grew very noisy. Against a formidable array of English noblemen and

English lawyers, Mary stood alone, and for two days maintained her defence. Then the trial was adjourned, and ten days later the commissioners met in the Star Chamber to re-examine such evidence as they thought relevant. They declared Mary guilty of compassing divers matters tending to the destruction of the English Queen. For three weeks Elizabeth temporised, then the Star Chamber's verdict was announced, and at last, on the 7th February, 1587, the Earls of Kent and Shrewsbury arrived at Fotheringay with a warrant for the execution.

Guards and a crowd of spectators filled the great hall of the castle. The scaffold, two feet high and twelve feet broad, with rails about it, was draped in black, as were a low stool and the block. There were prayers and more prayers, there was a conflict of prayers—English against Latin—but except in the excitement of that controversy Mary was calm, cheerful, seemingly indifferent to death. She forgave her enemies, prayed all saints to make intercession for her, and kissed the cross. Her executioners, kneeling before her, besought her to forgive them her death, and she answered, "I forgive you with all my heart, for now, I hope, you shall make an end of all my troubles."

Her two women took off her outer clothing, and Mary, with the courtesy of an almost incredible good humour, covered their nervous clumsiness with a pretended complaint that never before had she been compelled to disrobe before such a company. They were crying loudly, but she bade them be quiet, and one of them tied a cloth about her head. She knelt, and groping for the block, put her chin across it. She lay still, but cried loudly, three or four times, *"In manus tuas, Domine!"* One of the executioners held her lightly, the other struck twice and severed her head, save a little gristle of the neck. That he cut, lifted up her head, and cried "God save the Queen."

Her headdress fell off, and her hair, cropped close, was as grey as if she had been seventy. Her face was so changed by death that few could recognise it. Unnoticed by any there, one of Mary's little lapdogs had come in with her, and hidden beneath her skirts. It was discovered when an executioner bent to pull off her garters, but would not leave the Queen's dead body. It ran to her bleeding neck, and had to be carried away and washed.

James was twenty-one when his mother was executed. He had been separated from her when he was a year old. He can have had no memory of her, and in boyhood little knowledge other than the tales Buchanan may have told him, or that he had read in the *Detection.*

He had, after boyhood, turned against Buchanan, and bitterly rejected his charges. But he must often have thought of his murdered father, whom he so closely resembled. Though he no longer believed in his mother's guilt, she had married Bothwell, whose guilt has never been doubted; and the fact that she married in fear of her life may not have reconciled him to the union. During her imprisonment, moreover, Mary—ever the politician—had listened to a proposal for her return to Scotland which, had it been acceptable, would have subordinated James's authority to hers; and it is possible that her son had not relished the prospect.

It would be pharisaical to pretend that James must or should have felt an affection for his mother so strong as to overcome reason and blind him to reality. The tie of blood had been reduced by time and distance, and he, like his mother, was a politician. There were those who feared that Mary's death would mean war with England, and if James IV had been the king, war there would have been. But James VI, though pleading most earnestly for his mother's life, insisted that nothing should be said or done that would endanger his succession to the English throne. A dynastic purpose had dominated Mary's whole existence, and he had inherited her purpose. Her curious motto, "In my end is my beginning," is a testimony to her Christian faith, but so lively a mind as hers must also have been aware of its political implication. The throne of England would have given her a new sort of life, as it gave a second life to James.

4

In 1588 Philip of Spain launched his Invincible Armada, but his ponderous ships were outmanoeuvred by English seamen whose Queen grudged the cost and maintenance of her fleet. The Catholic crusade, the great campaign of the counter-reformation, was resoundingly defeated, but in the farther parts of Scotland there still remained some conservative magnates who professed a stubborn or romantic attachment to the Spanish cause. James did nothing to antagonise the Gothic north, yet stood firmly behind the Protestant league with England, and got, as a reward, a useful addition to his subsidy. He was a realist who understood that if Philip of Spain conquered England, he could easily subjugate Scotland.

Policy as well as nature now suggested that he should look for a wife, and, as was customary with Scottish kings, his thoughts turned first to France, where Henry of Navarre, Huguenot heir to the throne, had a disposable sister. She was a good deal older than James, however, and Henry was too poor to give her a dowry. In Edinburgh and the sea-port towns of the east coast there was strong feeling—that grew loud in expression—in favour of James's marriage to a Danish princess, for Denmark was an affluent and respectable Protestant power, with which Scotland did profitable business. The elder of King Frederick's daughters was already betrothed to the Duke of Brunswick, and perhaps to compensate for the relative unimportance of a younger sister, James's envoy made such extravagant demands for endowment, and military assistance at need, that his prospects were seriously threatened. The match was saved, however, by Anne herself, and apparently by a gathering enthusiasm in the genial Danish court for the splendour and merriment of a royal wedding.

Anne, the younger princess, was a gay, good-looking girl, barely sixteen, and the more James heard of her attractions, the more resolute he became to marry her. The bookish young man, whose own youth had been harsh and loveless, fell in love with the imagined charms of a youthful bride, and proudly declaring that he did not regard her as merchandise, abandoned his plea for a dowry. In Denmark there was busy preparation for the wedding, but in Scotland very little, for James lacked money. Elizabeth of England came to his help, however, and sent him £1000.

In August 1589, his proxy married Anne in Copenhagen, but strong westerly winds spoiled her voyage to Scotland, and the Danish ships found shelter in Oslo. James waited impatiently, and solaced his disappointment by writing poetry which, though its literary merit was small, was undoubtedly sincere and occasionally graceful. But poetry could not console him through a long winter, and with a splendid assertion of independence, and considerable skill, he made in secret his own plans. He nominated governors for his realm, left instructions for its defence, and from Leith, with a large retinue, put to sea in the last week of October, and by a fair wind was carried to Norway. Thereafter the voyage was slow, but in mid-November he met Anne, and fell in love with a reality that did not disappoint imagination. She was tall and slender, a girl of graceful carriage, with golden hair and smooth white skin. James was tall enough to match her, thin at that age, and regally clad in red velvet embroidered with gold under a cloak of black velvet and sables.

They were married on the 23rd November, and for a month enjoyed the hospitality of Norway. It was by then too late to return to Scotland, and a few days before Christmas the royal couple and their retinue set out by sledge for Denmark. They drove down and along the coast, through Bohuslän, were noisily entertained at its great castle, and somewhere south of Gothenburg put to sea, and crossing over to Elsinore were received at the castle of Kronborg with "a flourish of trumpets and ordnance shot off," as if to anticipate a performance of *Hamlet*.

James, with his young wife, remained in Denmark for four months; and it may be assumed that his kindly hosts often told him, as Hamlet told Horatio, "We'll teach you to drink deep ere you depart." It is very pleasant to think of the pedantic King, on holiday from the perils of his own land, relaxed and easy in mind under the great battlements of Kronborg; and to balance the tales, later current, of his homosexual tendencies, his love-affair with a well-grown girl of sixteen deserves attention. She was not his intellectual equal, but she had a gaiety that must have been refreshing, and his gratitude for something more than physical endearments is evident in a poem, of a rather later date, in which James calls her his "only Mediciner," and writes:

> "Your smiling is an antidote agains
> The melancholy that oppresseth me,
> And when a raging wrath into me reigns,
> Your loving looks may make me calm to be.
> How oft you see me have an heavy heart,
> Remember then, sweet Doctor, on your art."

Their affection, moreover, was no brief, transient emotion, but endured—as a kindly intimacy, if no more than that—until seven children were born.

Not all the King's time at Kronborg was spent in "heavy-headed revel," for he attended lectures in Copenhagen, argued in Latin with a learned theologian about predestination, and discussed the Copernican theory with Tycho Brahe. That he had a gift for statecraft as well as for scholarly conversation—that he had impressed upon fractious subjects his value on their throne—must here be admitted; for when he and Anne returned to Leith, on the 1st May, he found that the provision he had made for Scotland's government had been sufficient, that his realm was still whole, relatively peaceful, and ready to give him and his bride a welcome that culminated, amidst elaborate ceremony, in the young Queen's coronation at Holyrood.

The Kirk and its ministers, however, were something less than warm in their reception of the Queen. They thought her frivolous, and she found presbyterianism, or the presbyters, so little to her liking that eventually she became a convert to Rome. The Kirk had little respect for temporal authority, and some of James's nobles, who had hardly more, were quick to resent any attempt to extend it and enforce, on them as well as on common folk, a rule of law. James was well served by his Chancellor, Sir John Maitland—a brother of Maitland of Lethington, that enigmatic man who had served his mother when it suited him—but Maitland had many enemies, and when he and the King professed a desire for better administration and reform of the law, they encountered immediate opposition in which there was an element of real danger.

In the Gothic, conservative north the Catholic earls were unwilling to admit the magnitude of Spain's defeat when the beaten Armada was wrecked by the gales that followed sea battles in the Channel. They renewed a treasonable correspondence with Philip of Spain, and their letters were intercepted in England. Elizabeth, whose realm they threatened to invade, demanded their immediate punishment, and James was sorely perplexed because the leader of the Catholic faction was George Gordon, Earl of Huntly and Captain of the King's Guard. Huntly, whom his friends called the Cock of the North, was young, gay, good-looking, and as reckless as any of his clan. It was James's fond belief that he had rescued Huntly, as a brand from the burning, from the clutches of Rome, and made him a good Protestant. He may not have believed in Huntly's treachery, and certainly he had no wish to humiliate the northern earls in whose strength he had once found refuge from the Earl of Gowrie; and who might yet be needed to redress the balance if, on the other wing of politics, the Kirk and its ministers showed their hostility.

Unable to defy Elizabeth, James arrested Huntly and imprisoned him in Edinburgh castle; then weakly released him, and under nominal banishment dismissed him to his own lands in Strathbogie. Suddenly there was a threat of rebellion. The Earls of Huntly, Errol, and

Crawford rose in the north, and Francis Hepburn, Earl of Bothwell, was preparing to join them from the south. But before they were ready to move, James had taken the offensive. That unwarlike monarch, that timorous man, mustered an army and having led it to Aberdeen, offered battle. But daunted by such speed and resolution, by the King's own presence in the field, the rebel clansmen melted into the heather, their chiefs surrendered, and James in triumph returned to Edinburgh with the insurgent leaders in custody. But again he was lenient. Found guilty of treason, the culprits were imprisoned, but released within a few months. And Huntly was quickly in trouble again.

The Regent Moray, Mary's half-brother, had had no love for the Gordons, nor they for him. A daughter of Moray married another Stewart, who thus acquired the title to his late father-in-law's earldom. Huntly and the new Earl of Moray inherited an old feud, exacerbated by local rivalry, and Huntly was given an unexpected opportunity to humiliate a traditional enemy when Moray's arrest was ordered on a charge of abetting the Earl of Bothwell in sedition. Huntly was sent to apprehend him, and found him in the castle of Donibristle on the north side of the Firth of Forth. Huntly laid siege to the castle, and set it on fire. Moray broke out through a ring of flames, but was followed to the darkness of the seashore, and there stabbed to death. He who dealt the final stroke was thought to have been Huntly himself, and his victim—who had been known as "the bonny Earl of Moray"—is said to have mocked him in his dying speech: "Ye hae spoiled a better face than your ain, my lord."

The only enduring consequence of that fierce affray was a ballad which has preserved, not only the dead man's fame, but the iniquity of Huntly who had misused the King's authority for his own purpose:

> "Now wae be to you, Huntly,
>   And wharfore did ye sae?
> I bade you bring him wi' you,
>   And forbade you him to slay!"

But it was an event of contemporary importance, and roused a storm of anger, because it uncovered the lordly anarchy that could still erupt in the last decade before James's translation to the throne of England. Without military resources—without the standing army that none of them could afford—a king of Scotland could hope to retain his throne, and make his rule effective, only by exercising a sense of balance and discreetly using force when force was available.

More serious than Huntly's intransigence, and far more sinister, was the manic behaviour of Francis Hepburn, Earl of Bothwell. His father was a bastard son of James V and brother to the Regent Moray; his mother was a sister of Mary's Bothwell. His mind was cultivated, his education superior, and he may have been mad. He was James's cousin, a member of the family, and James, who could not deny him a certain respect, had good reason to be afraid of him. He was brave as well as wicked, and not without attractive qualities.

His uncle, the old Earl of Moray, had been leader of the Protestant Lords, and Bothwell, professing their faith, posed also as its champion. But he had joined the northern earls in their nonsensical rebellion, and tried to create trouble on the Border. He had broken into the Tolbooth in Edinburgh to abduct a witness against one of his Liddesdale men, about to be tried for some indefensible act of violence; and before the end of 1591 he had acquired a more fearful notoriety. He was thought to be a warlock who ruled with Satanic authority over several covens of witches.

In the Nineteenth Century, when the sciences of the time seemed to be as settled and assured as the Christian faith, it was easy to deride what did not fall within the circumference of science or Christianity, and historians of that century made mockery of King James for his profound interest in witchcraft. But no one today is likely to be so easily amused. Nowadays it is widely recognised that when the Reformation unfastened from a multitude of imprisoned minds the old despotism of Rome—in many ways a benign despotism—it gave release, over much of Europe, to obscure, long-hidden allegiances to ancient pagan beliefs and half-forgotten rituals, most of which had guilty association with fertility rites. Witches, self-made, and a dire faith in witchcraft rose up from the darkness of doubt that Luther and Calvin and Melanchthon cast as their shadows. How much of pagan thought and pagan practice had persisted under Christian governance cannot be assessed; but when Christian governance was divided, and the domination of Rome denied, witchcraft emerged as a mental plague which created insane fears and had to be suppressed or cured. Where the Inquisition ruled, witches were burnt in thousands. In the Germanic parts of the empire suppression was indiscriminate and ruthless. In England and Scotland witches were sought out and persecuted with a zeal dependent on local circumstance: there were many instances of horrible brutality, the consequence of a credulity that now seems absurd, but nowhere a wholesale, panic persecution.

North Berwick, a few miles from Edinburgh, is nowadays a pleasant and highly respectable retreat for golfers and elderly people in prosperous retirement; but in April 1591 it acquired a sudden notoriety when several women were there accused of witchcraft, one of whom boasted that she could repeat the King's pillow-talk to Anne of Denmark on their wedding night. Learned in theology, and devoutly interested in the mystery of God's providence, James had not eschewed enquiry into Satanism, and he was naturally attracted by reports of the trial in North Berwick.

The women, moved perhaps by a ludicrous exhibitionism, confessed to the common obscenities of a recognised ritual. The Devil himself, either black by nature or disguised as a black man, had preached from the pulpit of the parish church in North Berwick, and they, obedient to his will, had worshipped him with the customary indecencies. That blasphemous occasion, however, had been informed by a purpose of uncommon importance. The congregation of witches had been assembled to curse and confound the King, who was sailing to Oslo to meet his Danish bride; and the black man in the pulpit, the Devil who commanded the witches' worship and hoped for James's death, was Francis Hepburn, Earl of Bothwell, cousin of the King and well qualified, by art and nature, to succeed him.

Bothwell was arrested and imprisoned; but quickly escaped. Then, for a little while, the royal palaces and the life of the King were like a great house plagued by a poltergeist, by an almost irresistible and quite incomprehensible power of evil. On the Border Bothwell had many friends, and openly defied the King. At Christmas he broke into Holyroodhouse, tried to assault the Chancellor, whom he hated, and hammered on the door of a turret in which James had found refuge. The alarm was raised, people of the town came running to the palace, and Bothwell fled. But at Falkland he reappeared at the head of three hundred men, and his attempt to kidnap the frightened King nearly succeeded. He returned to Holyrood, and demanded to be tried on a charge of witchcraft; but his demand was refused and he was disappointed of the public attention that he wanted.

Irresponsibility again erupted in the Gothic north, and a lordly vacancy in the minds of Huntly, Errol, Angus, and some others was revealed by the ineptitude of George Kerr, their chosen agent. Kerr was on his way to the Spanish King to offer help from the bemused earls if the King would be so obliging as to send an army to the Atlantic coast of Scotland; but Kerr let himself be arrested, and in his possession were found some sheets of paper that bore noble signatures and nothing else: the earls had entrusted him with blank cheques to be drawn against a treasonable account. James took action, but the punishment he inflicted was not severe, and his leniency offended both Elizabeth and the Kirk.

Holyroodhouse was once more invaded by its poltergeist, and James, though terrified by his cousin's manic behaviour, kept dignity enough to assure the townspeople—who again came to his rescue—that all was well. Bothwell then made an attack in force, which was beaten off, and fell into grievous error when he tried to make alliance with the Catholic earls. That lost him the Kirk's support, whose ministers, quite incomprehensibly, had previously favoured him. He left Scotland and died in Naples.

In their own way the Reformed kirk and its ministers were as intemperate, as arrogant in their self-sufficiency, as the Catholic earls. Not content with dictating a necessary faith for the people of Scotland, they tried to dictate its policy. They denounced trade with France and Spain, and offered their own terms for relations with England, whose Queen they described as an atheist. James was rebuked for using improper language, Anne for her continued frivolity, and at Falkland palace Andrew Melville, having reminded the King that he was only "God's silly vassal," reasserted the Kirk's claim to divine authority and its monopoly of divine wisdom.

But the ministers showed something less than wisdom when, a little while before Christmas, 1596, they pretended to discover a popish plot to murder the King and his Council. The plot was a presbyterian fiction, but to give them some acquaintance with reality its authors were imprisoned in Edinburgh castle, there to await the King's clemency; and Edinburgh was fined for contumacy. Andrew Melville was discredited, and the King—as earnest a theologian as Melville himself—proclaimed that he and none other was head of the Kirk, and his was the right to convene its General Assembly when and where he pleased.

James was like the reed that bends in the wind, but never breaks. He had survived the menace of faction and rebellion because his own ability and native intelligence gave him roots, and he knew when to be pliant. He had been patient, and sturdy enough to feel fear but refuse to be defeated by it. In the contest between Kirk and King, which was to dominate and impoverish so much of the Seventeenth Century, he was as deeply committed as that minister of St. Andrews who declared that all monarchs were children of the Devil; though his commitment was more practical. His interest was persistent, his purpose stubborn, his belief in episcopacy unchanging. In the ebb and flow of policy bishops and presbyters had gone in and out, but in the last decade of the century James, quietly and without offence, added to his authority in ecclesiastical affairs, and before he rode to greater comfort in England he had appointed new bishops to the sees of Aberdeen, Ross, and Caithness.

He suffered, in 1600, a last demonstration of Scotland's volcanic temper—of the capacity for eruption that lay under a thin crust of conformity—when, from stag-hunting in the great park at Falkland, he was persuaded to ride to the Earl of Gowrie's house in Perth. Gowrie's young brother, the Master of Ruthven, told him that on the previous evening he had met a suspicious stranger who, he discovered, was carrying under his cloak an urn full of foreign gold pieces. He had taken the man into custody, and now wanted the King to question him.

The stag was hunted to its death, and the King rode off with young Ruthven; but he was not so foolish as to ride alone. In Perth, after a perfunctory meal in Gowrie's house, he was taken up a narrow stair to a room in a turret, to meet the man with the foreign gold, but found, instead, a man in armour. Ruthven threatened the King, and argument was followed by an angry struggle. A window was broken, and the King, with Ruthven's arm about his neck, called loudly for help. The man in armour stood quietly watching. Elsewhere there was consternation, for none knew where the King had gone. Gowrie said he had mounted his horse and ridden off to the North Inch, but that was denied, and when clamour and the King's voice were heard from the turret, there was a hurried sally to rescue him. Locked doors impeded his rescuers, but a young man, called John Ramsay, broke into the turret and killed Ruthven. A little while later, as others were pressing in and there was confusion on the stairs, he also killed Gowrie.

By that time the whole of Perth was in a state of roaring excitement, and the King and his party had no little difficulty in restoring order; for Gowrie and his family were both popular and influential in the town. There were those, inevitably, who doubted the King's story, and in later years many argued, and doubtless believed, that James had elaborated a daring plan to destroy Gowrie, who was, in some sort of way, a leader of the more extreme presbyterian faction.—It was not a way that can have commended itself to all presbyterians, for Gowrie, like Bothwell, was suspected of practising witchcraft.—But though James had stoutly defended himself, it seems unlikely that he, a man known to be timorous, would have chosen to lead so rash and dangerous an enterprise; and when an offer of pardon and a reward were offered to the mysterious man in armour—who had disappeared— he revealed himself as Andrew Henderson, chamberlain to the Earl of Gowrie, and said he had been overcome by "a dread of evil" when he learnt of the part he was supposed to play in the plot confected by Gowrie and his brother.

Gowrie was the grandson of Lord Ruthven, one of Rizzio's mur- derers, and son of the first Earl of Gowrie, who had led the "Ruthven Raid" to seize the King in 1582, and been executed for his treason. The most probable explanation of the affray at Perth is that Gowrie was attempting to repeat the Ruthven raid and gain possession of the King's person for political advantage; though it may be that long smouldering hatred had burst into flame, and his chief purpose was to take revenge for his father's death.

In England the Queen still refused to name her successor, but few doubted that James would be the next king, and Robert Cecil—son of William, Lord Burghley, Elizabeth's previous Secretary of State—was in correspondence with him and making ready for his reception. James grew impatient, for Elizabeth, that indomitable woman, was literally standing up to death, and not until the early morning of Thurs- day the 25th March, 1603, was her defiance quelled.

A messenger, Sir Robert Carey, set off in vulgar haste and rode with astonishing speed to reach Edinburgh on Saturday night. James was asleep, but Carey woke and hailed him as "England, Scotland, France, and Ireland!" Carey had not waited for letters from the Privy Council, and James showed a seemly caution. Nothing was said, beyond the walls of Holyroodhouse, until two days later, when Carey's news was officially confirmed.

With a great train of attendants, both Scots and English, James left Edinburgh on the 5th April, and one may assume, with some confidence, that he crossed the Border in high anticipation and with little regret for the land he left behind him.

5

At Berwick the migrant King was received with hospitable pomp, and he flattered the garrison artillery by expertly firing a cannon for them. Then he mounted a fine horse and rode thirty-seven long miles in something less than four hours, leaving his attendants panting behind him. His retinue grew as he went south, for there were time-servers on both sides of the Border. At York a conduit from the gate to the Minster ran claret wine, and at Durham the Bishop waited on him with a hundred gentlemen in tawny liveries. His Majesty charmed everyone with his geniality, and was always ready to delay his progress if there was a deer to be hunted. Once he fell heavily and dangerously bruised his arm, but he said it was nothing, and remounted. The next day however, he was too stiff to ride. At Hinchinbrook Priory he was magnificently entertained by Oliver Cromwell, uncle of the future Protector. Sir Oliver (so he was before the King left) presented James with a gold cup, horses, hounds, and hawks of excellent wing; and an acute observer noted there that the new sovereign regarded all who approached him with a straight and seeing eye.

England was a rich country: in comparison with Scotland immensely rich, and in the temper of the age ostentatious in its wealth, superbly aware of the uses to which money could be harnessed. Architecture had become domestic without losing sense of style or memories of grandeur. Tailors exploited damask and satin, silks and velvet, with exuberant anarchy. Poetry had conquered the theatre, and the splendours of Marlowe's verse had paved a resounding stage for the heroism, lyrical humour, and victorious tragedy of William Shakespeare. William Byrd was writing his madrigals, Bacon his *Advancement of Learning*. Walter Raleigh, justified in arrogance, put off his silver armour to record, with comparable display, battle at the Azores, the discovery of empire in Guiana. The imprisoned fortune of the Catholic church, released by Henry VIII, had poured into the arteries of Elizabeth's England and quickened its ebullient pulse, amplified imagination; and imagination had bred in its teeming mind a vocabulary bright as new-minted leaves and opulent enough to pay for all the extravagance of its invention.

The immigrant King was a scholar too, author of a shrewd and learned book, called *Basilikon Doron*, lately published in London, that recommended him to the literate as warmly as his wife and growing family commended him to a majority of his lieges who were thankful to have on their throne, in place of a barren Queen, a King whose children promised, in peaceful succession, a dynasty born and pledged to the Protestant faith. That James, emerging from the harsher dignities of Scotland, should find opportunities for enjoyment and excuse for relaxation in his new and larger province is not surprising; that he should retain a sense of purpose, an inspired opinion of his own authority, and a constant perception of the overarching importance of intellect— of words which are the mechanism of intellect—is proof of inherent principles which no clumsiness of behaviour should be allowed to obscure.

In everyday association, however, he did not advertise his principles nor parade his dignity, and his claim to respect was dubiously maintained by the exercise of a genial, irreverent humour that was bred of the rude egalitarianism on which the throne of Scotland was so precariously balanced. To a sceptical English parliament he boasted, at unseemly length, of his divine right to rule as he pleased, and in more amiable company he showed too frankly his appreciation of the luxuries denied to his earlier years. But much of his pleasure was strenuous, much of it most laudable. He hunted with a passionate delight in hard riding that made him conspicuous even in a country that was said to be paradise for women and hell for horses; and to the theatre he gave far more lavish patronage than it had known under Elizabeth.

Shakespeare's company, the Chamberlain's Men, were enriched and enfranchised as the King's Men, and with royal godparents to favour it the masque was born of the genius of Ben Jonson and Inigo Jones. To pose as a peacemaker in Europe was, perhaps, an exercise in pleasure —a virtuous exhibitionism—rather than practical politics; but when opportunity occurred for a new translation of the Bible, it was James's deep and persistent interest in literature and theology that innervated the enthusiasm which pushed the project to magnificent conclusion.

All that, however, lay in the future. The richness of the future became ever more obvious as he rode deeper into the green comeliness of the south, but all his kingdom was not yet open to him. His progress

—his triumphal migration into England—came to a temporary halt at Theobalds, Sir Robert Cecil's house in Hertfordshire. There was plague in London, and it was inadvisable to go farther.

With Cecil he was already on friendly terms. For some years they had engaged in discreet correspondence, and his "little beagle"—whom he created Earl of Salisbury in 1605—served his King with a devotion untrammelled by high principle. A small misshapen man with a noble countenance, his abilities were disparaged by his cousin, Francis Bacon, who said he was "fit to prevent things from growing worse but not fit to make them better." Like Bacon he accepted bribes without being influenced by them, and did not allow a Spanish pension of £1500 a year to modify his distrust of Spain. Despite mutual irritation he maintained an uneasy peace with parliament, and shared James's belief in pacific policies abroad. Though handicapped by royal interference he worked incessantly, and in his own way worked for England.

Also at Theobalds were Lord Henry Howard, Earl of Northampton, and his brother Lord Thomas, Earl of Suffolk. Lord Henry had been another of James's secret correspondents, and had wearied the King with the prolixity of his letters, that were like "Asiatic and endless volumes." The Howards were rich and influential and friendship with them was to involve James in an episode—the most discreditable of his reign—of stark criminality. For the moment they seemed useful, they knew everyone who moved in the great world about the court, and beyond question they were assiduous in advising their new King to put no trust in that magnificent but dangerous man, Sir Walter Raleigh. Before he left Theobalds, James showed some impatience with the humbler sort of his new subjects: they crowded about the gates of Cecil's great house to applaud their King, and James, unaccustomed to such demonstrations in Scotland, soon grew tired of the noise and stench of vulgar loyalty.

He and his Queen were crowned in July, but ceremony was curtailed by the plague which, so far from abating, had grown more deadly. He found refuge in the well stocked deer-parks which were an English amenity, and in learned conversation with ambassadors, who were impressed by his knowledge, and churchmen who were gratified by his insight into the scriptures. But England had its troubles as well as Scotland, and the absurd Bye Plot, which proposed to dethrone King James, gave Raleigh's enemies excuse to have the last Elizabethan imprisoned in the Tower; and after that came the notorious Gunpowder Plot, which was prompted by James's failure to show the favour to his Catholic subjects that was expected of him, and which may have owed its design to the plotters' memory of the explosion at Kirk o' Field which eliminated their King's father, Lord Darnley. James and his parliament survived the menace of gunpowder and Guy Fawkes; and the plot and its discovery have survived three and a half centuries in which forty more important events, or non-events, lie drowned in forgetfulness. But nowadays there are those who suspect that Cecil's secret service had as much foreknowledge of it as its doomed conspirators; and there is, perhaps, a more rewarding interest in the relationship that grew up between the scholarly King and his erudite subject, Ben Jonson.

Jonson was descended from a family domiciled in Annandale, in Scotland. He had fought in the Low Countries, and he became a scholar more formidable than any pikeman. He made no concession to popular taste, but gave to the theatre plays of classical severity or comedies fashioned, with brilliant device, on the grim pattern of tragic reprisal. He found, in the Scottish King, a true enthusiasm for the erudition which was his own pleasure, and for James's amusement made erudition playful. He elaborated—with the King's favour and the help of an architect as richly gifted as himself—the art of the masque: a charade or palace comedy compact of muscular fancy and scholarship twisted to baroque design. He had, as adjuncts to his genius, a Queen who delighted in dressing-up, and the Palladian enthusiasm of Inigo Jones. He and Jones eventually became enemies—Jones insisted on the supremacy, over mere words, of costume and scenery—but in the beginning they were potent allies, creative in alliance.

Queen Elizabeth, when she died, left a dressmaker's fortune of two thousand gowns "with all things else answerable." Her wardrobe had grown at the expense of her subjects, who found it politic to give her handsome presents—perhaps a petticoat of yellow satin, fringed with silver, silk-lined with tawny sarsnet; a velvet suit powdered with pearls; or a kirtle with Venetian gold lace and seven buttons "like the birds of Arabia"—and all were recorded in the inventory of her wardrobe, nothing was thrown away. But now Anne and her ladies rifled the treasure house and took scissors to refashion the old Queen's dresses and array themselves in splendour for *The Masque of Blackness*, *The Masque of Beauty*, or *The Masque of Queens*.

The first of them was inspired by the Queen's frolicsome desire to blacken her face, and Jonson found occasion to indulge her in a fable he set on the banks of the Niger; whose inhabitants, according to some classical author, were the blackest nation on earth. Under the direction of Inigo Jones the old banqueting hall, in the palace of Whitehall, was transformed into a landscape bordered by a sea on which floated a great shell, like mother-of-pearl, and in a heaven of blue silk a silver throne was built for the moon. Costumes were designed for sea nymphs and mermen, for negroes and the daughters of Niger, and the Queen and her ladies rehearsed their dances. On Twelfth Night—the year was 1605—the masque was presented with unexampled splendour, and though some were offended by a blackamoor queen and ladies too airily clad, the majority of spectators were well pleased with the strangeness and grandeur of the scene. At suppertime, indeed, enthusiasm passed all restraint, and so lustily was the great chamber invaded, where a banquet was spread, that every table was upset. The masque and the subsequent entertainment cost the exchequer £3000.

The temptation to expensive amusement, so compulsively offered by the richness of England, was heavily reinforced by the visit, in the summer of 1606, of Christian IV, King of Denmark and brother of Queen Anne. He came too late to see the enthusiastic reception of Jonson's *Volpone*, but in time for a postponed pageant at Greenwich at which, in mock heroical imitation of tournaments long ago, the Earls of Lennox, Arundel, Pembroke, and Montgomery challenged the world, in high, astounding, but not quite serious terms, to deny the four Indisputable Propositions:

"That in service of Ladies no Knight hath free will.
"That it is Beauty maintaineth the world in valour.
"That no fair Lady was ever false.
"That none can be perfectly wise but Lovers."

Though the age of chivalry was over, there were sceptics willing to do battle for their lack of faith, and the Danish King, wearing blue armour touched with gold, rode with distinction and was generously applauded. His month in England was thirty days of hard drinking, heavy feasting, untidy revels, and constant discharge of cannon. Up and down the Thames went the two Kings, drinking each other's health while peals of ordnance, proclaiming their emptied glasses, startled the swans and drowned the lusty "Westward ho!" of the watermen. At Greenwich, in the City, and at Theobalds, banquets were spread and amity, national and domestic, pledged in tipsy kindness. Men who were life-long abstainers till that time forsook sobriety and drank with Danish throats.

At Theobalds after a great feast there was a pageant of Solomon's Temple and Sheba bearing gifts. But Sheba forgot the steps leading to the Kings' dais and fell headlong into Christian's lap, spilling her caskets about the throne. He, laughing, got up and would have danced with her, but fell at her feet and once down could not rise again. So he was carried to an inner room and laid upon a bed of state, all smeared with jelly and cream and wine, the cates of Sheba's offering. A little later Faith, Hope, and Charity appeared to congratulate King James. But Hope was speechless and Faith reeled in her gait. Only Charity bore her gifts in safety, and to some extent covered the multitude of her sisters' sins. Victory and Peace followed these three, but Victory was tearful and Peace so angry that, when the crowd would not part quickly enough, she laid about her with a stout olive branch.

He who left that description of a royal occasion was Sir John Harington; and Harington, it must be admitted, was a celebrated wit. But there are no good witticisms without some foundation in fact—and still the cannon pealed, trumpeters blew for empty bottles, and drums beat to every toast. Cheerful Londoners crowded about the court, and when the Kings went hunting followed in noisy droves to fling their caps in the air. But graver minds condemned the royal folly. Even some who were no Puritans looked angrily at such heavy-headed revel, and frowned when new clamour told:

> "The king doth wake to-night and takes his rouse,
> Keeps wassail and the swaggering up-spring reels
> And, as he drains his draughts of Rhenish down,
> The kettle-drum and trumpet thus bray out
> The triumph of his pledge."

The Danish visit gave head to some unfortunate tendencies already apparent at court. A kind of loose brilliance had begun to invade it. Favourites acquired large estates, and intrigue flourished. Scots courtiers quarrelled with English, and the English lampooned the Scots. Vast sums were spent on jewels and weddings and wedding gifts, and foreign visitors were received with prodigal display: grandees of Spain, the princes of Moldavia, Vaudemont, Hesse, and Anhalt, nobles of Portugal and the Rhine, were entertained with wanton generosity. £500 a year was spent on velvet coats for the palace guard, and £1300 for the royal shirts and sheets. The King's Embroiderer bought twenty ounces of small pearls for the King's saddle, and three hundred and twenty fair round pearls for his Majesty's hose. And the King went hunting at Royston and Newmarket, leaving Salisbury at home to find the money: his little beagle, whose shrivelled body was always full of pain.

Londoners, though they began to grumble at the King's extravagance, were no more careful of their own money. The Puritans might rail and prophesy tribulation, but London was too rich to care. It bought feather beds and Venetian silk curtains and pearl necklaces. Coaches grew as common, some said, as those who rode in them. Cooks flavoured their dishes with ambergris. Foreigners of many nations came to sell their alien products and share in the city's wealth, so that London bawds, twirling their death's-head rings under the blind Cupids on their doors, could count upon French, Dutch, Spanish, and Italian customers to keep away impoverished captains from Ireland and "two-shilling Inns of Court men"; and yet the best clients were honest English flat-caps, who paid for their pleasure more liberally than any foreigner. What was the use of saving? When the weather grew warm again the sickness would come, and the sickness took miser and spendthrift with equal hands.

Wealth multiplied, and court and city flaunted their luxury like ensigns against the June solstice of recurrent plague. In this air, now perfumed and now stinking of death, *Othello* was acted, the monstrous passion of *Timon*, and the huger agony of *King Lear*. For part of the year London might live fearfully under the threat of plague, but for the other months, such lust and life were in them, the golden shade of Priapus, like a canopy, might have stretched from Finsbury Fields to Southwark. Lurid history, roaring comedy, bawdy interlude, and incessant poetry flowed from Dekker and Middleton, Webster and Drayton; Bacon's lean-fleshed essays swelled roundly, and *The Advancement of Learning* was born (like Gargantua) with provision for future growth; Burton was gutting libraries for *The Anatomy of Melancholy*; the springs of enormous invention were feeling for issue in Beaumont and Fletcher. Mild-seeming Shakespeare, in whose bald head volcanic fancy threw up its fertile continents, sucked for their procreant air the heat and cold of London's crowded streets, and side by side with Shakespeare was Jonson, turning now with brilliant strength the antique machinery of tragedy to comic use. Their plays would never have been written in the doldrums of time, or a land with peace in its heart. Othello and Volpone came to life because intrigue, jealousy, and violence were at home in London, and London was glutted with gold and too proud for prose.

So also the court and King redeemed their looseness and luxury by feeding art and literature, and while the King brittled his deer, scholars by his command worked diligently in Oxford and Cambridge and Westminster to make one true and lasting Bible out of the chaos of existing texts. The President of Corpus Christi College had first suggested such a work, and James, quick on a true scent as his good hound Jewel, instantly professed his dissatisfaction with every extant version of the Scriptures, and outlined a scheme for a uniform translation to be done by the best learned of both universities, reviewed by the bishops, submitted to the Privy Council, and ratified by his own royal hand. Let special pains be taken, he said, and wisely bade the translators refrain from adding such comments of their own as marred the Geneva Bible. So now, in the universities and elsewhere, nearly fifty chosen scholars, High Church and Low Church and laity working together, "sought the truth rather than their own praise," and often conferring together did not disdain "to bring back to the anvil that which they had hammered."

The Bible no longer enjoys the veneration paid to it when it was universally regarded as the inspired exposition of God's purpose and promise to the world, and of the imminent fulfilment of that promise. There is today no general acceptance of the prophetic significance of the Old Testament, or of the literal truth of the Gospels. But none has denied, nor could deny, the sublimity of language in King James's Bible which gives to a profession of historical purpose and its culminating faith not only supremacy over all other versions of the ancient texts, but a majesty which compels reverence of a creative mystery that criticism cannot dispel nor scepticism dispute.

It was James's good fortune to live in England when the English language had the freshness of spring water and a magnanimity bestowed on no other age. It was James's good sense—a shrewdness quickened by his own painful education, his laboured excursions into literature—that persuaded him to take advantage of a season in history coloured equally by April green and August gold, and compel, by a king's authority, a concourse of his scholars to ennoble Holy Writ with their native tongue.

Beside the awful simplicity of "Be still, and know that I am God," they wrote in pious hope: "They shall beat their swords into plowshares, and their spears into pruning hooks; nation shall not lift up sword against nation, neither shall they learn war any more." They gave enormous moment to the sort of speech common in castle and cottage—"Unto us a child is born, unto us a son is given"—and found lordly execration for their enemies: "Howl, ye ships of Tarshish," and "How art thou fallen from heaven, O Lucifer, son of the morning!" "All flesh is grass," they declared, and uttered comfort as well: "A bruised reed shall he not break," and "How beautiful upon the mountains are the feet of him that bringeth good tidings." They commended Stoicism: "God is in heaven, and thou upon earth; therefore let thy words be few." They silenced mockery: "As the crackling of thorns under a pot, so is the laughter of a fool." They could be down to earth— "Be not righteous over much" and "A living dog is better than a dead lion"—and they could rise above travail to the serene acceptance of mortal end: "When they shall be afraid of that which is high, and fears shall be in the way, and the almond tree shall flourish, and the grasshopper shall be a burden, and desire shall fail: because man goeth to his long home, and the mourners go about the streets." They could be utterly dismissive—"Let the dead bury their dead"—and march from an apparently domestic concern with "a piece of broiled fish, and a honeycomb" to abbreviate epistemology into the resounding epigram, "In the beginning was the Word, and the Word was God."

In the greatest age of English writing King James's Bible—regarded as literature, not as revelation—cannot be bettered by *Hamlet* or *Lear*, by Bacon or Donne; and in the oldest sense of "author"—of him who gives existence—the King must be accepted as its prime and motivating author. The professing Christian will readily admit that no other clerical writing has had a tithe, or one tenth of a tithe, of its influence in the propagation of his faith; and the non-professing critic can hardly deny the impact, on believers or unbelievers, of an imagery presented in a style that might substantiate divinity though no other proof of it could be found. Nothing that King James confused or misused, mishandled or vulgarised, can obscure the fact that he gave to the world the treasure in a treasury that none before him had properly illumined.

6

Henry, Prince of Wales, and Robert Cecil, Earl of Salisbury, both died in 1612. The Prince was a young man of strong and redoubtable character: to all Britain his death was a loss beyond assessment. Cecil —Elizabeth's pygmy and James's beagle—was no more than forty-seven or forty-eight, but overwork may have hastened his end. In his essay on *Deformity* Bacon had painted, it was said, "his little cousin to the life," and Cecil had certainly enriched himself while serving his master. But to the King he was indispensable. A couple of years before his death, James had met an attractive, worthless youth, Robert Kerr, who involved him in scandal and may have prompted his unfortunate quarrel with parliament. It seems unlikely that Cecil could have warded off the scandal, but if he had lived he might have prevented the breach with parliament.

Elizabeth had always been able to persuade or coerce her parliaments to do her will. She could dissimulate and flatter, she could appeal to the patriotism of her faithful House, and declare most nobly that she loved her country better than all its members did. But since the Reformation the House of Commons had been gradually and at intervals acquiring some new ideas about its power and responsibility, and the relative authority of the crown; and Elizabeth, if ever she was aware of changing thought, had never found accommodation for it. She was head of the Anglican church, but though in her time England had been menaced by an extreme Puritanism, and Catholicism was still a political danger, her church's policy had never been defined, and its discipline remained uncertain. To her successor she left, as well as the riches of her kingdom, some awkward problems, and James, with his stubborn belief that monarchy was "the supremest thing upon earth," was ill equipped to deal with them.

Parliament had grown in power, and when he came to England it was as warmly convinced of its importance as was James of his divine right to rule. Though the House of Commons spoke of privilege, a king was God's lieutenant and his Commons could not teach him how to govern: so James believed. He quarrelled with his Chief Justice, Sir Edward Coke, a bitter man, a headstrong defender of liberty, as he understood it. James told Coke that he, the King, was the protector

of the law. No, said Coke, it is the law that protects you. It was unfortunate for James that his extravagance—with which even the
ingenious Cecil could not cope—compelled him to seek help from
parliament; and though parliament proved more amenable than the
King—in return for the surrender of certain feudal rights it was willing
to vote him an annual income of £200,000—James failed to recognise
advantage when it was offered him. He talked too much; he uttered
threats, or seemed to utter them, against freedom of speech; and when
the Commons protested, James lost his temper and dissolved his parliament. His lack of judgment may have been stimulated by the flattery
of Robert Kerr.

Kerr's influence did not last for very long, but long enough to let
him be ennobled as Earl of Somerset. He was the son of a respectable
Border family, and blood may have entitled him to advancement.
But he had no other claims except good looks, high spirits, and a
genial temper. He allied himself with the pro-Spanish party at court,
and became friendly, and more than friendly, with that great Catholic
family, the Howards. The Earl of Suffolk had a beautiful and vicious
young daughter, Fanny, who at a tender age had been married to
the young Earl of Essex, son of Queen Elizabeth's favourite. Essex,
himself only fifteen, was sent abroad, and Fanny remained at court to
fall in love with Somerset. He returned her passion, and Fanny, or
her scheming relatives—Suffolk her father, Northampton her uncle—
decided to bring a suit of nullity against Essex, and so obtain her
freedom to marry the reigning favourite.

Somerset, however, had earlier enjoyed the friendship of a very
clever, insolent young man called Sir Thomas Overbury, who hotly opposed his projected marriage. Overbury belonged to the anti-Spanish
faction, and disapproved of Somerset's alliance with the Howards. His
language was intemperate, he called Fanny a strumpet, her relations
bawds; and his abuse was the more painful because it had some
flavour of truth. His enemies decided to get rid of him, and the King
was persuaded to offer him an embassy in Muscovy or the Netherlands.
He refused, with no better excuse than his admission that he knew no
foreign languages and hated writing letters. The King held serious
views about the importance of foreign relations, and had lately been
offended by Sir Henry Wotton, a diplomat who declared that "ambassadors were good men sent to lie abroad for their country."—Wit has all
too rarely been a doorway for advancement; too often an *oubliette* for

the bright promise of untaught youth.—Overbury, by his insolence, aggravated Wotton's offence, and was committed to the Tower.

In June 1613 the Globe Theatre went on fire, and Fanny's nullity suit was postponed because of a rumour that she was employing witchcraft to bring about the death of Essex. She was still frightened of Overbury's hostility, and when a new Lieutenant was appointed to the Tower—a man who was under some obligation to both Somerset and the Howards—she sent, to attend him, an apothecary and a physician's widow, called Turner, who was locally famous for her invention of yellow starch. Overbury's health deteriorated, but his constitution was robust, and four months after his arrest his physicians were compelled to use more decisive methods than powdered glass.

Overbury died, but his arrogance had deprived him of friends, and his death excited no concern. Fanny's uncle, the Earl of Northampton, put out a story that he had died of the pox. The nullity suit was continued, and John Donne was bribed to join Somerset and his faction. The King's influence was exerted on behalf of the petitioner. The King, softened by late sorrow, could deny nothing to those whom he loved. The royal family had grown small since Prince Henry died and his sister, the Princess Elizabeth, had married and gone abroad with her husband; and kindness increased daily in the royal household. The Queen even escaped rebuke when, shooting at a deer, she missed her mark and killed Jewel, James's favourite hound. The King fell into a rage at first, but as soon as he learnt whose hand was responsible, his anger vanished, and he begged the Queen not to be troubled by the accident. The next day he gave her a great diamond as a legacy from the dead dog.

The Essex marriage was dissolved, and Fanny came to court looking more beautiful than before. She wore a robe of green velvet, lined with white satin, patterned with gold. Under her yellow ruff—stiffened with Mrs. Turner's starch—her breasts were almost bare, and their whiteness was made more white by the red beads about her neck. She had yellow feathers in her golden crisply curling hair (brushed from a smooth forehead) and she carried a yellow fan. She and Somerset were married on the day after Christmas, she with her hair unbound in the fashion of a virgin, and all the court attending. At night a masque of Campion's was performed, and on the following day there was a tournament preceded by Jonson's *Challenge at Tilt*. Jonson had no suspicion of the criminal prelude to the marriage, and Somerset himself, on his wedding-day, may not have known the whole truth of Overbury's death. Fanny, her uncle Northampton and the other Howards, Mrs. Turner and the apothecary, kept their secret secure.

Masques and feasting still went on. *The Tempest* and *The Winter's Tale* were specially performed; Ben Jonson showed his *Irish Masque*, that the King liked so well he ordered it to be repeated; the City entertained the bride and bridegroom—and the ever-ready court—to a banquet and a masque by Middleton; and the gentlemen of Gray's Inn, under Bacon's patronage, presented their *Masque of Flowers*. Then festivities began to slacken, and there was little excitement till spring, when a parliament was summoned and the King made an eloquent speech in which he requested the Commons to show their good affection to him in such sort that this parliament might be called the Parliament of Love. But men were growing weary of the threefold dominance of Somerset, Northampton, and Suffolk, and the Commons proved so contrary that the King, though his patience with them lasted two months, at last sent them packing.

Then, in 1614, Northampton died, and after his death Somerset's arrogance turned to anxiety. His influence was waning—James had found a new favourite—and Somerset's ingenuous plea for a general pardon for all misdeeds, past and present, proved and unproved, was refused by the Lord Chancellor. One of the lesser agents in Overbury's murder confessed his guilt, and Somerset went to the Tower; where Fanny presently followed him. Sir Walter Raleigh had lately been released from long captivity, and they occupied his old rooms.

It may not be extravagant to see in Fanny Howard such a character as Beaumont and Fletcher might have conceived for another of their plays, or started Webster's imagination to see

> "Envy and pride flow in her painted breasts,
> She gives no other suck."

The London theatres were opening to more terrible fantasies than the simple thunder-and-horror of Elizabethan drama, and Somerset, by the brilliance of his figure, the glitter of his power, had drawn into his service good men as well as bad. But murder could not be tolerated, and wearing a yellow ruff Mrs. Turner also came to trial for her part in the death of Sir Thomas Overbury. She was condemned to death, and the hangman wore a yellow band and yellow cuffs starched by her invention. Yellow went out of fashion in London.

Largely owing to the inventions of Sir Anthony Weldon—that ingenious but malicious gossip—King James has often been accused, and widely believed to be guilty, of a besotted attachment to his favourites that obviously implied an active homosexuality. It is worth noting, however, that in his relations with Somerset he was quite immune from the jealousy that is commonly, if not always, associated with homosexual attachment. Somerset's marriage to Fanny Howard was not a marriage of convenience, but a union demanded by natural, though perhaps excessive passion. Yet James, so far from opposing it, did all he could to promote it. It seems unlikely—to put it mildly —that an elderly man, bound by perverted love to a young, gay, and handsome man, should exert his influence to bring about the marriage of his lover to a girl of remarkable beauty and vivid sexuality. It is infinitely more probable that James's attachment to Somerset was perverted only in so far as an excessive sentimentality can be called perverse.

The Scots, axiomatically dour, proverbially rugged, traditionally unemotional, have in fact often been wide-open—and, indeed, still are —to the most tearful sentimentalities; and the truth may be that King James was, by nature, more closely akin to that admired dramatist, the late J. M. Barrie, than to any of the omnifutuent heroes of the Arabian Nights. He had lost his older son, the defiant but adored Prince Henry, and in Somerset's good looks and gaiety he sought a surrogate for the gifted, handsome heir of whom he had been so cruelly robbed. That he fondled Somerset in the public view, while conniving at his marriage to a wicked little honeypot of a girl, is surely proof of a simple emotionalism and native innocence.

7

Raleigh, the last Elizabethan, had been released in response to mounting clamour from those opposed to friendship and alliance with Spain. Raleigh was inspired by a dream of empire and his memories of Guiana and the Orinoco; and his hope of mining gold in the river valley commended his proposals to the King. He told James that he had no intention of turning pirate, that he would explore in peace and traffic in friendship with the river tribes. He knew, however, that there was no chance of founding an empire, to stretch westwards to the Pacific and divide Mexico from Peru, without a Spanish war.—War with Spain, said the King, would cost him his life.—But Raleigh was a bold and fluent liar, he spoke convincingly of trade and the gold-bearing quartz he had found twenty years before; and he was allowed to muster ships and men. He was sixty-five years old, and his own ship was the *Destiny*.

James was not always idle, and for a long time he had worked, with considerable imagination but little success, to form a confederacy of states, pledged to peace, in Protestant and northern Europe. He had signed a treaty with the German Protestants, he had sent his ambassadors to Denmark and Holland, to Sweden and Brandenburg, Poland and Russia. But though fertile in ideas, he lacked the power to energise and make them work. The alliance for peace never came into being—Holland, a strong and stubborn rival for overseas trade, was a great obstacle—and James returned to his earliest hope of creating a friendly understanding with Spain.

Gondomar, the Spanish ambassador, was a man of exceptional gifts who carried his learning lightly to mask a formidable character. James enjoyed his company, and Gondomar favoured a proposal to marry Charles, Prince of Wales, to the Infanta. But the Spanish court was no more tractable than the stubbornest of English Protestants, and it was during a long period when negotiation seemed to have foundered that James let the aged Raleigh make his desperate bid for fortune on the Orinoco. But Gondomar was told of the expedition and the hope that fathered it.

Negotiations for the marriage were renewed, and the Spaniards demanded that the English penal laws be repealed, and worship according to the rites of Rome openly permitted in London. No English parliament would agree to that, and again there was deadlock. Then Raleigh came home, to admit defeat and the breaking of his promise. His good captain, Laurence Keymis, had attacked and taken the Spanish settlement of San Thomé, but young Walter Raleigh had been killed, Keymis had committed suicide, and there was threatened mutiny in the surviving ships. Raleigh wrote to his wife, "I never knew what sorrow meant until now. My brains are broken and it is a torment for me to write."

Gondomar demanded his execution, and James appointed a court of inquiry. The commissioners, who included Francis Bacon and Sir Edward Coke, reported that Raleigh had misled the King, plotted with France, and his purpose had been to plunder the Spanish settlements in America. He had, in fact, been under sentence of death since his imprisonment in 1603, and the commissioners decided that the sentence could now be carried out. He was executed in 1618, on the day of the Lord Mayor's Show: the day was deliberately chosen to prevent overcrowding at the bloodier spectacle.

James had no cause to love Raleigh—who had always made enemies as well as friends—and there is little doubt that Raleigh had deceived him. But the old Elizabethan was a gallant and learned man—arrogant beyond endurance, fiercely patriotic in a style outmoded—and a more magnanimous king might have treated him differently. Raleigh had friends who could have contrived his escape if they had been given some quiet encouragement.

During the two years of the Orinoco adventure a new favourite had risen like the sun in splendour. He was George Villiers, son of a poor knight in Leicestershire. He was uncommonly handsome, he had better qualities than Somerset, a livelier intelligence, and his rise to power was more spectacular. Created a Viscount, then Earl of Buckingham, he became a Duke in 1623, when he was thirty-one. He celebrated his elevation by the absurd proposal that he and Prince Charles should ride incognito to Madrid to woo the Infanta in person. James, ill with arthritis and the stone, reluctantly agreed, and in their absence was a prey to anxiety.

He sent them a collar of ballas rubies and knots of pearl, as a present for the Infanta, and wrote affectionately, "God bless you both, my sweet babes, and send you a safe and happy return." Buckingham—whom he called Steenie—had a young wife, and for comfort in his loneliness he invited her and Steenie's sister to sup with him. They discussed the weaning of Steenie's child, and lenitives for toothache: its four small teeth had been giving it some pain. His attachment to Buckingham, if indeed it was passionate, could also express itself in a scene of cosy domesticity, and for a little while they were not unhappy together, despite the absence of their dear boys. Then Charles wrote to say that the collar of ballas rubies was hardly good enough for the Infanta, and a chain of two hundred and seventy-six Orient pearls was sent as a more fitting gift. The Spaniards were astonished at its magnificence and they in their turn promised gifts. But in spite of these courtesies the match fell through.

In the last years of his life the King's temper grew more and more genial. When Dr. Abbott, Archbishop of Canterbury, unhappily shot a beater while hunting in Lord Zouch's park, James quickly forgave him, declaring an angel might have miscarried in that way. He went to look at Stonehenge, and was so interested that he commanded Inigo Jones to find out all he could about it; with the result that Jones informed him it was a Roman temple built after the Tuscan order to the god Caelus. At Steenie's country house he was entertained by Ben Jonson's masque, *The Gipsies Metamorphosed*, much of it rough and rude comedy, but out of rustic jocularity there bloomed a lyric of pure enchantment:

> "The faery beam upon you,
>   The stars to glister on you;
>   A moon of light
>   In the noon of night,
>   Till the fire-drake hath o'ergone you!
>   The wheel of fortune guide you,
>   The boy with the bow beside you
>   Run aye in the way
>   Till the bird of day
>   And the luckier lot betide you!
>
> "To the old, long life and treasure,
>   To the young, all health and pleasure;
>   To the fair, their face
>   With eternal grace,
>   And the soul to be loved at leisure.
>   To the witty, all clear mirrors,
>   To the foolish their dark errors;
>   To the loving sprite
>   A secure delight;
>   To the jealous his own false terrors."

Though old and ailing the King still dined and gossiped with his friends, and made small, unseemly jokes. There was a day when his guests were the Bishop of Winchester, the Bishop of Durham, and the young poet Waller. To them came a certain lord, whom the King greeted with a disconcerting question: "They say, my lord, that you lie with Lady X?"—"No, sir," replied the embarrassed visitor, "but I like her company because she has so much wit."—"Then why," asked the King, "do you not lie with my lord of Winchester?"

In the long catalogue of his dynasty—a catalogue of gifted, unlucky kings—he is the only one, until his time, who could be called fortunate, and the only one who has attracted derision. He does not deserve derision, but the untidy good humour, the lack of open and apparent dignity, the undeniable sentimentality and self-indulgence of his years in England invite it; and the scholarship that earned respect from his contemporaries has been submerged in a general recollection of his interest in witchcraft and detestation of tobacco. It should be remembered, however, that his early fear of witches, and abomination of their craft, yielded to a more realistic view of their pretensions and alleged activities. He grew adept in detecting fraudulence, he persuaded magistrates to share his scepticism, and finally seems to have decided that all who pretended to practise witchcraft were mere impostors, and those who believed in it were simply deluded.

His opinion of tobacco and those who smoke it will still seem excessive to many. Smoking he denounced as "a custom loathesome to the eye, hateful to the nose, harmful to the brain, dangerous to the lungs, and in the black stinking fumes thereof nearest resembling the horrible Stygian smoke of the pit that is bottomless." But many doctors now agree with him that tobacco may be harmful to the lungs, and even addicts—"tobacco-drunkards," he calls them—must admit that they "cannot abstain from that filthy stinking smoke, because, forsooth, they are bewitched by it."

He had been born in the immediate aftermath of the Reformation in Scotland; he was about to die in the antecedence of revolution in England. But the conclusion of his life was peaceful; except for the increasing incidence of physical pain. Early in January 1625 he watched yet another masque, *The Fortunate Isles*, in which Ben Jonson had compounded, with cheerful skill, good rhyming, good clowning, and an abundance of learned reference such as the King had always enjoyed. But by March he was sick of a fever that he and those round him recognised as fatal.

He took the physic his doctors ordered and composed himself to die like a Christian. He suffered the old Countess of Buckingham to wrap plasters of her own concoction on him, and grew worse because of them without complaint. He took the Sacrament with zeal, and having recited the Creed, said earnestly: "There is no other belief, no other hope!" He forgave his enemies and desired to be forgiven of them; but through this charity spoke once more the dogmatic voice that had wearied bishops' ears and shouted against the General Assembly of the Kirk in Scotland; for when he was asked if he would hear the Absolution he answered, "As it is practised in the English Church I ever approved it, but in the dark way of Rome I do defy it!" Then the chaplains about his bed spoke pious sentences, and though the pangs of death were on him the King lay still and took comfort from their words.

His funeral, like his reign, was extravagant and untidy, but his reign had been long—he had been a king for fifty-seven of his fifty-eight years—and he cannot be denied a capacity for survival that demands respect for the intelligence, resolution, and resilience on which it was founded. The most learned and literate of British kings, he was also—in a practical or worldly sense—the most successful of the Stewarts, and of all that talented family he enjoyed the strangest gift bestowed on any: he had a robust sense of humour that he found compatible with his ingrained belief that he ruled by divine right and God's own favour.

8

Hope Untimely Perished

1

Of the three sons and four daughters of James and his Danish Queen only two sons and a daughter survived their infancy. Henry, the elder, was born at Stirling castle in February 1594; his sister Elizabeth and Charles, who was to succeed as Charles I, at Dunfermline, the former in August 1596, the latter in November 1600.

The birth of Henry was the occasion for great joy in Scotland and a celebration of typical extravagance by his father; news of his tragical death, in the autumn of 1612, came with the shock of dismay and brought grief to England. He had grown with precocious speed into a young man of the most forceful character—a character that deeply impressed all who knew or heard of him—and to history he remains an enigma. Would he, by strength of mind and force of character, have learnt to exercise and govern the growing temper of his House of Commons, and so avert the war his brother could not win, the revolution that doomed his brother to the axe? Or would his lofty spirit and zealous interest in ships of war have led Britain to ambitious ventures and victories that crippled those who won them? He was, most certainly, the sort of prince whom men would have followed, but where he might have led them must be left to speculation.

His father educated him for greatness, and grumbled a little when Henry showed too soon his independence and his aptitude for rule. *Basilikon Doron*, the best of James's essays, was written for the Prince, and though much of it is sanctimonious, more of it is lively and vivid. James mocked "the preposterous humility of the proud Puritans" who, while proclaiming that all men were as worms, dictated to their King and would not let their own conduct be judged by anyone. He warned Henry to avoid affectation, in speech and clothing, in writing and eating. At table he should be neither gross nor too fastidious; he must dress neither like a whore nor a minister; in speech he was to avoid both crudity and "book language, ink-horn terms."

"Laws," he wrote, "are ordained as rules of virtuous and social living, and not to be snares to trap your good subjects.

"Learn also wisely to discern betwixt Justice and Equity; and for pity of the poor rob not the rich.

"Where ye find a notable injury, spare not to give course to the torrents of your wrath.

"But above all vertues, study to know well your own craft, which is to rule your people."

At the age of seven Henry began "to apply himself to, and take pleasure in active and manly exercises, learning to ride, sing, dance, leap, shoot with the bow and gun, toss the pike;"* and on his ninth birthday he was reading Terence, Cicero, and Aesop's fables Latinised by Phaedrus. When the royal family removed to England, Henry shared with his sister Elizabeth a household at Nonesuch or Hampton Court, where they were attended by seventy servants. A little while later that number was increased to a hundred and forty-one, of whom fifty-six were said to be above stairs, eighty-five below. And James wrote to his son: "Nothing will be impossible, if ye will only remember two rules; the one: *aude semper* in all virtuous actions: trust a little more to your own strength: and away with childish bashfulness. *Audaces fortuna juvat, timidosque repellit.* The other is my old oft-repeated rule unto you; whatever ye are about, *hoc age.*"—Or "Do it with thy might."

At Chatham the King's master shipwright was Phineas Pett. He was instructed to build a sailing-boat for the Prince, and in March 1604, a vessel was launched with a keel twenty-eight feet long, twelve feet of beam, "adorned with painting and carving, both within board and without." Flying ensigns and pennants she was brought to Whitehall, and Henry, in high delight, "with a great bowl of wine" christened her *Disdain*.

With Phineas Pett he formed a lasting friendship, and about this time it was observed that he showed an equal esteem for soldiers and men

* Thomas Bird: *The Life of Henry, Prince of Wales.*

of learning. The King took him to Oxford, where he was entered at Magdalen, and they listened to "disputations and civil law." Their entertainment now seems strange, but revives some of the topics of their day. There was debate on "whether saints and angels know the thoughts of the heart." On "whether the pastors of churches are not obliged to visit the sick during the plague." On "whether children imbibe the temper with the milk of their nurses." There was talk about tobacco, and "whether gold can be made by art." The King himself instituted a political debate, asserting "that it is greater to defend than to enlarge the bounds of an empire."

It was customary for royal persons to exchange and solicit gifts, and to the Dauphin—afterwards Louis XIII—Henry sent "a pack of little dogs," with which the Dauphin was not allowed to play; and asked, in return, for "a suit of armour well gilt and enamelled, together with pistols and a sword." His uncle of Denmark gave him a good fighting-ship with £2500; Mr. John Bond, "a learned editor of Horace," dedicated a new edition to him; and the States General of the United Provinces gave him a set of table linen.

In 1606 the French ambassador, M. de la Boderie, wrote of him: "He is a particular lover of horses and what belongs to them; but is not fond of hunting; and when he goes to it, it is rather for the pleasure of galloping, than that which the dogs give him. He plays willingly enough at Tennis, and at another Scots diversion very like mall; but this always with persons elder than himself, as if he despised those of his own age. He studies two hours a day, and employs the rest of his time in tossing the pike, or leaping, or shooting with the bow, or throwing the bar, or vaulting, or some other exercise of that kind; and he is never idle. He shews himself likewise very good-natured to his dependants, and supports their interests against any persons whatever; and pushes what he undertakes for them or others, with such zeal as gives success to it. For besides his exerting his whole strength to compass what he desires, he is already feared by those who have the management of affairs, and especially the Earl of Salisbury, who appears to be greatly apprehensive of the Prince's ascendant; as the Prince, on the other hand, shows little esteem for his lordship."

By his fourteenth year Henry was showing a surprising maturity. He took a great interest in foreign affairs, studied the patterns of military fortification, and became a connoisseur of sermons. His New Year gift to his father was a Latin thesis, but when he thanked the French ambassador for a more expensive present, he wrote: "You have sent me a present of the two things which I most delight in, arms and horses." He seems, however, to have reserved his warmest and most lasting affection for ships and the navy. In the summer of 1608 he sent word to Phineas Pett that he wanted to visit the royal dock at Woolwich. He went by barge from Blackwall, inspected the *Royal Anne*, and Mr. William Bull, Master Gunner of England, brought "thirty-one great brass chambers" from the Tower, and discharged them in salute. Some little while later complaint was made against Pett for his excessive expenditure on ships, and throughout the enquiry Henry stood near him "to encourage and support him under his anxiety and fatigue."

There is a portrait of Henry by Isaac Oliver—that miniature painter of marvellous accomplishment—which shows a young man of grave and memorable beauty: a profile of daunting severity, eyes of piercing directness under auburn hair, a fastidious mouth, a gull's-egg chin. He was well built, broad of shoulder, and narrow-waisted, and above the middle height. His smile was said to be gracious, his frown terrible. He was serious but affable, easy to approach but reserved of speech, fearless, and perhaps a little priggish. He was certainly self-willed, and immensely popular.

That James, on occasion, resented the independence and popularity of a son so different from himself, is no matter for surprise. But Henry's education had been devised and determined by James—he had been groomed for greatness—and he cannot have been unaffected by his education, or by the grandeur of his first household in England. Though he had little fondness for reading, he must have remembered some parts of *Basilikon Doron*, and the gift of a sloop that he called *Disdain* was not without its influence. He admired Raleigh, and might have led England into Elizabethan ventures. Of Raleigh he said, "Only my father would keep such a bird in a cage."

But Henry died untimely, and reticence hid the ambitions he may have nursed. It was in the late summer of 1612 that he fell ill, of a lingering distemper, and a strange listlessness alternated with bouts of feverish animation in which he tried to fight off his growing weakness by playing tennis and swimming in the Thames. The doctors had no advice to give until it was too late, when they tried to draw out his "corrupt and putrid fever" by applying newly killed pigeons to his shaven head, and cocks, split open, to his feet. Raleigh in the Tower had concocted an elixir, which made him sweat, but could do no more. He died on the 6th November, having recovered from delirium to ask, in a sensible voice, "Where is my dear sister?"

2

From the lavish household that James had initially provided for Henry and his sister, Elizabeth was soon removed to Combe Abbey, near Coventry, where her guardians were Lord and Lady Harington, known as staunch and pious Protestants whose piety did not prevent them from living in a princely fashion. Elizabeth was encouraged to rise at four or five in the morning, read and study till dinner-time—she learnt French and Italian but was spared Latin and Greek—and in the afternoon she was able to indulge a family passion for riding: Harington kept about twenty horses for her use. The major excitement of her childhood was the Gunpowder Plot, which roused so much fear in the neighbourhood of Combe that Elizabeth was taken to safer lodgings in Coventry. In Warwickshire it was thought that the purpose of the plot was "to blow the Scots back into Scotland."

Between Elizabeth and her elder brother there was great affection —they were forever writing little letters to each other—and after the Haringtons took Elizabeth to their house at Kew, she and Henry met every other day. When she was thirteen or fourteen suitors began to appear, and she was courted by dukes or princes from Brunswick, Würtemberg, Hesse, and Savoy; while the newly widowed Philip III of Spain—eighteen years older than she, virtuous and sadly stupid —made discreet enquiry about her willingness to exchange her church for a crown. Her father had hopes of a French marriage, but when that possibility vanished he chose, as her husband, Frederick V, Elector Palatine of the Rhine; and Henry her brother approved his choice.

Frederick, when negotiations began, was a healthy-looking boy of fifteen—the same age as Elizabeth—and said to be virtuous, physically sound, lively of spirit, and an accomplished horseman. He was not a reigning monarch, but his ancestry was distinguished, and as Count Palatine he was the senior prince of those who elected the Emperor. He would become, moreover, the leader of the German Protestant Union, and he would make no such unreasonable demands as Catholic princes did. In England the proposed union was loudly welcomed, dowries were agreed without undue delay, and in October 1612, Frederick arrived at Gravesend with a numerous train. The voyage had been stormy, and of his fleet of eight ships three had been forced to turn home.

Frederick, as it appeared, fell instantly in love, and Elizabeth received him with great kindness. But their happiness was overshadowed by Henry's illness, and when Henry died there was some doubt as to whether the marriage would take place. Charles, now heir to the throne, was a delicate child, and Elizabeth was next in succession. They were, however, formally betrothed, and mourning for Henry merged into rejoicing for his sister's wedding. The Palsgrave—the Count Palatine—was rich and generous and spent lavishly. He and Elizabeth saw a dozen plays,* among them *The Tempest, Othello,* and *The Merry Wives of Windsor.* Elizabeth went riding at Hampton Court and Hyde Park, and every would-be poet in England wrote a threnody for the dead prince or an epithalamium for his sister. In great pomp and splendour the young couple were married on the 14th February, 1613, and a little more than two months later embarked at Margate in the *Prince Royal.* Sailing in a fleet of fourteen vessels they crossed to Flushing in fine weather. Their progress through Holland to the Rhine was a long, continued triumph, and when they at last reached Heidelberg, in June, they were received with pageants and tumultuous pleasure.

On the 2nd January, 1614, Elizabeth gave birth to a male child, christened Frederick Henry, and there was uproarious rejoicing both in the Palatinate and in Britain. Elizabeth had to endure the burdens of royal domesticity, the disputes and jealousies of a large household, the unfortunate consequences of her own extravagance; but for half a dozen years she kept the light-heartedness of her youth, and it may be said that she was happy. The Palsgrave, however, was thought to show signs of melancholy. His responsibilities, as head of the Protestant Union, already bore hardly on him, and as if to invite disaster, he, who had not the capacity for major adventure, involved himself in the quarrels and complexities of the Empire and religious war.

The Holy Roman Empire had long ceased to be Roman, and when the Hapsburg emperors tried to reimpose the unity of holiness—on a Catholic basis—they provoked the Thirty Years' War. Dissent and dis-

* Carola Oman: *Elizabeth of Bohemia.*

content flared into violence in Prague, and Frederick enlarged the conflagration.

The childless Emperor Matthias, hereditary Archduke of Austria and King by election of Hungary and Bohemia, secured the accession of his cousin, Ferdinand of Styria, to the two thrones, and roused the Bohemian Protestants to extreme anger. Their leaders broke into the imperial palace in Prague, and from an upper window threw the Emperor's principal officers into the moat sixty feet below: to the vocabulary of international diplomacy the word "defenestration" was added, and local fighting became the prelude to wide-spread war.

Matthias died, and Ferdinand of Styria was elected Emperor. But the Bohemians rejected him, and to their own throne elected the Palsgrave. From the walls of Prague cannon roared in salute, and Elizabeth, daughter of James I of Great Britain, became Queen of Bohemia. Her father, though gratified by the enlargement of her estate, was deeply embarrassed when asked for help in maintaining it.

Frederick and Elizabeth entered Prague in triumph, and in November 1619 were crowned with splendid ceremony. A few weeks later Elizabeth gave birth to her second son, Prince Rupert, but her unhappy fate was prophesied when Frederick was nicknamed the Winter King. It quickly became known that she was in danger—great Catholic armies were mustering—and there was intense anger in England, much talk of intervention, and fiery volunteers demanded opportunity to fight for her. But nothing was done—nothing of that sort—and the devotion she undoubtedly inspired found no expression of any value other than a poem by Sir Henry Wotton which gave the Queen of Bohemia an immortality guaranteed by the Oxford Book of English Verse:

> "You meaner beauties of the night,
>   That poorly satisfy our eyes
> More by your number than your light,
>   You common people of the skies;
>   What are you when the moon shall rise?
>
> You curious chanters of the wood,
>   That warble forth Dame Nature's lays,
> Thinking your passions understood
>   By your weak accents; what's your praise
>   When Philomel her voice shall raise?

You violets that first appear,
        By your pure purple mantles known
Like the proud virgins of the year,
        As if the spring were all your own;
        What are you when the rose is blown?

So, when my mistress shall be seen
        In form and beauty of her mind,
By virtue first, then choice, a Queen,
        Tell me, if she were not design'd
        Th' eclipse and glory of her kind."

Her gaiety and high spirits earned the tribute of romantic love, but
nothing more substantial. In Prague, even during the short season of
her triumph, her lightheartedness had astonished and offended some
of its more solemn citizens, but when the Imperialist forces routed the
Bohemian army at the battle of the White Mountain her courage was
undimmed. Frederick had left the army to find comfort with his wife,
and through panic-stricken crowds they drove away from the city to
find refuge, at last, with Prince Maurice of Orange at the Hague. That
was in 1620, and a little while later the Spaniards were in occupation of
both the Upper and Lower Palatinates.

The Winter Queen got no help from her father. In his old age—a
decrepitude of mind and body that his years could not quite excuse—
James had lost almost all power of decision, and his devotion to the
cause of peace—his common-sensible abhorrence of war—had become a
tetchy and terrified aversion from all thought of military action. He
was, moreover, given some excuse for refusing his support when, before
Spanish intervention, there came a Spanish suggestion that he could
usefully act as mediator between the Emperor and the Bohemians.
Promptly he sent an embassy to which neither side paid much attention, and the Spaniards continued their preparation for war.

That the Bohemians' rejection of a duly elected Emperor was wanton rebellion—that Frederick's rash acceptance of a dubiously vacant
throne was usurpation—these are opinions that braver and better men
than James might, in all honesty, have held. But the Winter Queen was
his daughter, and much of England was hotly opposed to the Catholic
Emperor and its natural enemies in Spain: a king who thought less of
himself, more of his subjects—and, in an old-fashioned way, more of
honour—would, at the very least, have given indignation a voice of

thunder, and the menace of lightning before the next peal might have kept the Spaniards out of the Palatinates.

Spain invaded the Palatinates, and still James did nothing. Parliament, in a surly mood, refused to grant the necessary supplies for war, and abetted the King's inaction. But war would have been justified, and could have been effective. The Spaniards, who had to feed and supply an army in the Netherlands, were open to sea-borne attack, and idle though it is to measure the *ifs* of history—to speculate on what might have happened—it is difficult not to suppose that history would have run in a rather different course if Prince Henry had lived.—Would Spanish ships have sailed into the English Channel? It seems unlikely. And much less likely that they would have sailed out again.

Elizabeth, though given no help, was not without friends. She lived at Rhenen on the Lower Rhine, in Dutch Gelderland, which she had visited on her honeymoon and where Frederick built a palace for her. She had many English visitors, and it may have comforted her to be called the Queen of Hearts. Recurrent disappointment did not destroy her health—she was able to bear thirteen children, though she grumbled at the pain of the ninth—and straitened means could not defeat her high temper, though poverty reduced her hospitality and her household. The payment of her English annuity of £12,000 ceased when Charles I and his parliament fell out, and a pension from the house of Orange also came to an end. Then she began to quarrel with her children.

Frederick Henry, the eldest, had been drowned in the Haarlem Meer on a frosty morning early in 1629. Her second son, Charles Louis, refused to receive her when he regained his Electorate, and Charles II, restored to his English throne, showed no great willingness to give her house-room. Parliament, in 1660, voted her £20,000 to pay her debts, but the money did not arrive, and the following year, taking matters into her own hands, she sailed from the Hague and in Drury Lane found shelter, of a magnificent sort, at the house of an old admirer, the rich and gallant Lord Craven. Then Charles II relented, treated her with kindness, and gave her a pension. But Elizabeth was sixty-six, and for nearly half a century her life had seldom been easy. Within less than a year of her coming home—forty-nine years after she had left it—she died, and was buried in Westminster Abbey.

By life she had been defeated, but with Mary, Queen of Scots, she could have said "In my end is my beginning." Of her thirteen children Charles Louis, Count Palatine of the Rhine, Duke of Bavaria, was the father of a daughter, Elizabeth Charlotte, who married Philip, Duke of Orleans, from whom descended the royal house of Orleans; Sophia, born in 1630, married Ernest, Duke of Brunswick, Elector of Hanover, and their son George, Elector of Hanover, in 1714 ascended the throne of Great Britain and Ireland, from whom is descended Her Majesty Queen Elizabeth II. From Charles Louis the kings of Italy, Belgium, and Bulgaria fetched descent; from Sophia, as well as British sovereigns, the kings of Denmark, Jugoslavia, the Netherlands, Norway, Roumania, and Sweden. From the fertile womb of the Winter Queen—"the eclipse and glory of her kind"—came tenants for most of the thrones of Europe.

9

The Anglican Martyr

1

It is recounted that Prince Henry once said to his young brother Charles, "When I am King, you shall be Archbishop of Canterbury."

Henry did not live to be King, and Charles as Archbishop could only have survived under an unchallenged despotism whose first charge was his security. But in Henry's joking there was percipience, there was shrewd criticism; for Charles, even as a boy, was devout and grave, responsive to ceremony and observant of decorum. From Canterbury he might have devised, for the Anglican church, a ritual of intricate and solemn beauty; but he would have alienated worshippers by insisting on an adherence to it more closely disciplined than mere piety required.

He must be admired for a small but resolute courage that let him defeat the many ailments of his childhood. When he first came to England observers were shocked by his sickly appearance, his uncertain walk, and an inhibiting stammer. But he was so fortunate as to acquire a competent and devoted governess in Lady Carey, wife of him who had ridden so fast to Edinburgh to advise King James of his enlargement. His health improved, and he began to grow up in the stimulating company of his pretty, vivacious sister and his brilliant brother. It was, perhaps, in emulation of Henry that he learnt to ride well and play tennis. But when he was twelve his brother died, Elizabeth married, and Charles appears to have been left strangely friendless. His stammer had been cured, but it may have made him shy. He was earnest and intelligent, but he had no sense of humour, and by his

loneliness he was deprived of sympathy with others, of that understanding of other men which, in an age of irascible change, was of the
first importance to anyone who, born to authority, wished to maintain
it.

When George Villiers—who became Duke of Buckingham—first won
the old King's favour, Charles was intensely jealous of him. But Buckingham, quick-witted and shrewd enough to see where his own advantage lay, deliberately paid court to the lonely boy, and won his
friendship. To his mother Charles had been bound by close affection,
and after her death in 1619 he grew dependent on Buckingham; and
when Buckingham turned a diplomatic somersault—he ceased to campaign for Elizabeth of Bohemia and argued the case for a Spanish marriage—Charles was led into ludicrous misadventure.

The prospect, always unsubstantial, of his marriage to the Infanta,
was temporarily obscured by invasion of the Palatinate, and Charles,
like so many indignant young men, was hotly in favour of war: his sister
meant more to him than a Spanish princess. But James had no liking
for war, and parliament, without whose willing help war could not be
waged, had no love for James. The Winter Queen and her defeated
husband were left to shift for themselves, and presently—to James and
Buckingham and Charles himself—the thought recurred that an alliance with Spain might be of advantage to all. Gondomar, Spain's clever
and pertinacious ambassador, prompted the thought, and after negotiations had stumbled ineffectually from month to month, Charles grew
impatient and decided to be his own ambassador. That Buckingham
encouraged him is not to be doubted. That Buckingham proposed
their ridiculous journey is highly probable. The King was persuaded
to give them permission to go, and, ludicrously disguised, they put to
sea at Dover, rode to Paris, and still incognito hurried to Madrid.

It was in February they left England, and not till October did they
return. Then there was infinite rejoicing when it became known that
Charles was still unmarried, the Infanta still in Madrid. Charles had
promised toleration for English Catholics, he had promised more than
he should have done. But no reasonable concessions could satisfy
Spanish demands, and Charles's own convictions, rooted in the doctrine of the English church, were too deep to be moved, too strong to
be shaken. The Infanta was equally resolute in faith: she had a
charming disposition, but, it was said, her chief pleasures were meditating on the Immaculate Conception and preparing lint for the use of

hospitals. Her unwillingness to accept a Protestant bridegroom was matched by England's reluctance to welcome a Catholic princess, and the end of the unrewarded wooing was bonfires on Blackheath, hogsheads of wine in the streets of London, and the plaudits commonly reserved for victory.

Charles himself, however, was deeply offended, announced his hostility to Spain, and with some success took part in debate in the House of Lords. War was declared, and Buckingham disastrously assumed control of policy. Several thousand untrained men were enlisted to serve under an adventurer, the Count Mansfeldt, in an attempt to expel Imperialist troops from the Palatinate. The expedition was tardily mounted, and did not put to sea until January 1625. Permission to land at Calais and Flushing was refused, and the men—they could hardly be called soldiers—began to die of plague and famine. Most of them died.

That was the first of Buckingham's military failures, but almost simultaneously he was arranging another marriage for Charles, and in the negotiations for a marital alliance he may have omitted some military instructions and overlooked the casualty lists for which he was responsible.

The chosen bride was Henrietta Maria, the youngest child of the gallant Henri IV—murdered a year after her birth—and sister of Louis XIII. Marriage to a princess of France entailed almost as many secret concessions as the Spaniards had demanded; and a Catholic queen on the throne of a land whose Catholic subjects were forbidden the comfort of their priests was an anomaly even in a country so ingenious in compromise as England. But in June 1625, less than three months after Charles's accession to the throne, Henrietta was made welcome in London with noisy protestations of loyalty and pleasure. She was a light-hearted, frivolous, loving girl of fifteen, whose frivolity hid a strength of character, not always timely and seldom discreet, which the years would reveal; and after some months made hazardous by misunderstanding and an intrusive host of French priests and courtiers, it became a marriage truly secured by love; and therein lay its danger.

Henrietta never ceased to be French, never understood the apparent contradictions which subsist without difficulty in English minds. After Buckingham's death Charles had no one to love but his wife, and because he loved her he trusted her. In one respect she never failed him— she loved him too, and abused him for his weakness with the frankness of love—but he believed in the advice she gave him, and her advice was always wrong. When the King and his parliament drifted unwillingly into war, Henrietta wanted to wage total war. But in the early phases of the war neither the King nor his parliament had any wish to destroy those whom—each according to opinion—they had the right to rule or represent. Henrietta was brave and simple—once only did her spirit fail—but Charles, though no coward except on that same occasion, was both stubborn and changeable, faithful and faithless. He needed a wife whose mind was subtle enough to understand the nature of his weakness, and tolerant enough to sympathise with the alien problems of the English constitution and the curious conscience of the English. But few kings have deserved such a paragon on their pillows.

Buckingham continued his maladroit foreign policy, and in 1626 a singularly ill-equipped expedition essayed an attack on Cádiz. Its leaders were inefficient, the troops were undisciplined, the ships sailed under canvas that was said to have been first hoisted against the Spanish Armada; and the result was ignominious failure. Huguenot rebellion compelled France to make peace with Spain, and in 1627 Buckingham, who had so lately negotiated a French alliance, swung like a weathercock to hostility, and led a fleet to Rochelle, then in possession of the Huguenots. His ships were not allowed to enter the harbour, and his troops attempted an assault on the nearby Ile de Ré. Buckingham had no military sense or education, and his untrained conscripts were soundly beaten. Buckingham returned to England, and when about to launch a new attack on Rochelle he was fortunately assassinated by John Felton, a soldier embittered—perhaps driven crazy—by the Duke's calamitous ineptitude.

In 1628, the year of Buckingham's death but some time before it, Charles confronted his third parliament and came very close to that conflict of interest which finally provoked the great drama that so tragically colours his reign. His first parliament had granted him two subsidies—income tax and property tax—but contrary to usage had voted tonnage and poundage—the duties on wine, beer, and dry goods—for one year only. In 1626, when the expedition to Cádiz brought shame and defeat, Buckingham was impeached by Sir John Eliot and another member. "Our honour is lost," said Eliot, "our ships are sunk, our men are perished." Charles refused to admit their right to question or criticise his servants, and Eliot was sent to the Tower. He had to be released when the Commons protested, but the House refused to grant supplies. Charles threatened a dissolution, and when the Lords asked him to delay his decision he answered "Not a minute," and parliament was dismissed. To permit conscription martial law was proclaimed, and five knights who declined to pay a forced loan were refused bail and imprisoned by the King's special command.

Charles's third parliament gave history a cue by presenting its Petition of Right, a protest against unparliamentary taxation, arbitrary imprisonment, and martial law, that followed a long list of grievances and asked for an immediate reply. Thomas Wentworth, a Yorkshire member who was to play a leading part in the Caroline drama, had tried to postpone a definite answer to the question that now underlay all debate—whether Charles was above the law, or the law above Charles—but Charles himself spoilt that well intentioned effort by vainly demanding a vote of confidence in his honesty and goodwill. He accepted the Petition of Right on being assured that it would not infringe his real power, and continued his collection of tonnage and poundage. His financial difficulties might have been eased if either he or his parliament had recognised what principally caused them. For the last fifty years the value of money had been falling.

Another member, who became more famous in later years, joined in debate, and the debate was enlarged to include a topic ever present, in that age, in men's minds: ecclesiastical politics. The member was John Pym, and what perturbed him was the influence of Arminianism: the doctrine, in Milton's words, of those who set up "free will against free grace." Eliot and Pym impeached an Arminian member for defending unparliamentary taxation, and Charles insisted on his right to the old liberties of the throne and his royal conscience. Tempers rose, and the Commons, not content with denouncing tonnage and poundage, added Popery to their grievances; and a new member, Oliver Cromwell, was heard for the first time. There were those who observed the rough country-cut of his clothes, but in the House there was a worse roughness than that of rustic tailoring, and as debate deteriorated the Speaker moved to adjourn. He was held in his chair, and behind locked doors the Commons voted that innovators in religion—all who favoured Popery and Arminianism—were equal enemies of the kingdom with those who, lacking parliamentary authority, exacted or paid tonnage and poundage.

In March 1629 parliament was dissolved, and did not meet again for eleven years.

2

In the reign of Queen Elizabeth, which lasted from 1558 till 1603, nine parliaments were summoned. One had a life of eleven years, but no more than three sessions; each of the others enjoyed one short session only. England was governed by its Privy Council, which included the Lord Treasurer, the Queen's Secretary of State and other officials, the Archbishop of Canterbury, and as many as twenty members in all. It met several times a week, and dealt with all administrative problems.

James summoned four parliaments, and the members of his House of Commons were more independent, and increasingly more critical, than Elizabeth's parliament-men. For that, in some degree, he had himself to blame—he could not bluff or cajole them, as Elizabeth had; he could not, like that great, unscrupulous Queen, summon their patriotism and move them to tearful agreement—but if Elizabeth had lived only a few years more she too would have found a growing reluctance to accept the near-absolutism that she so cleverly disguised. Her disguise would have been penetrated.

Neither James nor Charles had the skill—and Charles had not the wish—to conceal their belief in a monarch's divine right to rule, and both were foolishly explicit in asserting it. Their assertion was offensive to all who had accepted by faith the teaching of the Reformation, and by experience had acquired some knowledge of the increased importance of parliament. The Reformation had taught men to believe in their right to immediate contact with God—the priests who had posed as essential mediators had become redundant—and experience had shown that monarchs were no longer able to sustain regality from their own resources, but—especially in time of war—were utterly dependent on parliament and its willingness to grant supply.

In Charles's mind there was no thought that his kingly state had been diminished: it had been established by God, and God is not mocked. There was, on the other hand, the certain knowledge in the minds of his parliament-men that their powers had been enhanced; and to them also God had spoken, and spoken clearly—so one may assume—in the vernacular tongue which the Reformation authorised. A belief in God's association with the everyday affairs of life, with foreign policy and the collection of taxes, must be accepted as a characteristic of the age. It is notorious that the Scots were utterly convinced of God's declared preference for the Presbyterian form of worship, but it was an Englishman—an Englishman still revered for his lofty genius —who asked if God had not revealed himself "as his manner is, first to his Englishmen?" It was John Milton who said that; and Cromwell, a few years later, showed even greater familiarity with the Deity. He was in correspondence with the General Assembly of the Church of Scotland, and wrote: "I beseech you in the bowels of Christ think it possible you may be mistaken." To men so neighbourly with their Creator the authority of a king was of small account.

The young Lord Falkland—soldier and scholar, one of the most amiable men of his time—trod the middle way and believed in the Church of England because that was where it stood. He defended Anglicanism as the cause of reason against the claims to infallibility put forward with equal vehemence by Rome and Geneva. That, at first sight, seems modest enough; but Falkland, though more gently than the extremists on either flank, was as sure as they of the rightness of his position, and of God's preference for Canterbury. The Pilgrim Fathers who had sailed from Plymouth in 1620 were Separatists from the Church of England who took their faith aboard the *Mayflower* to worship God in what Cromwell called the "howling wilderness" of America, where they would have exclusive rights in him.

The professed faith of schismatics and "precisians," of one sort or another, is now suspect because of their insistence on the importance of what later ages have dismissed as trivialities.—There was a man devout and otherwise reasonable, who for two years refused Holy Communion because he was not allowed to receive it standing.—But schisms and sects were a natural consequence of the Reformation which had brought God so much closer to man that men, by nature independent and dogmatic, were encouraged to believe that they alone could see the truth he revealed and hear his own prescription for worship. It has been widely observed that Puritanism often went hand-in-hand with prosperity—that well-to-do merchants tended to a pious non-conformity—and the religion of the rich has often excited doubt. But the Old Testament abounds in texts that promise rewards to the righteous—"Yet saw I never the righteous forsaken, nor his seed begging their bread"—and in the re-awakening of faith that followed the Reformation the mere possession of riches may well have seemed the mark of God's favour, and been accepted as an incentive to yet greater piety.

The King and the wildest Anabaptist were alike dominated by religion, and more and more of the King's subjects were finding reason for a self-importance that encroached on the traditional importance of the monarch. In one respect Charles was a man of his own time, but in another he was a man out of his depth. He was more virtuous than most men, but his virtues were private virtues and all his faults were public. He had exquisite taste, but no talents. He collected pictures with perception and enthusiasm, but he had no such judgment for politics nor liking for the forum.

There may be some significance in the fact that Queen Elizabeth, a supreme politician, had no taste in art—her appalling clothes are evidence of that—and little interest in theology. But Charles the theologian was also an outstanding collector of pictures in an age of great collectors. Francis I, Charles V, Philip II, and the Emperor Rudolph II were all patrons and lavish purchasers, but even among his fellow sovereigns Charles was conspicuous for the virtuosity of his munificence. He bought Mantegna's *Triumphs of Caesar*—a present for Henrietta—and Raphael's cartoons. He persuaded Van Dyck to settle in England, who painted portraits of Charles, his family, and many courtiers: Van Dyck lived at Blackfriars, and Charles is said to have built a jetty below his house, so that he might easily visit him. Both Van Dyck and Peter Paul Rubens were knighted, and Rubens was commissioned to paint the ceiling which Inigo Jones had designed for the banqueting hall in the palace of Whitehall. In 1625, before Charles's accession, Rubens had written of him: *"Monsieur le Prince de Galles est le prince le plus amateur qui soit au monde."*—Add to that Milton's jealous complaint that the King spent too much time reading Shakespeare, and there is good reason to deplore the fate that gave him an uneasy throne instead of a country seat and the ducal domain to which he had been born.

3

As in Elizabeth's time—but now with less agreement—England was ruled by the Privy Council, and an ingenious Treasurer extracted from a rich country a revenue sufficient for Charles's needs, but insufficient to let England exert any influence in foreign affairs. The peace that followed Buckingham's death encouraged trade, but the crown interfered with trade by creating new monopolies in tobacco and gunpowder, and corporations that controlled the sale of such domestic necessities as coal and salt and soap. For two or three years, however, England presented an appearance of prosperity; the King—now warmly in love with a wife who had dismissed her French priests—was reasonably happy; and those who found Anglican rule intolerable were not merely free to emigrate, but encouraged to do so by heavy investment in New England properties.

As well as his able Lord Treasurer Weston, Charles had now a valuable servant in Thomas Wentworth, the Yorkshire member who, in Charles's third parliament, had tried to postpone presentation of the Petition of Right. Wentworth was made President of the Council of the North, and in York proclaimed his belief that kings must be indulgent fathers to their people, and their authority accepted. Later he went to Ireland, and there imposed his own authority. He was a man of great vigour and high ideals, and it is possible that Charles could have made more use of him. It is equally possible that if he had been given power, not in Yorkshire and Ireland but in Whitehall, his fierce ability and autocratic temper would have precipitated the great rebellion which a less purposive government put off until 1642. Wentworth advocated a policy that he called "Thorough"; but Charles had no appetite for the absolute rule of a dictator.

Within ten years the Queen bore eight children, and retained her happy temper while acquiring a new self-reliance. Charles, who was to become Charles II, was born in 1630, a vigorous and ugly baby who was christened by William Laud, then Bishop of London. In 1633, at the age of sixty, Laud became Archbishop of Canterbury, and with the noblest of motives but by niggling means precipitated the tragic conflict to which Charles was doomed. Like Charles, his royal master, he was in love with the beauty of holiness, and found it enshrined in the Church of England. He and Charles hoped to create a unity of spirit "in the bond of peace and in righteousness of life," and to do so tried to extirpate Calvinism in England and Presbyterianism in Scotland in order to exalt, in lonely authority, the Anglican rites and dogma. Laud was a scholar, utterly devout, and his private life was exemplary; but his large ambition was spoiled by a pettiness like that of a house-proud woman who cannot bear to see chair or picture removed from where she thinks proper to it. The position of the communion table was vital to his purpose, and the sanctity of the name of Jesus depended on the inclination of a communicant's head. He was a good man, but unduly irritable, insufferably bigoted, too warmly addicted to punishment, and as insistent on ritual as the Genevan on predestination. He was also an advocate of censorship, which, however justifiable, has always been unpopular.

In an old-fashioned way King James had kept a professional fool, a court jester, called Archie Armstrong: a man of character and considerable wit. He lived until Charles was king, and was then thrown out of court for giving voice to popular feeling, and exclaiming, with reckless impudence, "All praise to God, and little laud to the Devil!"

A prescribed manner of worship, the imposition of taxation unwarranted by parliament—which had the greater moment in hastening resistance to Charles's unconstitutional government? It was not unduly extravagant—it cost less than Cromwell's, in later years—but it antagonised many who were not, by nature, hostile to the throne's established authority. Ship-money had traditionally been levied on seaboard towns and counties for the provision of coastal defences in time of need; but when in 1634 the receipt from maritime areas was insufficient, Charles's government enlarged its demand to include inland areas, and John Hampden, a country squire who had already been in prison for refusing to pay a forced loan, repeated his peremptory "No!" and was again arrested. Resentment was aggravated; resistance grew against an arbitrary and seemingly illimitable power to mulct men of lands and money which they regarded as their own.

Disaffection, seeping in from many quarters, found the impetus of a spring tide in Scotland. Charles rode north in 1633, and ill-advisedly took Laud with him. They were horrified by the untidiness of divine worship in the Godliest part of their dominion, and to rectify disorder commanded the clergy to wear surplices. Then they ordered removal of the communion table to the east end of churches, and advised the adoption of a new prayer book, more ritualistic than Knox's, without submitting it for approval to the General Assembly. The consequence was a riot in St. Giles, gross disorder in Edinburgh, and an attempt to lynch its Bishop. In what was very like a prelude to revolution neither side showed any inclination to give way, though from many parts of the country, and from all classes of the community, the Privy Council was bombarded with pleas that the King by grace would rid his Scottish subjects of Laud's hated liturgy.

The rebellious petitioners appointed committees, called "Tables," representing the four orders of noblemen, lairds, burgesses, and ministers, which then demanded withdrawal of the liturgy and removal of bishops from the Council. Charles rebuffed the Tables, maintained the liturgy, and declared the petition treasonable. The Tables showed their strength by devising a "National League and Covenant," and inviting the whole Scottish nation to sign it.

In 1581 James VI had pledged his word to uphold the Presbyterian system and defend the state against Romanism. That earlier covenant and various statutes supporting the Reformed religion were quoted, to give the document historical substance and legal authority, and signatories would promise to maintain the Scottish form of worship to the utmost of their power and "against all sorts of persons whatsoever." By the 1st March, 1638, the Covenant was ready for signature, and to Greyfriars churchyard, where it was exposed, the people of Edinburgh came exuberantly to endorse it. All over the country, except in the Celtic north and Aberdeen—where episcopacy and a tradition of scholarship flourished—there were similar demonstrations, and with the utmost enthusiasm the Scots of all classes swore by the great name of God, and with some lack of logic, to resist unconstitutional innovation, to ignore "foul aspersions of rebellion," and to maintain both royal authority and true religion.

Charles was shocked and angered, but listened, as it seems, to both Laud and the Queen. Henrietta, with unusual good sense, advocated concessions; Laud spoke in favour of Wentworth's "thorough" policy, and protested too much; for Charles took Henrietta's advice. He revoked the prayer book, and permitted a General Assembly—the first for twenty years—to meet in Glasgow. Election to it was carefully manipulated, and Covenanters packed it. It defied the Marquis of Hamilton, the King's Commissioner, when he ordered its dissolution; and with a flamboyant gesture abolished episcopacy. Early in 1639 an invitation was issued, to sympathisers in England, to join in a war against Papists and bishops, and the Covenanters occupied Edinburgh castle. Charles mustered an army and marched to Berwick.

Scotland enjoyed a military advantage that Charles could not ignore. The Covenanters had the services of Alexander Leslie, a "little old crooked soldier" who had risen to the rank of Field-Marshal in the wars of Gustavus Adolphus of Sweden, and a host of others who had learnt their trade as mercenaries abroad. The whole country—except Aberdeen and the north—was united in arrogant assurance of its virtue, rich merchants gave their money, and officers lately returned from Swedish or German regiments drilled their levies under standards that proclaimed their new loyalty to Christ and the Covenant. But despite enthusiasm the Scots retained a useful prudence. They thought it unlikely that England would welcome invasion, and hoped to win a war without fighting.

Charles shared their hope. His English army was untrained, unwilling to fight, and poorly supplied because London had refused to lend him the money he required. At Berwick a truce was arranged that neither side intended to honour. Charles refused to accept the Assembly's high-handed abolition of episcopacy, and the Assembly, again convoked, found the office of bishop contrary to God's law and enforced acceptance of the Covenant on all.

In Ireland the workmanlike Wentworth—advocate of a "thorough" policy—had not only established the rule of law but recruited and drilled a small army. He returned to England, was created Earl of Strafford, and advised Charles to discontinue the collection of ship-money and summon parliament. Against Scotland he advocated decisive war, but parliament refused to vote supply before it had discussed its grievances, and its grievances were many. John Pym, that redoubtable squire, emerged as its leader, and in the temper of the age combined complaint against unparliamentary taxation with an attack on the growing Popery of the church. Charles asked for subsidies, and when he found that the Commons were more interested in Scottish demands, threw away the last chance of constitutional reform by dissolving the Short Parliament: it sat for three weeks only.

Strafford, the lion-hearted Yorkshireman, declared that parliament had failed the King, and the King, in consequence, would be justified in doing whatever he had the power to do: there was, he said, an army in Ireland which could be used to subdue Scottish dissidence. The Privy Council gave new authority for the collection of ship-money, the Church defended the railing-in of altars and damned all who took arms against the King. These intemperate decisions provoked widespread resistance. There was rioting in London, soldiers mutinied, and an army that Charles again led to the north refused to fight. The Scots under Leslie entered Newcastle, and the city of London made common cause with the House of Lords in demanding peace. Strafford, still advocating no surrender, was in a lonely minority, and the Scottish terms were accepted: Leslie's defiant army—drawing closer to the King's enemies in England—was to occupy the northern counties and receive a subsidy of £850 a day.

To find the subsidy Charles had to summon parliament, and in November the Long Parliament came into being and quickly showed its temper. Pym was again its leader, and as urgent in their demands were Hampden, young Harry Vane, and Cromwell the solid squire from Huntingdonshire. Cromwell had not yet discovered his gift of eloquence, and was still conspicuously ill dressed. Very different was Harry Vane. He was a fiery young Puritan of uncommonly broad experience, for he had emigrated to America where, at the age of twenty-three, he became Governor of Massachusetts. Defeated for re-election, he returned to England where his father was now the King's Secretary of State. It was they who brought about the downfall and execution of Strafford.

The Long Parliament attacked old grievances with a new vehemence. Its policy was as "thorough" as Strafford's, and because Pym was a better parliamentarian and a stronger man than Charles its policy was put into practice, and grievances were pulled up from the roots. It abolished irregular courts such as the Star Chamber—first established by Henry VII—and all extra-parliamentary exactions. It asserted its right to sit until it should be pleased to dissolve itself, and thereafter a parliament must be summoned every three years. By the Root and Branch Bill it again abolished episcopacy, and Archbishop Laud, now sixty-seven, was impeached and imprisoned in the Tower; where he remained until his execution five years later.

It was the presence of a Scottish army in the north of England that gave Pym and his associates the power to enforce their demands, and Strafford, summoned to London, boldly proposed to arrest them on a charge of treasonable correspondence with the Scots. Charles hesitated, and then drew back. He still hoped for compromise, he abominated the thought of drastic, irreversible action. But Pym suffered no such inhibition. The House of Commons locked its doors and framed charges against Strafford. Then, in the Upper House, those who there supported Pym accused Strafford of treason and demanded his arrest. Strafford was with the King, and refusing to seek safety in flight, went down to face his accusers. In the House he was humiliated, forced to his knees, and made prisoner. Then he joined Laud in the Tower.

In February 1641 he was impeached, and in March stood his trial in Westminster Hall. Charles had assured him of support, and was ostentatious in showing him favour and sympathy. He and his Queen attended the trial, as did ladies of the court, and Strafford rewarded them by the stubborn ability of his defence. He stood alone against eight who represented the Commons. In the case for the prosecution there was wild inconsistency, witnesses were intimidated, and a vulgar clamour filled Westminster Hall. It was crowded with spectators who argued, quarrelled, and ate and drank as lavishly as if they were picnicking. The trial lasted for three weeks; and though gross confusion clouded its proceedings, the heart of the case beat strongly. Strafford had proposed war against Scotland—perhaps England too—because "the commonwealth was sick of peace: it will never be well till it be conquered again." That was the charge against him, but evidence was lacking to substantiate it, and at one time the trial seemed to break down. Then Pym produced a copy taken of some notes on a speech that Strafford had made in Council on the 5th May, 1640; and that was conclusive.

Sir Henry Vane, though the King's Secretary, was Strafford's enemy, and had already testified to his having told the King: "You have an army in Ireland, you may employ it to reduce this kingdom." But no other councillor would corroborate Vane's statement, and he could not produce written evidence. He had burnt his notes at the King's command, he said. But his son Harry—that ardent young Puritan—had seen them before they were burnt, and made a copy which he gave to Pym.

A Bill of Attainder was introduced, declaring Strafford guilty of treason. He made a final speech, at great length, with a power that hardly faltered. Pym replied, briefly but with compelling effect, and in due course the Bill passed its third reading in the House of Commons. But the King's assent was necessary before the Bill became an Act, and for a little while there was a tantalising possibility that he could evade a terrible decision. Could a government of moderate, middle-of-the-road temper and opinion be formed? The Earl of Bedford was well qualified and apparently willing to lead it. It was rumoured that Lord Saye and Sele, a Puritan peer, would join it; and even Pym might accept office. Bedford tried to save Strafford from the axe, arguing that banishment would serve a parliamentary purpose as well as death; but found little support. He was harshly rebuffed by the Earl of Essex—Essex, in his youth, had been married to Fanny Howard, and led the disastrous expedition to Cádiz—who told him, "Stone-dead hath no fellow." And Bedford's arguing was finally stopped by smallpox and death.

The King made a last effort on Strafford's behalf. It was ill-advised, but Henrietta was urgent in persuasion. In the army of the north, that faced the Scots and got no pay for their trouble, there were many Catholic officers, and she had friends with some of whom she was fondly weaving plots and plans to rescue the prisoner in the Tower. So Charles went to the House of Lords and summoned the Commons to hear him. He denied all intention of using the army of Ireland, and asked them to be merciful to Strafford. Let him be found guilty not of treason but of a misdemeanour, he said. Both Houses were offended by this apparent invasion of their privilege, and Charles gained nothing.

Then an attempt was made, and defeated, to rescue Strafford from the Tower. London was suffused with anger. Outside the House of Lords a dense crowd of respectable citizens shouted for death, and a howling mob terrified the royal household in their palace of Whitehall. Even Henrietta, that foolish, gallant woman, was frightened. She had her young children about her, and could say nothing to stiffen fortitude in the King. Neither could his councillors and bishops. All except one —honest William Juxon, Bishop of London—advised him to give assent to the Bill, though some must have asked themselves how Strafford, for reminding the King that he had an army in Ireland, could be thought more guilty of treason than Pym and his friends, who openly relied, for their own purposes, on Alexander Leslie and his army of Scots.

Strafford himself tried to ease the King's agony of mind. Charles would do better, he wrote, to sacrifice his servant than his kingdom. But Charles, when he asked Strafford to come down from the north and help him, had promised that not a hair on his head should be hurt. Could he forget that promise because his Privy Council advised him to let the Commons have their way, and his wife and children, as well as his kingdom, were in danger?

On his own confession he sinned against his conscience, and saved his kingdom rather than his friend. He let a commission, appointed for the purpose, give assent to the Bill of Attainder, and on the 12th

May Strafford went to execution on Tower Hill. From his prison cell old Archbishop Laud reached out to bless him, and in the high temper of the age Strafford died without flinching.

4

The King had maintained peace at the expense of his conscience, and there were many in both Houses who began to feel they had done enough, and gone as far as discretion could approve, to repair the faults and malpractice of eleven years of unparliamentary rule. It was unfortunate, therefore, that Henrietta chose to initiate new plots and plan to go secretly to Holland, taking the crown jewels with her. Her intention was discovered, and she was forbidden to leave the country.

Misfortune, or a menace of it, was renewed when Charles decided to visit Scotland. That again roused suspicion, for Scotland was a strange land and there were many in England who distrusted both its goodwill and its docility. It may be that Charles wanted only to escape for a little while from London, where he had suffered intense humiliation and known the bitterness of spiritual conflict; he hoped, perhaps, to renew himself in the livelier climate of his own country. He may have thought, however, that he could find, beyond the Border, a surviving loyalty and a new source of strength; but if that were so, his hope was defeated.

His most powerful subject in Scotland was, in effect, subject in no discernible fashion. Archibald Campbell, Earl of Argyll, supported the Covenant and had been instrumental in assuring for his party a revolutionary authority at the expense of the royal prerogative. But his appetite for power was excessive, and among the enemies he had made was James Graham, Earl of Montrose, who also had signed the Covenant but later had found cause to doubt the Covenanters' honesty and suspect Argyll of reaping private profit from public policy.

At Newcastle the King found the Scottish army disbanding, and seems to have established very friendly relations with "the little crooked general," Alexander Leslie, whom he raised to the peerage as Earl of Leven. Leslie entertained his King in the handsomest style, and promised never again to take up arms against him. In Edinburgh, too, Charles was received with apparent warmth and passing kindness. He attended service at St. Giles and sessions of the Scots parliament, but amity was short-lived. The Covenanters' hostility was deep-seated, and Argyll showed his capacity for intrigue by seducing—on the low level of politics—the King's Commissioner, Hamilton. Montrose was in durance, and Charles achieved nothing except an amnesty for political prisoners that secured his release.

The King returned to London and an unexpected welcome. Politics had interfered with trade, corruption was rife, and the City had begun to realise that an ineffectual king might be preferable to an over-officious parliament. But the cheers that greeted Charles were soon silenced by terrible news from Ireland. Strafford had ruled by the strength of his own will, and in Ulster the removal of that iron will had released the pent-up hatred created by half a century of oppression. Land-hunger and religious fervour brought out the Irish in a fury of blood-letting, and wild rumours were spread that Dublin was captured, every Protestant would have his throat cut, that twenty thousand had already been murdered. The true tale was bad enough, but not so bad as that. Dublin remained intact, and measures were taken to suppress a rebellion which—like every other Irish rebellion—might have been foreseen. But in England old fears were wakened, fears of a Catholic rising, and hatred grew of the Catholic Queen who might be instigating another plot to bring England under the insufferable rule of Rome. Not all the English—not even a majority, or anything like a majority—were subject to such irrational fear and the emotion of hate, but enough were infected to create an atmosphere untypical of England and woe-fully destructive. A fatal division began to appear between those who were called Cavaliers, and the others, crop-headed in a puritanical way, called Roundheads.

In the House of Commons, where Charles had found new support-ers, Hyde and Falkland now faced Pym and Hampden. Edward Hyde had opposed Strafford but supported episcopacy. A learned and judi-cious man, who defended Charles against rabid parliamentarians and tried to protect him from the well-intentioned but deplorable intrigues of the Queen, Hyde—who instinctively disliked the Puritans but had no intemperate desire to punish them—won his immortality when, after being created Earl of Clarendon and suffering much persecution, he wrote his majestic *History of the Rebellion and Civil Wars in England*. Falkland acquired less fame, but was that "incomparable young man" who, totally honourable, did all he could to reconcile the inter-ests of King and Commons, and at the battle of Newbury, realising that scholarship was vain and his high hopes had been defeated, placed himself in the front ranks of Sir John Byron's regiment and rode forward to solicit death at the age of thirty-four.

Pym and Hampden, their opponents, were no less honest. Pym was a politician, a parliament-man who trimmed his sails to political breezes, but retained a fundamental integrity and good manners in defence of the sovereignty of parliament. He was never unwilling to negotiate with Charles or bargain with the Scots. Hampden, a country gentleman from Buckinghamshire, was wholly admirable though his opinions did not recommend him to the Royalists. Neither learned nor eloquent, he won the King's respect as well as the more easily earned esteem of his fellow parliamentarians. He stood stubbornly for what he conceived to be his rights, suffered in defence of a common right, and like Falkland died in battle for a constitutional principle. The great tragedy of the Civil War is not merely that there were good men on both sides—there always are, in any war—but that so many good men, arrayed in arms against each other, were essentially of the same sort. Clear-headed or muddle-headed, the majority were dignified by the degree of integrity that their intelligence made possible, and the war —in its earlier phases—was mollified by mutual respect and a disinclination to inflict unnecessary suffering. Before professionalism moved in and the extremists had their way, it was a very English war.

It came closer—perhaps became inevitable—when Pym took advantage of the evil news from Ireland and divided the House by introducing the Grand Remonstrance. An infinitely tedious measure that contained two hundred and four clauses, reiterating yet again all the faults of Charles's government, it made one positive demand: that Charles must choose ministers of whom the Commons approved, or they would find their own way of defending Ireland. The Remonstrance was carried by eleven votes, after debate that lasted into darkness. Swords were drawn, the House was full of turmoil before the end, and Pym came closer than was his habit to revolutionary sentiment when he put the wishes of the people before the studied enactment of a law. Authorising the raising of a militia, the House demanded a General chosen by parliament, and called for the execution of Catholic priests.

Hyde, Falkland, and others advised moderation; the Queen was all for action. A crowd of angry Londoners ran noisily about Whitehall, and the bishops—still extant, though often abolished—complained that parliament had lost its authority to the mob. For that they were impeached and imprisoned. There was a growing fear in Whitehall that Pym intended to impeach the Queen, and the King, moved by love to quite uncharacteristic decision, forestalled that fear by instructing his attorney general to impeach, for treason, Pym, Hampden, three other members of the House of Commons, and one peer. On the 4th January, 1642, attended by several hundred soldiers, he himself went to the House to demand surrender of the five members.

But the five had fled to shelter in the City, and London erupted in revolt. In a very untidy fashion, war had been declared. The King left London, the Queen fled to Holland. Parliament declared that sovereignty was exercised in its chambers, and issued nineteen propositions that asserted a somewhat intemperate authority. Not until then did Charles give orders to raise an army, and towards the end of August he set up his standard at Nottingham.

5

It was a war without fervour; a war from which strategy vanished, and intention was constantly subject to diversion of interest. England was unequally divided, with a huge preponderance of material advantage on the Roundheads' side: they had the money, they held London, the great armouries of Hull and the Tower were theirs, the fleet was of their party, and they occupied every major port except Newcastle. The Royalists had a cavalry arm which needed training, an abundance of what would now be called "officer material," but very little artillery; and for supply the King had to rely on the generosity of his rich supporters, who first donated their rents and then their silver plate. For their daily rations both sides plundered, but there was no wanton destruction.

East Anglia, the southeastern counties, and a large part of the Midlands were Roundhead territory; the King's strength lay mainly in the west and north. But there was no front on which to fight, no clear-cut division between social classes. There were almost as many country gentlemen on the parliament side as on the King's, and though London apprentices were Roundheads, the yeomen and farm-labourers of Cornwall were Royalists. The great men of a district rallied support for one side or the other; or remained neutral. Religious opinion dominated a majority, but was insufficient to recruit as many soldiers as would be needed; it had to be stiffened by conscription.

Prince Rupert of the Rhine was a major reinforcement for the Royalist army. He, a son of Charles's sister Elizabeth, the Winter Queen, was in both character and appearance the *beau idéal* of a Cavalier. As a boy he had seen service on the continent, at the age of twenty-three he became an inspired leader of cavalry, almost invincible in a charge of horse, but less certain of success when there was a chance to exploit advantage and win a battle. Without Rupert, however, the Royalist army would have lacked the leadership which made it fight before it was ready, and kept it fighting after any reasonable hope of victory had gone.

Despite obvious weaknesses the Royalists in the first year of war were more successful than their opponents, who may have felt some reluctance to oppose their King with naked force. Charles mustered a substantial army in North Wales and Lancashire, and sensibly decided to test the defences of London. Essex was the Parliamentary General, and in September 1642, Rupert routed the Roundhead cavalry near Worcester, and Charles advanced to Edgehill where, three weeks later, Rupert's cavalry were again successful. But the Royalist infantry faltered, Hampden brought up artillery, and night fell on a drawn battle. The advance on London was checked, and Charles marched south to Oxford. A more resolute command might have seized an opportunity that would not recur, and if Rupert's advice had been taken the advance would have been continued. But in an army where jealousy ruled as much as discipline, there was little hope of decision, so time was wasted, and when, in mid-November, Rupert took by storm Brentford, on the western fringe of London, he found, on the following day at Turnham Green, the trained bands of London—they had been well trained—in an army of 24,000, against whom the Royalists had only 15,000.

Prudently but sadly they turned back—London, if ever it had been vulnerable, was not open to attack—and found winter quarters in Oxford, in Banbury and Reading and Marlborough: to feed his army the King had to disperse it, and dispersal made nonsense of strategy, which required concentration. In the following year the fortunes of war were not obscured by the fog of battle, but by the mists which overhung intention. It was a war shaped by opportunity, not by plan; the Roundheads attempted to destroy such Cavalier forces as they found in circumstances tending to their defeat, and Cavaliers were impelled to attack where and when advantage appeared to be on their side. In the north the Earl of Newcastle held York, the Parliamentarians Hull. In February Rupert stormed Cirencester, in April he sacked Birmingham. The Royalists were short of arms, but the Queen evaded the Navy and landed with supplies at Bridlington in Yorkshire. The Parliamentarians were successful in the Welsh marches, and having taken Monmouth and Hereford stood between Royalist Cornwall and the King in Oxford. Fighting continued, but the war had become incoherent.

In the summer of 1643 the Royalists had an opportunity to retrieve their failure at Turnham Green, but failed to take it. In July Rupert had joined the Cornish army, and before the end of the month took Bristol by assault. That was his greatest victory, for Bristol, second only to London as a port, was rich in men and money: men who favoured the King, money that he sorely needed, for the supply of silver plate was dwindling. Now was the time to reassert the only strategy by which the war could be won, and advance on London from the north, the midlands, and the west. But Newcastle in the north laid siege to Hull, the King invested Gloucester, and half the Cornish army attacked Exeter. Strategy declared its bankruptcy, and the war seemed unlikely to be won, or lost, except by exhaustion.

In the last days of 1642 Charles in Oxford had written to the Earl of Newcastle, in York, a letter that shows clearly the amiability of his temper and the lack of that decision needed by a king fighting for a throne and his own existence: "Though I may propose many things to your consideration, yet I shall not impose anything upon you; as, for example, I hear General King is come; now I desire you to make use of him in your army. I am sure you have not good commanders to spare no more than arms, yet I confess there may be such reasons that may make this desire of mine impossible."—So he wrote to his commander in the north, and finished his letter with a small, endearing joke and a repetition of his preference for delegating authority: "My conclusion is to assure you that I do not only trust in your fidelity, which (as Charles Chester said of Queen Elizabeth's faults) all the world takes on, but likewise to your judgment in my affairs."

More agreeable to read is his letter to the Mayor of Newbury after the town had been taken in September 1643: "Our will and command is, that you forthwith send into the towns and villages adjacent, and bring thence all the sick and hurt soldiers of the Earl of Essex's army; and though they be rebels, and deserve the punishment of traitors, yet out of our tender compassion upon them as being our subjects, our will and pleasure is, that you carefully provide for their recovery, as well as for those of our own army, and then to send them to Oxford."

Compassion, in time of war, is not always so evident, and an equal regard for justice is revealed in a letter from the King to the Governor of Dartmouth, written at the end of the year: "Whereas divers ships and vessels of good value are brought in, as we understand, to our port of Dartmouth, which our and other ships have taken from the rebels and their adherents; and whereas it is like that many more will be hereafter brought in thither, concerning which it is fit that there be a legal proceeding before they be any way disposed of. Our pleasure and command therefore is, that you take effectual order that not only the said ships already brought in, but all that shall be hereafter, be first legally adjudicated by the judge of our Admiralty there who is or shall be for the time being, before you or any others whatsoever, offer to dispose of such ships, vessels, and prizes, or anything belonging to them, or any of their goods, and commodities aboard. Which rule we will and command you punctually to observe and cause to be observed for the avoiding of injustice, and the prejudice that would ensue to our service by the contrary."

That he was anything but a weak and unavailing king no re-reading of history, however weighted by affection, can sustain; but what a good man he often seems, and intermittently how likable! A letter to Rupert, written in June 1644, discloses with a charming gravity, not only the trouble he sometimes took to be a scrupulous and provident commander, but how far from military absolutism was his notion of a peremptory order: "I know the importance of supplying you with powder, for which I have taken all possible ways, having sent both to Ireland and Bristol, as from Oxford this bearer is well satisfied that it is impossible to have at present: but if he tell you that I may spare them from hence, I leave you to judge, having but thirty-six* left; but what I can get from Bristol (of which there is not much certainty, it being threatened to be besieged) you shall have.

"But now I must give you the true state of my affairs, which, if their condition be such as enforces me to give you more peremptory commands than I would willingly do, you must not take it ill. If York be

* 36 barrels, presumably.

lost, I shall esteem my crown little less, unless supported by your sudden march to me, and a miraculous conquest in the South, before the effects of the northern power can be found here; but if York be relieved, and you beat the rebel armies of both kingdoms which are before it, then, but otherwise not, I may possibly make a shift (upon the defensive) to spin out time, until you come to assist me: wherefore I command and conjure you, by the duty and affection which I know you bear me, that (all new enterprises laid aside) you immediately march (according to your first intention) with all your force to the relief of York; but if that be either lost, or have freed themselves from the besiegers, or that for want of powder you cannot undertake that work, you immediately march with your whole strength to Worcester, to assist me and my army; without which, or your having relieved York by beating the Scots, all the successes you can afterwards have most infallibly will be useless to me."

In that letter, which a lesser man could have read as an open invitation to choose his own course, Rupert recognised his uncle's need and his own duty. He had lately had great success in Lancashire—he had taken the town of Bolton after the bitterest fighting of the war—but the relief of York would bring him face to face with the Scottish army and a Parliamentary army too. He did not hesitate, and when Newcastle, in York, advised caution, replied "Nothing venture, nothing have." He rode out to Marston Moor, and with 17,000 men faced the combined armies of his enemies, under Leven and Manchester, who numbered 24,000. He was defeated in a battle that began under a storm of rain and hail, but the Parliamentarians failed to take advantage of a major victory, and instead of pursuing Rupert and the 6000 troopers whom he rallied, broke up into devious enterprises which yielded them little.

Then, when Royalist hopes sank into near despair, there was an astonishing revival of their cause in Scotland, where Montrose began a campaign of dazzling success. Let Rupert be accepted as the *beau idéal* of the Cavalier, but Montrose was both the advocate of sound constitutional monarchy and the most splendid of those military commanders who can be described—to differentiate them from the professional leaders of massive armies—as amateurs. It is not enough to say that he was brilliantly successful: he exhibited, in the military art, an incontestable genius. He, a poet and a man of principle, led his difficult little army—wild Irish and clansmen of unquestioned valour but not always of consistent loyalty—into a series of battles, over the mountains and into the lowlands again, that defeated the professionals, quelled Clan Campbell at Inverlochy after bitter marching through the snow, and was ultimately defeated at Philiphaugh, near Selkirk, by a Presbyterian army that outnumbered him by five to one, and celebrated its victory by slaughtering prisoners and camp followers.

That was in September 1645, three months after Fairfax's New Model army—in which Cromwell commanded the cavalry—had decisively beaten Charles and Rupert at Naseby in Northamptonshire: Fairfax had almost twice the Royalists' strength, Cromwell's cavalry were well handled and effective, and the King lost 5000 prisoners, all his artillery, and most of his small arms. The New Model fought a successful campaign in the west, and about the same time as Montrose was defeated at Philiphaugh, Rupert lost Bristol and the King's confidence. He was cleared by court martial, but the King was slow to forgive him, and Rupert took no more part in the war that was manifestly lost. The remaining Royalist strongholds fell in turn, and by the summer of 1646 the war, which had lasted far too long, was over at last.

6

Of peace, however, there was no visible prospect. In September 1643 the Long Parliament, dominated by Pym, had effected an alliance with the Scots—in earnest of which the Solemn League and Covenant was drafted—and obtained for its service an army of 18,000 foot and 2000 horse in return for a treaty that guaranteed preservation of the Reformed religion in Scotland and the Reformation of the church in England and Ireland "according to the Word of God and the example of the best reformed churches." The Scots anticipated the establishment of Presbyterianism throughout Britain, and the Westminster Assembly of Divines busily engaged in the compilation of catechisms, a confession of faith, and a directory of public worship.

In May 1646 Charles escaped from Oxford in disguise. He had decided to surrender to the Scottish army, which lay at Newark-on-Trent and was commanded by the Earl of Leven; who had once sworn never to take up arms against his King again. Charles ordered the garrison of Newark to surrender, and Leven led his army and his captive north to Newcastle. There the King engaged in theological argument, and was much plagued by Presbyterian ministers who prayed at inordinate length; but still maintained the Anglican cause. Under Fairfax and Cromwell—the only Roundhead generals who had kept and enhanced their reputation during the long raggedness of the war—the Roundhead army had discovered its own democracy, its own brand of Puritanism, and soldiers who called themselves Independents were now at odds with the Presbyterian majority in parliament. It was Charles's hope to take advantage of that division, and draw one or the other to his side; but though he pretended willingness to compromise he refused to forsake his church, his sovereignty, and his friends.

The Scots were as stubborn as their King: for them it was the Covenant or nothing. They distrusted the English Presbyterians, they would not listen to Charles's proposal for an experimental establishment of Presbytery with a guarantee of toleration for Anglicans; the English Presbyterians were as exigent as the Scots who distrusted them; and Roundhead soldiers, their occupation finished and threatened with discharge or service in Ireland, muttered their growing discontent. For six months or more Charles lived drearily in the Scottish camp, until, at the beginning of 1647, the Scots solved an intractable problem by exchanging their King for the arrears of pay that the Long Parliament owed them: it amounted to £400,000. Parliamentary Commissioners took delivery of him, and while the Scots returned to their own country, Charles was escorted to Holdenby House in Northamptonshire. Crowds gathered to cheer him as he passed.

From France the Queen and her advisers put great pressure on him to meet the demands made by the English parliament. That meant abandonment of the Anglican church, and Charles would not agree to so drastic a betrayal. But he was persuaded to accept a trial period of Presbyterian rule—the experiment which the Scots had refused to consider—on condition that it was followed by a settlement agreeable to both sides. Perhaps he remembered that Henrietta's father Henri IV, the Protestant King of Navarre before he became King of France, had said *"Paris vaut bien une messe"*; and thought that London was worth a Presbyterian sermon. The English Presbyterians, apart from their representatives in the House of Commons, were much less rigid than the Scots—they included many who disliked the narrow and more fervent sort of Puritans as much as they distrusted Anglicans—but their representatives in parliament served them badly. They alienated the army by their illiberal proposals for its disbandment, to reduce taxa-

Mary, Queen of Scots
James VI and I

Henry, Prince of Wales

Elizabeth, Queen of Bohemia,
'The Winter Queen'

Right:
Charles II

es I

Charles Edward Stuart 'Bonnie Prince Charlie' in old age

tion, and threw away the advantage they would have won by the accession to their ranks, temporary though it might be, of a King who would add his authority to constitutional innovation. Before parliament had composed its thoughts, the army had made up its mind; and the army moved quickly.

Cromwell, that staunch parliamentarian, lost patience with a House that seemed to have forgotten the great sacrifices which the Roundhead army had made, and was still unwilling to authorise payment of wages many months overdue. He knew how deeply the army felt, and feared the consequences if its feelings were ignored. So, acting promptly, he ordered Cornet Joyce to make sure that the artillery park at Oxford was in safe hands, and to fetch the King from Holdenby House in Northamptonshire. Holdenby was a great Tudor palace which Charles had found more comfortable than military quarters in Newcastle. He hesitated for a little while before consenting to see Joyce, but when the Cornet accepted his modest conditions, agreed to go with him. He paused again, and asked to see Joyce's authority. Joyce pointed to the five hundred troopers drawn up in the great courtyard of the palace, and Charles, most royally affable, said, "Indeed, it is one that I can read without spelling. As handsome and proper a company of gentlemen as I have seen this many a day!"

Cromwell had had a narrow escape from London, where angry Presbyterians were demanding his arrest. He rode to Newmarket, and there, with the army about him, received the King. There was a royal welcome for Charles, and he was received with all possible courtesy. Royalist officers came to kiss his hand, Fairfax let his chaplains return, and Cromwell said the King was the most upright and conscientious man in the three kingdoms. In the country as a whole—in London in particular—there was as much confusion as there had been in the most incoherent phases of the war; but now it was mental or moral confusion, political rivalry or religious bickering, social brawling and constitutional dispute. From the Anabaptists and Levellers on the left, to Royalists and Bishops on the right, there was every shade of opinion, all of it vociferous, and for several months the most broad-minded and conciliatory spokesmen of any party were the high-ranking officers of the Roundhead army: Fairfax, Cromwell, and Cromwell's son-in-law Ireton. That they failed to re-establish the monarchy as kingship by contract was due, in part, to the violence of hostile opinion, and very largely to Charles's own folly.

The army wanted to march on London and enforce its demands. Cromwell and Ireton suggested that a more sensible preliminary would be to decide what demands it proposed to make, and submit them to the King. Abolish the bishops and sell their lands; the Covenant should be optional; dissolve parliament and let the King rule through a Council of State—there was a start, and the officers of the army were disposed to agree. Cromwell opposed the march on London, but had to move in to restore order. Charles demanded amendments to Ireton's proposals—he could not agree to the abolition of bishops—and Ireton compromised. The proposals were published, and neither the army nor parliament liked them. Ireton was ready to purge parliament as thoroughly as might be necessary, and the King informed both Houses that the amended proposals had his approval. It was thought that Cromwell so warmly approved of the King's concessions that he would accept an earldom from him, but in September the House of Commons repudiated Cromwell's negotiations and rejected the King's message.

That most benevolent of scholars, G. M. Young, has written:[*] "Charles was the martyr to an ecclesiastical theory and the victim of a political theory, both of which he had, as it were, incorporated into his own personality. He never felt the least temptation, for the sake of a quiet life as a beloved and harmless sovereign, to surrender either the rights of the Church or the rights of the Crown; in which, as he saw them, the rights of his Christian people were involved."—That his royal prerogative was widely recognised as necessary for the defence of his people's liberty is open to doubt: the majority of his people preferred to rely on courts of law and a free parliament. But now there was neither law nor liberty in the land, and Young continues: "A third of the Commons had joined the King; their places had been filled by coupon, and few of the recruits had any reason to expect that if once they left Westminster the freeholders and burgesses would ever send them back there. If, that September, Fairfax had expelled the House of Commons and issued new writs in the King's name, steeples would have rocked and bonfires blazed from one end of England to the other, as they did thirteen years later when Monck at last opened his mouth and declared for a free Parliament."

But there was one obstacle which Cromwell recognised, and that was the army. The army was full of Independents, and Ireton's proposals had found favour only among its higher ranks. The army was

[*] *Charles and Cromwell.*

growing angry, and at a general council of officers and men Trooper Sexby declared: "We sought to satisfy all men, and it was well. But in going about to do it, we have dissatisfied all men. We have laboured to please a King, and unless we cut our own throats, I think we shall never please him. We have gone about to support a House of rotten studds, a House of Commons and its company of rotten members. And one thing I must say to General Cromwell and General Ireton themselves. Your credit and reputation hath been much blasted upon two accounts—your dealings with the King, your plan of settlement which was to satisfy everybody and has satisfied nobody, and your dealings with Parliament. The authority of Parliament is a thing which most here would give their lives for, but the Parliament to which we would loyally subject ourselves has still to be called."

Trooper Sexby is immortal, of course, and men of his sort are as common today as they were in the Seventeenth Century. Anger and dislike of authority are, in their eyes, the robust and evident proof of idealism—the rejection of established order is a policy sufficient for their day and purpose—and when Sexby and his friends issued a programme called *The Agreement of the People* it made manifest their hostility to the King and revealed, almost as clearly, their debt to the teaching of a remarkable man called John Lilburne. He was one of those unfortunate beings who invite misfortune, solicit disaster, and magnetise injustice. According to Young he "started his career of universal opposition at the age of twenty-two by helping to print and circulate unlicensed books." He was so cross-grained that it was said of him, "If the world was emptied of all but John Lilburne, John would quarrel with Lilburne and Lilburne with John." But a policy of universal opposition is not without attraction, and to men like Sexby appears to rationalise dissent and justify repudiation of all they dislike.

In the meantime rents were falling and prices rising. The Scots were grumbling because the Presbyterian triumph they anticipated had disappeared from sight. Ireton and Cromwell had lost the army's goodwill, they were warmly disliked in parliament, and since the defeat of Ireton's proposal they had been of little use to the King. A sense of insecurity was everywhere, and the King himself had been heard to say, "I really do believe we shall have another war." It was feared that he had given up hope of finding agreement in England, and was meditating another retreat to Scotland.

Then, in November, Charles was warned of a plot to assassinate him.

With simple assurance that escape would be easy, he and some companions walked away from Hampton Court under cover of darkness, and having crossed the river at Thames Ditton rode southwards and succeeded in reaching the Isle of Wight. From Carisbrooke castle he wrote to the House of Lords: "I appeal to all indifferent men to judge, if I have not just cause to free myself from the hands of those who change their principles with their condition . . . and with whom the Levellers' doctrine is rather countenanced than punished?" It was Cromwell at whom he pointed, as one who had changed his principles; but when the Levellers in a regiment mutinied, Cromwell had their leaders seized and one of them shot after drumhead court martial. And the King's flight from Hampton Court had absolved Cromwell of any remnant duty to him.

At Carisbrooke Charles lived very comfortably, and showed a reasonable mind when the draft of yet another policy-for-peace was presented. But parliament and the army were both intent on plans for their own survival, and with that in view Scotland was a factor far more important than the King. The consequence of their neglect, however, was that Charles also recognised the Scots' importance, and with their representatives signed an "engagement" by which they undertook to restore his throne by force of arms. England, to all appearance, was hopelessly divided, and their prospects seemed good.

In March 1648 the second Civil War began. The governor of Pembroke castle declared for the King, there was insurrection in Ireland. Royalist commanders took Berwick and Carlisle, in Kent and Essex rebellion flared. A threat of mob-law in London was suppressed by the army, but not before Cromwell and Ireton had narrowly escaped capture. The Scots, overconfident, despatched an ultimatum and demanded disbandment of the Roundhead army.

Fairfax stood firm. He, more than anyone, seems to have kept his head and seen how, by decisive action, to repair a fractured country. The Roundhead officers, after prayer and preaching at Windsor, were "hardly able to speak a word to each other for weeping"; but they were ready to fight. Cromwell marched into Wales, and met sturdy opposition. Fairfax set out for Berwick, but had first to deal with insurgent Royalists in Kent, then in Essex. Early in July the Scots crossed the Border, and a few days later Cromwell took Pembroke and with a reinforcement of artillery went north at speed. The Scots moved more slowly, and Cromwell, finding a few English regiments in the Pennines, added them to his army, stopped the invaders at Preston, and beat them decisively. Victory enhanced his eloquence, and his habit of speech began to show some affinities with the language of the Old Testament.

There were many who enriched their vocabulary from the same source, and as the more radical began to speak openly of putting the King to death—many kings in the Old Testament met a violent end—a phrase found opportunely in the Geneva Bible was transferred to Charles, who by extremists was called the Man of Blood. There was much argument both about the propriety and the consequences of executing a monarch, and Cromwell—though still opposed to the idea—conceded the possibility that it might become a duty. Fairfax said that if the King were killed the rights of the crown must pass to someone else; and asked what those rights were. Colonel Harrison, a brave, flamboyant, fanatical Puritan, was quite certain that the Man of Blood must be called to account; and Ireton, once so conciliatory, reinforced extremism with his legal mind.

The second Civil War was a less gentlemanly affair than the first: after taking Colchester Fairfax executed some of his prisoners, Cromwell sold his into slavery in the West Indies. There was an appetite for revenge, a hunger for destruction, and among the nominal subjects of the Man of Blood there were many who had grown accustomed to shedding it.

Cromwell drew closer to the Levellers, and agreed with them that Charles should be brought to trial. There were those who pleaded with Charles to escape while he could, but the King had given his parole and would not break it. He was removed to closer imprisonment at Hurst castle, and from there Colonel Harrison took him to Windsor. Charles, who had once been warned that Harrison meant to murder him, was frightened by his arrival, but, when he saw the man, took a liking to him—"He looked like a soldier"—and they talked pleasantly together.

Early in December Colonel Pride had purged parliament of "dissentients"—the Presbyterian majority of a hundred and fifty members, that is—leaving eighty Independents, who were then discussing the King's approaching trial. But Charles did not know that. He spent Christmas at Windsor, insisted on maintaining his kingly state, and reaffirmed his lifelong principles when he rejected the army's final attempt to bargain with him.

7

On the 20th January, in the Great Hall of Westminster, King Charles appeared before a High Court of Justice appointed by the eighty Independent members who remained in the House after Pride's Purge had removed the Presbyterian majority. Of the one hundred and fifty commissioners named by that minority, between sixty and seventy attended the meetings of the Court, and absent with both majorities was all the law of England. The army said it acted of necessity, and the Court claimed an authority derived from the people. "You never asked the question of the tenth man in the kingdom," replied Charles, and refused to plead. He was the ultimate guardian of law and the constitution, and to recognise such a Court would deny to all his people the protection which law had previously given them.

The president of the Court was John Bradshaw, a staunch republican born in Cheshire, and with him sat sixty-seven commissioners on benches covered with red cloth. The roll was called, and there was no response to the name of Fairfax until his wife, in one of the galleries full of spectators, boldly answered, "Not here and never will be. He has too much sense." The King, who had slept in his own bedchamber in the palace of Whitehall, was ordered by Bradshaw to listen to the charges against him: "Charles Stuart, out of a wicked design to erect and uphold in himself an unlimited power to rule according to his own will, and to overthrow the rights and liberties of the people, hath traitorously and maliciously levied war against the present Parliament and the people therein represented."

There was a Mr. Cook, appointed Solicitor for the Commonwealth, who said in conclusion: "Charles Stuart was a tyrant, traitor and murtherer, and a public and implacable enemy to the Commonwealth of England"; and Charles laughed openly in sight of the angry Court.

Bradshaw demanded his answer to the charge, and Charles replied: "I would know by what power I am called hither; I was not long ago in the Isle of Wight; how I came there, is a longer story than I think it fit at this present time for me to speak of; but there I entered into a Treaty with both Houses of Parliament, with as much public faith as it is possible to be had of any people in the world. . . . Now I would know by what authority, I mean lawful; there are many unlawful authorities in the world, thieves and robbers by the highways; but I would know by what authority I was brought from thence, and carried from place to place, and I know not what: and when I know what lawful authority, I shall answer. Remember, I am your King, your lawful King. . . . I have a trust committed to me by God, by old and lawful descent; I will not betray it, to answer to a new, unlawful authority."

Bradshaw made a foolish mistake. He claimed authority for the Court, "which authority requires you, in the name of the people of England, of which you are elected King, to answer them."

Promptly the King replied: "England was never an elective kingdom, but an hereditary kingdom for near these thousand years. . . . I do stand more for the liberty of my people than any here that come to be my judges."

There was more debate, all inconclusive; the Court was adjourned, and reassembled on Monday the 22nd. Charles still refused to plead until the Court's authority had been proved, and argument became irate.

Said Bradshaw, in defence of the Court: "They sit here by the authority of the Commons of England, and all your predecessors and you are responsible and you are responsible to them."

Bradshaw's anger had made him a little incoherent, and Charles replied curtly: "I deny that; show me one precedent."

Said Bradshaw: "Sir, you ought not to interrupt while the Court is speaking to you. This point is not to be debated by you, neither will the Court permit you to do it: if you offer it by way of demurrer to the jurisdiction of the Court, they have considered of their jurisdiction, they do affirm their own jurisdiction."

The King replied: "I say, Sir, by your favour, that the Commons of England was never a Court of Judicature; I would know how they came to be so."

A little while later Bradshaw showed again the shortness of his temper. The King had said: "I do require that I may give in my reasons why I do not answer, and give me time for that."

Said Bradshaw: "Sir, it is not for prisoners to require."

"Prisoners!" exclaimed the King. "Sir, I am not an ordinary prisoner."

"The Court hath considered of their jurisdiction, and they have already affirmed their jurisdiction; if you will not answer, we shall give orders to record your default."

"You never heard my reasons yet."

"Sir, your reasons are not to be heard against the highest jurisdiction."

"Show me," said the King, "that jurisdiction where reason is not to be heard."

To which Bradshaw made the unfortunate reply: "Sir, we show it you here, the Commons of England." And the day's proceedings came to an end when he added, "Serjeant, take away the prisoner."

Till the end of the week there was agitated debate as the Court tried to justify itself, but before Saturday the sentence had been decided, and on Saturday, in a crowded hall, Charles was summoned to hear his doom. He came in quietly, dressed in black, and one thinks of him as Van Dyck painted him, full-face and in profile too: stubbornness in the brow, nobility in the eyes, the grace of an assured majesty in all his lineaments, and the *panache*—agreeable to his Cavaliers—of the small trimmed beard and moustache brushed proudly up.

"Shall I be heard before the judgment be given?" he asked, but Bradshaw ignored him, spoke to the Court, and again repeating the crimes charged against the prisoner, said, "In the name of the people of England!" And again he was interrupted by the loud voice of Lady Fairfax: "It is a lie! Not half or a quarter of them!"

There was an adjournment, the Court met again, and Bradshaw spoke at great length, accusing the King of guilt for all the blood shed in the war. The King was allowed to reply, and said: "I conceive that a hasty sentence once passed, may be sooner repented than recalled; and truly, the selfsame desire that I have for the peace of the kingdom, and the liberty of the subject, more than my own particular, does make me now at last desire, that having something for to say that concerns both, I desire before sentence be given, that I may be heard in the Painted Chamber before the Lords and Commons."

That request was not granted, and the Clerk of the Court read the sentence: "For all which treasons and crimes this Court doth adjudge, that the said Charles Stuart, as a tyrant, traitor, murderer, and a public enemy, shall be put to death, by the severing his head from his body."

A scaffold was erected in front of the palace of Whitehall. The King busied himself with letters, his last bequests, his little dogs. He said goodbye to Elizabeth and Henry, his children, and told them they must forgive their enemies. Good Bishop Juxon came to pray with him, and he remembered dead friends. For the Prince of Wales he left a long letter, full of solemn advice and adjurations to piety.

Tuesday morning, when he had to dress for the last time, was bitterly cold, and under a waistcoat of Garter blue he put on two shirts lest he should shiver and let people think he was afraid. Walking briskly from St. James's to Whitehall, he went out to die as his grandmother had died, and as he knelt bade the headsman to wait for his signal before he struck. "I shall say but very short prayers," he said.

It was Andrew Marvell, most melodious of Cromwell's admirers, who wrote the lines about Charles's death that have never been forgotten, and for the Anglican martyr—martyred for a Church that has not greatly encouraged martyrdom—composed an epitaph that sings like a requiem. Marvell eulogised Cromwell, writing an Horatian ode for him on his return from Ireland. He also extolled Charles's bearing on the scaffold, and into the ode inserted eight lines in praise of the King whom Cromwell's army had condemned to die:

> "He nothing common did or mean
> Upon that memorable scene,
>   But with his keener eye
>   The axe's edge did try;
> Nor called the gods with vulgar spite
> To vindicate his helpless right,
>   But bowed his comely head
>   Down, as upon a bed."

10

The Glorious Restoration

1

The interregnum lasted from February 1649 till May 1660, when Charles II was restored to his throne. In this biography of a family, concerned only with the character and activities of the Stewart (or Stuart) rulers of Scotland and Great Britain, there is no place for an assessment of Cromwell's achievements, nor of the manner of life imposed or permitted by him and his associates in their government of the three kingdoms of England, Scotland, and Ireland. It will be useful, however, to include a brief chronicle of the eleven years to fill the gap.

Parliament had been reduced by Pride's Purge to a "rump" that eventually numbered about fifty members. They, unabashed by the vacancy in which they sat, abolished the House of Lords and declared England a Commonwealth. It was a Commonwealth that had to live in a hostile world. The regicides were detested on the continent; the royalist colonies of Virginia and Maryland refused recognition of the Rump; Prince Rupert had taken to the sea and was privateering in the Channel; and in Ireland and Scotland—where Charles II was made uncomfortably welcome after he accepted the Covenant—there was open war.

Cromwell went to Ireland with 12,000 troops, stormed Drogheda and Wexford, and invoked God's judgment to warrant massacre of their garrisons. War and famine reduced its population by a third, and Ireland became a province under an army of occupation which sent its own soldiers to represent a desolate land in parliament. Cromwell, leaving ruthless subordinates behind him, then went into Scotland and at Dunbar, in September 1650, decisively beat an army which pious ministers had weakened by purging it of "malignants." The following summer Charles and another army marched into England, pursued by Cromwell, who routed them at Worcester. Charles escaped, but Worcester was Cromwell's "crowning mercy," and north of the Border General George Monck, with exemplary efficiency, completed the subjection of Scotland. The endangered Commonwealth was equally well served at sea by Robert Blake: he, a middle-aged country gentleman, had shown redoubtable qualities as a soldier on the parliamentary side, and when he sought a new career on blue water he achieved successes, from the Atlantic coast of America to the Mediterranean, that created fame for himself and a new tradition for the Navy.

The infant Commonwealth found a military strength sufficient to guarantee its safety, but a Puritan government taxed its people more heavily than its royal victim had ever done—closed the theatres, punished every indulgence from profanity to adultery—confiscated lands and sold the pictures that Charles had bought with such judicious taste. Everyone hated the Rump, and demanded reform of the law. Corruption was rife, and religion splintered into furious segments: Socinians, Anabaptists, Antinomians, sects that permitted female preachers and offered their pulpits to corporals of horse.

There was war against the Dutch, who were traders in the Far East, and whose mercantile ambition was aggressive and dangerously successful. Blake and Monck won useful victories against them, and from Westminster the Rump was expelled. Cromwell and a few musketeers dealt harshly with the Long Parliament's indurate bottom and its symbol of authority, the parliamentary sceptre, the Mace. "Take away that bauble," said Cromwell. But the parliament which the Army Council selected from nominees of Congregational churches—it was called Barebone's Parliament—was fatuously inept, and resigned its power to Cromwell. He refused the title of king, but as Lord Protector became head of a limited monarchy under which England revealed a constructive energy long suppressed by faction, an efficiency hitherto unsuspected.

Cromwell was a country squire who carried to supreme authority the common sense of a man long accustomed to the contrariness of people. His patriotism was Elizabethan in temper, his overt Godliness was agreeable to the spirit of the time—his God spoke with an English roughness—and his practical view of society permitted no sympathy with Levellers and other insensate theorists.

Nor was he more sympathetic with parliament than James I or Charles I, and for a year or more divided the country into districts ruled by major-generals. But under his authority equitable or politic agreements were concluded with the Dutch; Jews were permitted to come in, Quakers tolerated; Episcopalians and alehouses were protected. England regained prestige and importance on the continent, and a formative alliance with France. In the West Indies Jamaica was captured, Spanish treasure-fleets intercepted: Milton was the Protector's Latin Secretary, and when both English and French protested against the massacre of the Protestant people called Waldenses, in Piedmont, Milton gave to English foreign policy an uncommon distinction by expressing it in a sonnet that began:

> "Avenge, O' Lord, thy slaughtered saints, whose bones
> Lie scattered on the Alpine mountains cold."

On the 3rd September, 1658—the anniversary of his victory at Dunbar in 1650, of the "crowning mercy" at Worcester in 1651—the Lord Protector died while a great storm raged over England, having prayed to God to give his people "consistency of judgment, one heart, and mutual love."

None of those bequests was realised by his beneficiaries. Cromwell had done much for those he ruled, but Royalists had always plotted against him, Levellers hated him, and after little more than a year it became evident that he had neither created a sustaining tradition of military government nor sufficient agreement to perpetuate a political system. He was a great, unlikable man whom no one who respects virtue can fail to respect, and whom no one averse from uncomely virtues can applaud without reserve. He left for common men a larger liberty than they had previously known, he served England, and he was cruelly mocked when Charles II returned to sit on the throne he had abolished; for all Britain rose to greet its true monarch with exuberant delight.

2

The King who came home was a man who had suffered all the insults and privations of exile. Circumstances had used him hardly in his wanderings, and as travellers lost in a perilous country may throw away unnecessary burdens, so Charles had discarded such impedimenta as idealism; any excess of probity that initially he may have had; belief in the probity of others; and faith in the high seriousness of politics. He was a cynic, but cynicism had not destroyed his amiability. He retained, indeed, more good qualities than others, only half as cynical as he, would expect to find in him.

He had known zealots in England and Scotland—"They are all quite mad" said his aunt Elizabeth, the Winter Queen—and learnt to distrust enthusiasm. As a corollary to that, he doubted the wisdom of action when inaction seemed to serve a better purpose, and thereby kept his popularity in a land that disliked taxation and unnecessary wars. But, in a very English way, he showed a lively interest in the Navy, and a very un-English interest in science. As a king he was careless of personal honour, but contrived to reign in such a manner that England was able to expand the boundaries of its influence, to acquire New York on the one side, Bombay on the other, to build its commerce oversea and power in the Mediterranean, to found the Royal Society and create a new dramatic tradition of scandalous brilliance. It would be foolish to deny him ability, and even his detractors have never refused him an intellectual gaiety, a native and persistent wit, such as seldom grace those doomed to wear the burden of a crown.

Born at St. James's on the 29th May, 1630, he was physically precocious and looked a year old at the age of four months. Big, dark, and ugly as an infant, he grew to exceptional strength and height—he was a full six feet—and his childish ugliness acquired a handsome, saturnine distinction. Like all his family he was an accomplished horseman, he danced and fenced well, carried himself gracefully, but had no appetite for scholarship, and when his mother hoped to marry him to *la Grande Mademoiselle,* daughter of the Duke of Orleans and the richest heiress in Europe, he was much handicapped by his inability to speak French.

While still a child, or little more than a child, he was exposed to events which, according to contemporary thought, must have been traumatic and might have been disabling. At the age of ten he was so oppressed by the political situation—the Scots had invaded England —that he wept for days on end to think that he would grow up without a kingdom; and a few months later, when Strafford had been condemned to die, he was made to take his seat in the House of Lords and present his father's petition for mercy. Then, after the break with parliament, he and his father marched with the Royalist army and at Edgehill, when Charles was only twelve and his brother James three years younger, they were both spectators of a battle where Prince Rupert led his cavalry in a galloping thunder that scattered his opponents but could not save the day. Pistol in hand, Charles tried to join the final confusion of the battle, and a few days later revealed his immaturity by falling ill with the childish complaint of measles.

To modern eyes it was a calamitous introduction to life, but Charles recovered from measles, battle, and Strafford's death to take his place in the Royalist parliament at Oxford, and in another campaign; and when he was sent into the west country he exhibited, in Somerset, a lofty indifference to his elders that did no good at all to the Royalist cause. He appears to have been immune to traumatic experience.

He could not, however, avoid the fugue which politics composed for him. In 1645 he fled to the Scillies, thence to Jersey, where he was warmly welcomed and his good nature endeared him to the islanders. But politics drove him to France, where his mother, who had been selling her jewels to buy arms for the King, expected their son to live without pocket-money. Hopefully she introduced him to *la Grande Mademoiselle*, who thought he had a beautiful head and "a very tolerable personality"; but their conversation was sadly limited because she spoke French and he knew no language but English.

He had a tutor, and he studied mathematics under the philosopher Thomas Hobbes, also a refugee. Hobbes was a rationalist for whom religion was merely a department of state; he believed in the universal validity of Galileo's laws of motion and the absolute necessity of government. Any government, however bad, was better than anarchy, said Hobbes. He and his theories may have left a small but lasting impression on his pupil's mind; but Charles's studies were interrupted when there came an invitation from the Scots army at Helvoetsluys, commanded by the Duke of Hamilton. He went to Holland and there joined the little Royalist fleet which, under Prince Rupert, had broken away from the Roundhead navy. There were negotiations with Scotland that came to nothing, and Rupert took the fleet to Ireland. Charles remained at the Hague with young Prince William of Orange and Mary his wife, Charles's sister, who had married ten days before Strafford went to his death. Also with them were Elizabeth, the Winter Queen, and her children; and elsewhere in the town was an attractive young woman, called Lucy Walter, with whom Charles had a very happy association.

Early in January he heard that his father was in imminent danger, and after appealing in vain to Fairfax he sent to the House of Commons his signature on a sheet of paper, otherwise blank: they might write above it, he said, whatever conditions they chose if they would spare his father. To that there was no reply, but a few weeks later came news of the King's death, and though Charles had realised that dreadful possibility, "yet the barbarous stroke so surprised him that he was in all the confusion imaginable, and those about him were almost bereft of their understanding." So says Clarendon.

Later in February a distinguished visitor came to the court in mourning, and offered his service. He was James Graham, Marquis of Montrose, whose campaign in the Highlands had been the prime glory of the Royalists' war. In the Winter Queen Montrose found a woman of kindred spirit, and she as warmly recognised the charm of his person, the gallantry of his mind. He fell in love, it is said, with Elizabeth's daughter Louise, and she with him. It does not seem, however, that Charles was equally impressed.

In March, as Lieutenant-Governor of Scotland, Montrose left the Hague for Denmark and Sweden, there to find money, and troops if he could, for an attempt to raise the Highlands and seat Charles on his father's throne. He had warned the young King against the commissioners, Covenanters all, who were on their way from Scotland, where Charles had already been proclaimed. They would compel him, in return for their support, to accept the Covenant and impose it on Scotland; and certainly they would not tolerate the presence in their country of the banned and excommunicated Montrose. Only by force of arms, indeed, could Montrose have achieved his purpose, and there was never a possibility of his mustering a sufficient force. As well as Covenanters in the Lowlands there were Campbells in the Highlands, and Archibald, Earl of Argyll, was his bitter enemy. To have given him a commission as Lieutenant-Governor of Scotland was an impolitic decision for which, before long, Charles probably blamed his impetuous aunt Elizabeth, sometime Queen of Bohemia.

The Covenanters came, and the Queen of Bohemia entertained her grim guests. They begged her to use, on their behalf, her influence with her nephew; but she gave them no encouragement, and Charles was more interested in plans to join Prince Rupert in Ireland. If the Covenanters would refrain from interference in England, they could have their way in Scotland, he said; and set out on his intended journey to Ireland. But *en route* he paid a visit to his mother at St. Germain.

Again she impressed on him the advantages of marrying *la Grande Mademoiselle*, but Charles could the more easily resist her enticements because he had taken Lucy Walter with him to Paris. He continued his journey, but, with his brother James, waited in Jersey for news and instructions from Prince Rupert; and when news came it told of Cromwell's brutal visitation. Without money—he had not enough to pay his servants—and without an army, there was now no possibility of an Irish venture, and to Charles it seemed that his only hope of advantage lay in Montrose's gallant devotion. Could Montrose, by a display of force, overawe his stubborn subjects in Scotland? He was again in communication with the Covenanters and their leaders.

He had forgotten or ignored Montrose's warning against them, and with the optimism of youth—or so it seems—thought himself able to compel agreement between those whom no power on earth could reconcile. After advising the Covenanters to show "a just and prudent moderation," he told Montrose that from him he expected measures that might produce "a present union" of the nation of Scotland. Seldom in its history had anyone produced union in Scotland, and no one who knew anything of Covenanters would expect moderation from them. But Charles was only nineteen, and again he failed to appreciate Montrose's advice. Montrose had written to him on the 20th March—it was his last letter—and declared his readiness to give his life for his King, but earnestly entreated him to beware of the craftiness of Argyll and his friends. It is a pity that Montrose was too courteous to speak plainly and tell Charles that the agreement he had made with those who claimed to be the "true government" of Scotland was sheer contradiction of the authority he had given to his Lieutenant-Governor. Charles could not offer "formal recognition" to the Covenanters, and still expect Montrose to rule in his name with the acquiescence of his enemies and the warrant of his title.

But Charles was young and the Covenanters' leaders were old in intrigue. He had signed an agreement with the commissioners sent to him, two of whom—Jaffery of Aberdeen and Livingstone, a minister—later admitted that they had deliberately entangled him in specious argument: the whole nation, they said, should accept the guilt of forcing him to accept conditions that he hated in his heart. Argyll had told him that political agreements often meant less than they appeared to mean, and Charles had failed to recognise the craftiness which Montrose knew well. Some of his own friends, moreover, added their persuasion: the Prince of Orange advised him to be "sensible," and the meaning of that was clear enough. When he realised, too late, that he had been foolish, and his folly must endanger Montrose, he made serious but ineffectual efforts to ensure his safety. But Argyll and his party had already put a price of £30,000 on Montrose's head, and declared they did it "in the King's name."

Before he sailed from Holland, on the 30th June, 1650, Charles had learnt the consequence of folly, the reward of impatience, the result of giving his trust to Argyll and the Covenanting establishment; for Montrose was already dead. With Charles, aboard ship, were weak and contemptible representatives of the kingdom he coveted, and when they put into Speymouth, on the Moray Firth, he was forced to take the Covenant before he was allowed to land. Then, as he rode south, he may have seen, here and there, fragments of Montrose's body that were exhibited as an example of what might happen to those who opposed the God-directed rule of Argyll and the church in which he worshipped.

Montrose, the nonpareil of sheer nobility, had sought arms, ships, and men in Denmark and Sweden; but rumour of Charles's correspondence with those who governed in Scotland deprived him of much that he had been promised. He sailed from Gothenburg with a fleet smaller than he had anticipated, and a great gale scattered his ships. In March he landed in Orkney, where Charles's letter told him of the "formal recognition" he had given to the existing government in Scotland; and Montrose, with too courteous a reticence, replied that his life was still at the King's service.

In Orkney he recruited some hundreds of men, untrained in arms, and crossed the Pentland Firth in small boats. He had a few experienced officers, and marched south towards Inverness. At Carbisdale, however, above the Kyle of Sutherland, he waited in the hope that some of the northern clans would join him, and was suddenly attacked by three hundred dragoons under a Colonel Strachan. The Orkney men had never seen cavalry before, and fled in panic from so fearful an apparition; and the northern clans joined the winning side. Some days later Montrose—who had fought his way out of confusion—was captured at Ardvreck, in the desolate lands of Assynt, and carried to Edinburgh where, after coldly brutal ill-treatment, he was hanged at the Market Cross from a gibbet of monstrous height.

His judges were not satisfied with death unadorned by vengeance. His sentence included the following stipulations: "To be hanged on a gibbet at the cross of Edinburgh, with his book and declaration tied in a rope about his neck, and there to hang for the space of three hours until he be dead; and thereafter to be cut down by the hangman, his head, hands, and legs to be cut off and distributed as follows—viz., his head to be affixed on an iron pin, and set on the pinnacle of the west gavel of the new prison of Edinburgh; one hand to be set on the port of Perth, the other on the port of Stirling; one leg and foot on the port of Aberdeen, the other on the port of Glasgow. If he was at his death penitent and relaxed from excommunication, then the trunk of his body to be interred by pioneers in the Greyfriars, otherwise to be interred in the Burrow Muir by the hangman's men under the gallows."

Those who believe that folly which amounts to criminal folly should be punished, will be happy to know that Charles for his youthful vanity—for his ignorance of politics—suffered punishment, not commensurate with Montrose's, but of a sort to humiliate his pride and exacerbate the wounding knowledge that he had been tricked by men he despised. His mother declared that she had been no party to his sacrifice of honour and conscience, and as a prisoner of the Covenanters—which, in effect, was his condition—he was forced to listen to endless praying, to interminable sermons of a sort that must have driven him into solitary confinement in a mental cell where he could neither stand nor lie. The clergy, says Clarendon, "reprehended him sharply if he smiled on these days (their Sabbath) and if his looks and gestures did not please them, whilst all their prayers and sermons, at which he was compelled to be present, were libels and bitter invectives against all the actions of his father, the idolatries of his mother, and his own malignity."

The poor young man! He had sinned against good sense, he cannot quite be absolved of double dealing though he had thought to play one hand against the other; he was shamed and humbled, but not quite defeated, for he learnt how to reply to his tormentors in an imitation of their own canting language; and it may be that when Cromwell won his great victory at Dunbar, Charles did not wholly mourn his success.

He was finally crowned at Scone on the 1st January, 1651, in an atmosphere of grotesque hypocrisy, of pretended contrition and humility, and solemn protestations of future virtue; at the end of which Charles was heard to murmur, "I should repent also that I was ever born." Having been crowned, however, he discovered a new authority. He had a charm of manner that his elevation made more evident; he had the great advantage that Cromwell was threatening Scotland's independence, and as Scotland's monarch he represented independence; and he was able to dismiss Argyll. Charles mustered an army, and when Cromwell advanced too deeply into Scotland, Charles moved into England. But he won no support in England, and at the battle of Worcester, where he himself showed great gallantry—gallantry worthy of his heroic grandfather, Henri IV of Navarre and France—he was utterly defeated, but lived to acquire a romantic halo as a hero of escape.

In the hearts of many there is a secret desire for the ability to escape oppressive surroundings, and he who does so, in circumstances of danger and by dint of courage and ingenuity, is assured of their favour and applause. Charles was ingenious, Charles was brave, and he did escape. On the 6th September he hid in an oak tree—a passport to approval—and then disguised himself as a groom to ride with a helpful and complaisant lady. By his ready wit he escaped recognition on several embarrassing occasions, and of those who did recognise him none betrayed him, though there was a price of £1000 on his head. At last he reached Shoreham in Sussex, and persuaded a skipper called Tattersall to give him passage to France. He landed at Fécamp north of Le Havre, and in Paris a friend gave him a clean shirt; but his indignant little mother told him that if they were to dine together he would have to pay for his share of the meal.

There followed nine years of humiliating expediency, during which time, to his infinite credit, Charles retained a large capacity for enjoyment, a cheerfulness, a strength of will, that preserved him from the exile's fatality of despair. There were many who thought his behaviour reckless, but light women and heavy drinking neither weakened his fortitude nor impaired his mind. The grandson of Henri IV had shown courage in battle, his skill in escape, and now he revealed a durable spirit that survived rebuff by France, disappointment in Spain, the recurrent annoyances of poverty, and the constant uncertainty that clouded his future.

In Paris, where he stayed until 1654, his mother aggravated his difficulties by her jealous and domineering temper, and he may have welcomed Cromwell's new friendship with France, which compelled him to leave. The allowance promised him by the French government was in arrears, but now the arrears were paid, and with a handsome gift from English loyalists he went to visit his sister the Princess of Orange, and spent a winter in Cologne. There he lived more quietly, reading French and Italian to repair a neglected education, and prudently refused an invitation to seek new adventure in the Highlands.

Among his supporters, indeed, there were those who complained that Charles showed little interest in their plans for his restoration. Cromwell's alliance with France had prompted an engagement with Spain, but the Spaniards showed no great enthusiasm for Charles's cause, and his only benefit was a promise of 6000 guilders, with 3000 for his brother James; but they had to wait for the money, and were in some discomfort before they saw it. His nominal duty was to recruit, for the Spanish service, Scots and Irish soldiers employed in France; and in Bruges, where he went to live, there was more gaiety than in Cologne. He saw some action in Flanders, where the Spanish defeat in 1658 was followed, within a few months, by the death of Oliver Cromwell. New hope, like a sunrise, lighted Charles's future, and his followers were wildly exultant. Charles himself, more realistic, was content to wait for the turn of the tide, and to exiles the English tide seemed reluctant and slow to turn.

Established by a man whose vigorous genius had given his creation a semblance of inevitability, the Cromwellian dictatorship lingered beyond his death as if, by mere weight, it defied removal. Oliver's son Richard was an inoffensive nonentity, but the Rump, which reappeared and ousted him, was supported by Monck in Scotland and by the Navy; and neither France nor Spain offered assistance to Charles. He had to wait till the uncomely remnants of dictatorship fell apart, and that happened when the Rump quarrelled with the Army, Presbyterians with Independents, and the good soldier Monck, who had "no fumes of fanaticism to turn his head," convened a loyalist

House of Commons—they had nothing to fear from Charles's return, he told them—and in accordance with its wishes made arrangements for the Restoration. The apparatus of dictatorship had, after all, lasted only a year and eight months longer than the Lord Protector.

3

To Sir Edward Montagu, subsequently Earl of Sandwich, was given the honour of bringing Charles II to Dover, and Montagu had recently appointed his young cousin, Samuel Pepys, to be his secretary. On the 3rd May a messenger brought Montagu a letter from the King and his "Declaration," dated from his court at Breda in Holland, which offered grace to "all that will come in within forty days," and was to be communicated to the fleet which Montagu commanded as General-at-sea. A council of war was summoned aboard the flagship and Pepys read the letter and the declaration to the commanders of some thirty ships. A vote was taken, and with Montagu and the commanders Pepys went up to the quarterdeck and again read both documents to the ship's company, who "did all of them cry out 'God bless King Charles!' with the greatest joy imaginable."

The news was carried from ship to ship, and the following day Pepys made many copies of the council's vote, and with one of them enclosed, for a friend, his own letter: "He that can fancy a fleet (like ours) in her pride, with pendants loose, guns roaring, caps flying, and the loud 'Vive le Roys,' echoed from one ship's company to another, he, and he only, can apprehend the joy this enclosed vote was received with."

Joy was profound—widespread though not general—for the Commonwealth had been heavily repressive as well as grievously expensive, and in England neither repression nor taxes have ever been popular. The King, moreover, was a man whom it was easy to like. On the homeward voyage to Dover, "before a fresh gale and most happy weather," he walked "here and there, up and down, very active and stirring," and on the quarterdeck entertained those who cared to listen —among whom was Pepys—with tales of his escape from Worcester: how for four days and three nights he had travelled on foot—footsore in country shoes—now forced to run, now to sup on bread and cheese from a poor boy's pocket—here to lie hidden in a priest's hole, and there, more agreeably, to drink heartily and prove he was no Round-head.

At Dover he was received by General Monck and a great, enthusias-tic crowd; and the Mayor presented him with "a very rich Bible, which he took and said it was the thing that he loved above all things in the world."—He was tactful as well as amiable, and it is interesting to compare Pepys's account of his easy, vigorous geniality aboard ship with that, in the *Memoirs of Count Grammont,* which refers to a period about two years later. Grammont, "accustomed as he was to the gran-deur of the court of France, was surprised at the politeness and splen-dour of the court of England. The King was inferior to none either in shape or air; his wit was pleasant; his disposition easy and affable; his soul, susceptible of opposite impressions, was compassionate to the unhappy, inflexible to the wicked, and tender even to excess; he showed great abilities in urgent affairs, but was incapable of applica-tion to any that were not so: his heart was often the dupe, but oftener the slave, of his engagements.

"The character of the Duke of York was entirely different: he had the reputation of undaunted courage, an inviolable attachment for his word, great economy in his affairs, hauteur, application, arrogance, each in their turn: a scrupulous observer of the rules of duty and the laws of justice; he was accounted a faithful friend and an implacable enemy."

Lacking the arrogance, implacable temper, and devotion to duty of his brother, Charles was well suited to be king of a people who wanted, above all, release from the austerities of the Commonwealth. Without James's "inviolable attachment for his word" and "great econ-omy in his affairs," he seems designed by nature itself to rule a court which, however loose its morals and absorbing its attachment to pleas-ure, retained a respect for what was practical in politics and liberally patronised both learning and the arts.

In the circumstances of the time England was prepared for the re-vival, with discretion, of royal authority, and Charles, disbanding the army except for a few favoured regiments, achieved a welcome econ-omy and made sure of the continuing loyalty of General Monck by creating him Duke of Albemarle. Edward Hyde, the staunch friend of Charles I—and remembered for his *History of the Rebellion*—became Earl of Clarendon and Lord Chancellor. Cromwellian laws were set aside, the Acts of Charles I reasserted. Parliament was deprived of its lately claimed right to continue until it decreed its own dissolution, and granted its new King a revenue, for the care of his realm, of £1,200,000 a year.

Charles insisted that the clemency announced in his Declaration be honoured, and indemnity granted to all who were not involved in his father's execution. Pepys observed that parliament had ordered the 29th May, the King's birthday, to be kept for ever as a day of thanksgiving for redemption from tyranny; that by the middle of August the King was tiring everybody with his energy and early rising; and in October that Major-general Harrison, about to be hanged, drawn, and quartered, looked "as cheerful as any man could do in that condition"; and by the 20th of the month that there had been a bloody week, with ten regicides suffering the same fate. But only regicides—those who had been immediately concerned in the death of Charles I—were condemned to that barbarous and revolting torment.

In Scotland the Restoration was welcomed as enthusiastically as in England. Good Presbyterians had grown weary of the pious Independents—many in uniform—who preached with such relentless enthusiasm, and long years of repression had persuaded all but the sternest of Covenanters that the mild disciplines of episcopacy were preferable to the militant theologians of a Cromwellian garrison.

An Act of Rescission, annulling all Acts since 1633, was accepted without open resentment, though it implied acceptance of a Church governed by the laws of James VI and Charles I; and the Covenant might have been forgotten had it not been for the folly of a measure that compelled all ministers ordained since the abolition of patronage to solicit the approval of their lawful patrons and their bishops. That was wanton provocation, and in the southwestern parts of Scotland there were many who responded with a blunt defiance. Charles himself had no sympathy with religious intolerance, but his Scottish parliament was less liberal than he. Charles refused to believe in a God who found pleasure in making his people miserable; but his parliament intended to give episcopacy a puritanical conformity.

He had long lost sight of Lucy Walter, whom he had loved in his impoverished youth, but she had had her successors, and a habit of life that never lacked the caresses of women whom he chose for their liveliness, charm, or beauty let him be persuaded to marry for political advantage. The bride recommended by Louis XIV—who had paid handsomely for the redemption of Dunkirk, captured in Cromwell's time, and given Charles a private gift of £80,000—was the Portuguese princess, Catherine of Braganza, whose dowry would include Tangier, Bombay, and the sum of £300,000. Cromwell had found advantage in a French alliance, and so did Charles. He permitted the marriage of his sister Henrietta to the Duke of Orleans, brother to Louis XIV, and continued to enjoy a French pension. But he was sadly disappointed in Catherine of Braganza.

He was in love with Barbara, Lady Castlemaine, whom he refused to discard even when Catherine was on her way to England; and the prospect of a diplomatic marriage cannot have been pleasant. He had, however, seen a flattering picture of her, and the reality was more unpleasant than he had anticipated. Poor Catherine was short and squat, with a dull brown complexion, badly dressed, and sadly unattractive but for innocently large and luminous eyes. The marriage was not a happy one, but Charles's good nature persuaded Catherine to make the best of it—as he was doing—and even to accept Barbara Castlemaine as a lady of her bedchamber. She became, indeed, very friendly with Barbara, and at one time the royal *ménage* included the King's mother, his illegitimate son by Lucy Walter, his Queen and his mistress, to whom his son—subsequently Duke of Monmouth—was warmly attached. Though lacking the moral qualities whose supremacy none disputes—though deficient in that high seriousness which all respect —Charles had an amiability of rare distinction, and within his own walls was capable of a diplomacy which few can have excelled.

On the last day of August 1661, Samuel Pepys was in a censorious mood and wrote: "At Court things are in very ill condition, there being so much emulacioun, poverty, and the vices of drinking, swearing, and loose amours, that I know not what will be the end of it but confusion." Poverty was not the most conspicuous feature of Court life, for elsewhere he writes of the King's progress to Westminster for his coronation: "So glorious was the show with gold and silver, that we were not able to look at it, our eyes at last being so much overcome with it." But there was, of course, great competition for favour and the profit of office, and where riches were so obvious the poverty of those who wished to better themselves may have made them desperate in "emulacioun." The King himself was not now a heavy drinker, and his "loose amours" were governed by a certain propriety: he never, says Pepys, kept more than one mistress at a time.

He was deeply attached to Lady Castlemaine, later Duchess of

Cleveland, by whom he had three sons and a daughter or two; but she did not reward his attentions and lavish gifts with fidelity, and her supremacy was dangerously menaced by the arrival at court of a remarkable young woman known as "la belle Stuart." Her beauty was acknowledged by all, her lack of sense was generally recognised. The author of the *Memoirs of Count Grammont* wrote, with an astonishment that still survives, "It was hardly possible for a woman to have less wit, or more beauty." Her features were fine and regular, she was tall and slender; she was very graceful, danced well, spoke perfect French; she had a passion for music and a singing voice. But she was "childish in her behaviour, and laughed at everything, and her taste for frivolous amusements, though unaffected, was only allowable in a girl about twelve or thirteen years old. A child, however, she was, in every other respect, except playing with a doll; blind man's buff was her most favourite amusement."

"At this time," the narrative continues, "the King's attachment to Miss Stuart was so public, that every person perceived, that if she was but possessed of art, she might become as absolute a mistress over his conduct as she was over his heart." Miss Stuart, however, had neither art nor inclination, and the King of a profligate court was tenderly considerate of her witless virtue. Her chastity was only fractionally impaired when, in 1667, she married the Duke of Richmond.

A French woman, Louise de Kerouaille, subsequently Duchess of Portsmouth, became the recognised favourite in 1671, but Charles, some years before, had relaxed his almost monogamous habit and found a new enjoyment in the theatre: not only as a playgoer, but as a patron of the young actresses who, since the Restoration, had added so much to the gaiety of the stage. There was Moll Davies, a dancer; there was the charming and ebullient Nell Gwynne; and there were some others. Only Nell Gwynne—pretty, witty Nell—was to gain, as well as the King's affection, the enduring respect of succeeding ages; but she, in popular esteem, has acquired a fame far exceeding that of his greedy duchesses, and probably deserved it.

"She is young," wrote Madame de Sévigné, "of madcap gaiety, bold, brazen, and ready-witted." "The indiscreetest and wildest creature that ever was in a court," said Bishop Burnet. Colley Cibber, actor and dramatist, declared she had no faults but frailty, cost less than other favourites, and "was as visibly distinguished by her particular personal inclination to the King, as her rivals were by their titles and grandeur."

Her beginnings could hardly have been humbler—daughter of a broken soldier, she sold fish in the streets, oranges in the theatre, sang in taverns—but from somewhere she had inherited true genius, and Dryden so admired her acting that he wrote parts to show off her daring charm. Pepys saw her as Florimel in Dryden's *Secret Love*, and wrote, "So great a performance of a comical part was never, I believe, in the world before." She had abounding success and won a vast popularity; but neither spoiled her. She rarely interfered in affairs of state, nor used her influence in matters which did not concern her; and throughout her life she valued wit above dignity.

Louise de Kerouaille, Duchess of Portsmouth, was a Catholic, much disliked by the ordinary people of England, and Nell Gwynne was once in some danger when an angry crowd mistook her coach for the Duchess's. She was being driven through Oxford, and a sudden mob surrounded her, rudely shouting their disapproval. She opened a window, smiling, and disarmed her audience. "Good people," she said, "you are mistaken. I am the Protestant whore." But a whore she was not. She is said to have been faithful to the King, and she bore him two sons, one of whom survived to become Duke of St. Albans.

It must be repeated, however, that a profligate court was inimical neither to science nor the arts. A memorandum of November 1660, records the incorporation of the Royal Society, which within a few days received the King's approval; who, in the following year, offered himself for membership. Among the original members were Christopher Wren, architect of the Sheldonian Theatre and St. Paul's; Robert Boyle, who adopted an atomic theory of matter and defined the chemical element as a substance which could not be decomposed into simpler constituents; and in 1671, when the King was showing more interest in Louise de Kerouaille, Isaac Newton, "professor of the mathematicks at Cambridge," was elected a Fellow. In 1663 the Society was entitled "The Royal Society for the improving of Natural Knowledge by experiments," and the King presented it with a mace. In its long history and its own field the Society has been of incomparable importance, and the prestige that graced its beginning has been constantly enhanced by the work of its Fellows.

In the theatre, in the reviving world of English literature, John Dryden—dramatist, satirist, critic, and Poet Laureate—was supreme. He was amazingly prolific, his range was immense, *Absalom and Achitophel* remains unmatched as portraiture-in-poetry, and his prose was incisive. In a literary judgment the reign of Charles II occurred in the Age of Dryden. But the theatre owed much to Charles. It was he who licensed Thomas Killigrew and Sir William D'Avenant to recruit two companies of players, which were known as the King's and the Duke of York's. Killigrew was a wit, a dramatist, and the King's jester. He and D'Avenant revived many of the great plays of Elizabethan and Jacobean times, and D'Avenant's *Love and Honour* was a work of real distinction.

George Etherege was perhaps more famous for foppery and indolence than for his dramatic successes, but for the first performance of *She Would if She Could* there was so long a queue—Pepys and his wife were in it—that a thousand people were still in the street when the pit was full. Sir Charles Sedley was another who, very successfully, defended his profligacy by his wit, and was a capable man of affairs. William Wycherley, born in 1640, lived until 1715 and enjoyed the Duchess of Cleveland's favour before he foolishly married Lady Drogheda, a rich but ill-natured young widow: *The Plain Dealer*, an admirable satire, is the best of his plays, and *The Country Wife* the coarsest.

There were other dramatists, no longer remembered except by scholars with a special interest; and the English stage was enriched with plots and characters filched from Molière, with *comedias de capa y espada*—cloak and dagger stuff—stolen from Lope de Vega. French opera made a tentative appearance, and Purcell's *Dido and Aeneas* was produced in 1680. Charles was dead before the London stage took on the elegance of Congreve, Vanbrugh, and Farquhar—the heirs of Wycherley and Dryden—but his reign enjoyed, among its major distinctions, the minor ornament called Aphra Behn.

Born in Kent, in 1640, Mrs Behn was the first professional female author in the annals of English literature, and in some ways a curiously modern figure. With a man appointed Lieutenant-Governor of Surinam, whom she called her father, she went to South America, and after the death of her protector married a Dutch merchant, with whom she returned to London. Her husband died, and Aphra found employment in Antwerp as a spy. Espionage was badly paid, however, and she took to literature instead. In her novel *Oronooko* she anticipated Rousseau's belief in the intrinsical nobility of savages; for her plays she found material by bold and ingenious piracy; and it has often been remarked that her lively and inventive dialogue was broader, more liberal—*risqué* used to be the favoured word—than that of her male contemporaries.

4

Dryden's poem, *Annus Mirabilis*, has, as its double theme, war with the Dutch and the Great Fire of London. His description of triumph and disaster is vivid and splendid, his explication of events less admirable; but the poem may be regarded as a symbolic illustration of the jeopardy in which England lived. In the twenty-five years of Charles's reign the danger often recurred of a new conflagration, political or religious, and though one may not believe in the heavenly fire-service which, according to Dryden, put out the flames of London, one cannot deny that Charles, by the coolness with which he played his kingly part, did much to discourage a latent incendiarism in many of his subjects and the circumstances of the time.

Bitter rivalry in trade was the cause of the Dutch war which broke out in 1664. Both nations were building empires oversea, and to each it appeared that the other's ambition was excessive, its practices insufferable. The English held their Navy in high esteem; the King and his brother James were warmly interested in their ships, expert in knowledge of them; the war at sea excited much emotion, and fortune varied from one side to the other. In 1665 the Duke of York won a decisive victory off Lowestoft, but in May of that year the Great Plague broke out, and in September, 1666, the Great Fire. In London alone the plague killed nearly 70,000, and the fire that began in Pudding Lane, east of London Bridge, burned for four days. Old London was timber-built, its lanes were narrow, there had been weeks of drought, an east wind blew fiercely; and from London Bridge to Fleet Street and the Inner Temple old London was destroyed.

A financial crisis followed; in Scotland the Covenanters rebelled; when winter came the Thames froze and the supply of sea-coal failed for lack of convoys. Only the press-gang could find recruits for the Navy, and France—though without much conviction—took sides with Holland in the war. Monck, hopelessly outgunned, fought in June a long and bloody battle in the Downs, but in July he and Prince Rupert drove the Dutch home to their harbours.

A treaty of peace was agreed with France. Bankruptcy dictated it, and to Louis XIV was left the task of dealing with Holland. Britain promised neutrality in France's war with Spain, and France returned some lately captured islands in the West Indies. The fleet was laid up, and when the Dutch came into the Thames, and sailed up the Medway, half its ships were burnt. The peace signed at Breda was ignominious, and Clarendon was dismissed and banished. The French were rewarded with Acadia, the Dutch with most of the West African coast and freedom for its commerce in the narrow seas; but Britain kept New York, New Jersey, and Delaware.

Clarendon, the Lord Chancellor, had followed Charles into exile, but his long fidelity was discounted by somewhat outmoded and reactionary opinions, and he made enemies who blamed him for the shocking humiliation that the Navy had suffered. He was also blamed, but unfairly, for the ecclesiastical code to which his name was given. The Church of England was declared supreme, its discipline absolute; and hope vanished of a peaceful accommodation with Protestant dissenters. Charles was more liberal than his advisers, more liberal than his parliament, and the ministry that succeeded Clarendon did little credit either to King or country. It is remembered because the initial letters of the names of its five members—Clifford, Arlington, Buckingham, Ashley, Lauderdale—happened to spell "cabal," a word that meant intrigue, and acquired a new and sinister connotation in an age when politics was riddled by intrigue. All western Europe was divided by enmities, open or concealed by shifting alliances. Spain was decaying, France was dominant, Britain and Holland were still at odds; and from the East Indies to South America there was frantic competition for the advantages of trade and new territory.

Arlington, more of a statesman than his colleagues, negotiated a triple alliance with the Protestant states of Sweden and Holland in 1668, but in 1670 Louis XIV, whose war with Spain had now terminated, concluded at Dover a secret treaty with Charles, by which Charles was to receive an annual pension of £200,000, declare himself a Roman Catholic, and restore Catholicism in Britain. Neither party took the latter clauses seriously; Charles made no declaration of his faith nor took steps to impose it on his people; and in the next eight years his pension amounted to rather less than half the promised sum. But Louis XIV secured an ally in his war against Holland.

It cannot be denied that Charles was guilty of chicanery; and what can scarcely be disputed is that chicanery was the current coin of international politics. England was jealous of French sea-power, and Charles himself shared a general belief in England's prerogative to command the sea. Both Elizabeth and Cromwell had recognised the advantage of alliance, or a close relationship with France, and so did Charles; who hoped to persuade Louis XIV to curtail his naval programme. Against an opponent of superior strength dissimulation was essential.

France had immense resources, and Louis XIV—called the Most Christian King and God's deputy on earth—was an absolute monarch. In comparison with him, Charles ruled from a tightrope and maintained his footing by the art of balance. Before the renewal of war against Holland he issued a Declaration of Indulgence that gave freedom of worship to Protestant Dissenters and permitted Catholics the luxury of worship within their own walls. A year later parliament refused to grant supply for the war until the Indulgence was withdrawn, and when Charles yielded, the House of Commons passed the Test Act, requiring all office-holders to take the Anglican sacrament and deny their belief in transubstantiation. The Catholic Duke of York was compelled to leave the Admiralty, and Charles to recognise the turmoil of religion, fear, and danger that underlay his tightrope. The new Anglicans were as intransigent as the Independents of Cromwell's time.

The Dutch war was inconclusive. There was heavy fighting at sea, and on land the French won large successes. But young William of Orange—William III, Charles's nephew—fought on heroically, found Hapsburg allies, and drove the French back to the Rhine. Peace was made at Westminster in 1674, the Cabal fell, and Lord Danby—Cavalier, Protestant, and no friend of France—formed a party which was greatly assisted by a revival of trade.

Charles continued to play Louis against his parliament, parliament against Louis, and obtain from one or the other an income almost sufficient for his needs. In 1677 he agreed to a marriage between the valiant, unscrupulous William of Orange and the Duke of York's daughter Mary: a marriage that had important consequences for Britain, pleased England and the House of Commons, and deeply wounded Louis. But peace between England and Holland persuaded Louis to sign the treaty of Nijmegen in 1678, with little advantage to Charles.

Domestic peace was quickly shattered by James, Duke of York, and the malignancy of a sinister adventurer called Titus Oates. The King's brother was a declared Catholic; England, as so often before, was nervously afraid of Catholicism; and when Oates, who had been studying in Jesuit seminaries abroad, returned to England with a fantastic tale of a Catholic plot to assassinate the King and massacre Protestants, London fell into a frenzy of indignation and terror. Before a magistrate, Sir Edmund Berry Godfrey, Oates swore to the truth of his story, and a fortnight later Godfrey was found dead in a ditch on Primrose Hill. Terror and indignation became a passionate hatred of Catholics and Catholicism, and the malignant Oates—who may have connived at Godfrey's murder—was exalted as a Protestant hero.

Excitement was aggravated by revelation of Charles's compromising relations with Louis XIV. A score or two of Catholics were executed, Danby committed to the Tower, and wild stories circulated that the Queen and her servants were guilty of Godfrey's murder and now proposed to poison the King. For two years England lived in a fever of wrathful suspicion, and at the centre of the storm Charles—Charles alone, as now it seems—remained tranquil and inactive. Contemptuous of slander, he ignored its calumnies as he ignored threats to his safety; but he showed conspicuous kindness to his slandered wife.

The country, of course, had reasons for apprehension. Charles had no legitimate children, and the heir apparent was his Catholic brother, whom the Commons wished to exclude. There were those who thought the Duke of Monmouth—Charles's son by Lucy Walter—a better candidate; but Monmouth's character was of doubtful sufficiency, though he commended himself by defeating the Scottish Covenanters, who were again rebellious. There was, indeed, a mutter of rebellion throughout England, and politicians plotted feverishly for advantage on the outskirts of civil war. Charles, in a virtual solitude, lived in imminent peril, and peril did not darken his intelligence or diminish his courage. He knew that his country did not want another war, and believed that his people preferred him to parliament: "Better one king than five hundred," he said.

England, at last, grew tired of its unseemly passion, ashamed of its excesses. The King had proved his strength, and demonstrated his constant wish for conciliation. The turmoil of the years had precipitated the two parties which, for the next couple of centuries, were to divide and dominate political activity: the Tories, so called after Irish outlaws, had gathered round Danby, and Danby had been defeated in 1678; the Whigs—a word which originally meant Scottish

Covenanters—were led by Ashley Cooper of the Cabal, now Earl of Shaftesbury and for ever Achitophel in Dryden's *Absalom and Achitophel*. As the King grew in favour, the Whigs lost it, and Shaftesbury —who had made rascally use of Titus Oates—fled from England to die in exile. In October 1682 there was a plot to murder the King and the Duke of York at Rye House in Hertfordshire, and when that failed Charles's triumph was complete.

For the remainder of his life he lived in the peace he had earned, he left administration to subordinates, but showed his apparent wish to secure the succession for James his Catholic brother by appointing him, in defiance of the Test Act, Lord High Admiral. Charles had once said of him, "I am much afraid that when he comes to the crown he will be obliged to travel again," but from the changed temper of England there had lately emerged a new regard for the Duke of York— there was, said Bishop Burnet, "an indecent courting and magnifying him"—and among the royal Stuarts family feeling had always been strong. What Charles intended, however, was hidden by death. He was only fifty-four, and may still have hoped for a legitimate son to follow him. Early in February 1685 he had an apoplectic fit, and died four days later.

From Father Huddleston, who had helped him in his escape from Worcester, he received the last rites of the Roman Church, and history, in a benign mood, has preserved his final command to his dull, insensitive brother James. "Let not poor Nelly starve," he said.

5

Charles, beset by foreign and domestic difficulties, had reigned for twenty-five years; James made his own difficulties and reigned for three. Unlike his brother, he had no charm, no judgment, but a strong sense of honour: habitually he kept his word and quickly lost his throne.

In his youth he shared exile and adventure with Charles. He fought with courage and verve under Marshal Turenne in his campaign against the Frondeurs, and later, less happily, with the Spaniards at Dunkirk. He returned to England at the Restoration, and was appointed Lord High Admiral and Warden of the Cinque Ports. As a naval administrator he was hard-working, honest, and efficient. In his earlier years he was amiable, easy of approach, but according to Bishop Burnet "lacked vivacity of thought, invention, or expression." As warm a libertine as Charles, he was less fastidious, and in his brother's opinion chose a mistress as if proposing to do penance.

Falling in love with Anne Hyde, daughter of the Earl of Clarendon, he got her with child and was inveigled into marriage, to the great displeasure of his brother and Anne's father. Both families were reconciled, however, and though Anne had no great physical attraction she soon evinced her dominating influence, failing only to control the ineptitude and indiscretion of James's love affairs. He continued to work diligently for the Navy, and when war was declared against the Dutch, in 1665, he commanded the fleet and set sail in the *Royal Charles* for the Texel. Brought suddenly into action in Southwold Bay, the *Royal Charles* was engaged by the Dutch admiral, and a single cannon-shot killed the Earl of Falmouth, Lord Muskery, and Richard Boyle: "their blood and brains," says Pepys, "flying in the Duke's face, and the head of Mr. Boyle striking down the Duke, as some say." The Dutch flagship was sunk by a shot from the *Royal Charles* which penetrated her magazine, and the English fleet took twenty-four of the enemy's ships. "Fat and lusty and ruddy from being in the sun," wrote Pepys, the victorious sailors came home to great feasting and rejoicing, and the Commons bestowed a grant of £20,000 on the gallant Duke.

When the war was renewed he again took command, but was less fortunate, and a very dubious victory brought his naval career to an end. In 1672 he withdrew from the communion of the Church of England, and when the Test Act was passed he submitted, weeping, the resignation of his commission as Lord High Admiral to the King. The sincerity of his conversion has never been doubted, but its ostentation may well be deplored.

He had eight children by Anne Hyde, who died in 1671. Three survived infancy, but the only son died in the year of his mother's death. Two years later Charles permitted his brother to marry Mary of Modena, an Italian princess recommended by Louis XIV. About fourteen years of age, she was "tall and admirably shaped, her complexion was of the last fairness, her hair black as jet, so were her eyebrows and her eyes"—but her eyes filled with tears when she learnt her fate, and she wept all the way to England. It was Charles who reconciled her to an unhappy marriage. "He was always kind to me," she said, "and so truly amiable and good-natured that I loved him very much." At court

Mary's charm and good looks won her many friends, but England no more welcomed the marriage than she did. As an antidote to his Catholic entanglement the Duke had to accept Charles's stipulation that Anne Hyde's two daughters, Mary and Anne, be educated as Protestants.

He was a hapless target for the abominable Titus Oates, who attacked him as a Papist and a traitor who deserved to be hanged. "And I hope I shall live to see it," said Oates. The Duke and his Italian Duchess retreated to Holland, but were soon recalled, and James was appointed High Commissioner to Scotland. Scottish emotion often conflicted with policy, and James and his Duchess were warmly welcomed to Edinburgh, and made themselves popular by reviving the vanished magnificence of Holyroodhouse. Recalled, for a period, in 1680, James returned to Edinburgh before the end of the year, and in his high office behaved with a studied moderation more typical of his brother. He took no action, and advised no action, against the private, household worship permitted to Covenanters; he was, like a good naval officer, impartial in justice; and he subdued by goodwill a great deal of Scotland's native antagonism to his religion. Such toleration was dictated by policy, for his purpose was to legalise acceptance of a Catholic monarch. An act was passed to ensure lineal succession irrespective of religion; another to combine preservation of "the true Protestant religion" with recognition of the King's supremacy "over all persons and in all causes" both ecclesiastical and civil.

Charles, in London, was unwilling to let his brother return to England unless he would conform to the Anglican ritual; but the stubborn Duke remained stubborn in assertion of his unpopular loyalty. He was encouraged by a wave of popular favour, and unexpected support, when the Rye House plot was discovered, and added to favour by permitting the marriage of his daughter Anne to the Protestant Prince George of Denmark. He was restored to office as Lord High Admiral, and in the final months of the King's life was much with him. When Charles died, England—still under the spell of his generous authority—quietly acquiesced in James's succession.

6

England had recovered from the unnatural excitement provoked by Titus Oates—there was, if not equanimity, a prudent disposition to peace in the land—and the throne to which James succeeded might have been comfortable enough had he shown a decent regard for the well-being and authority of the Church of England, a sensible recognition of the Protestant temper of England. He did indeed assert his intention "to preserve the government both in Church and State as by law established"; and in that assertion he—who had once been known for his "inviolable attachment" to the truth—lied prodigiously, and as if to proclaim his real purpose went ostentatiously to mass, and expected his ministers to attend him.

In his choice of ministers he was shrewd, and there is no reason for doubting his honesty when he told the House of Commons that his heart was English, and the Navy—"the strength and glory of this nation"—as close to his heart as it should be to theirs. In both England and Scotland his parliaments were generous, and voted him a lavish revenue. At court he may have given some offence by his professed determination to reform its manners, though he seems to have objected only to profanity and blasphemy. And the loyalty he had inherited was strongly reinforced when peace was threatened by a twofold rebellion.

The rebels were inept, they made no effort to co-ordinate attack, and neither in England nor Scotland had they any hope of success. In Scotland Argyll was defeated, in England the Duke of Monmouth and his wretched followers were brutally repressed and savagely punished. Argyll was sentenced to death and beheaded. Monmouth, marvellously handsome and exceptionally incompetent, had declared his legitimacy and true title to the throne; denounced James as a murderer and Popish usurper; and led a poor army of peasants to defeat. He was captured and executed, and Judge Jeffreys, after the "Bloody Assize" that tried his captured supporters, boasted of having hanged more traitors than any of his predecessors since the Norman Conquest.

Great anger was roused by the shocking punishment of rebels who had never presented a real danger to the country, and loyalty, so evident a little while before, began to seep away from a King who seemed intent on establishing authority by terror. That freedom might again be menaced by an intransigent ruler looked very probable when parliament assembled and James pressed the Commons to pay for a larger standing army, and proposed repeal of the Test Act and *Habeas corpus*. Both Houses protested, and parliament was prorogued. It did not meet again.

Had James intended nothing more than religious toleration, he could have satisfied a reasonable desire by reasonable methods. But his larger purpose began to reveal itself when he commissioned or re-commissioned Catholic officers; appointed Catholic councillors, judges, and heads of colleges; let a Catholic bench assert its power to repudiate acts of parliament, and brought an army to Hounslow Heath. In an attempt to promote a union of interest between Catholics and Dissenters an Indulgence was proclaimed, in both England and Scotland, that gave them freedom of public worship; the Catholic Tyrconnel was made Commander-in-chief in Ireland, where Protestant officers were dismissed; the Catholic Duke of Gordon commanded Edinburgh castle; and with consternation the country awaited the birth of a Catholic heir when it was announced that the Queen was pregnant.

The Tories who had supported the Restoration, and defeated the attempt to exclude James from the succession, were by James driven from office, and the Church of England, ever loyal to the throne, was insulted by a new Indulgence that James commanded to be read in every parish church. Archbishop Sancroft and six bishops denounced the Indulgence as a violation of law, and were committed to the Tower to be tried for seditious libel. Their counsel argued that the King could legislate only through parliament, and to a tumult of rejoicing the bishops were acquitted.

On the continent of Europe the balance of power was swinging away from France. The might and arrogance of Louis XIV had lasted too long, and now both Catholic and Protestant states were in league against him. William of Orange, whose wife was James's daughter, was foremost in that improbable coalition, but dreaded the possibility of attack from a new alliance between France and England. He had agents in England who knew of the growing opposition to James, and from England came an enquiry as to William's intentions which coincided with his discovery that James was reinforcing his Navy with the help of a French subsidy, and asking for the return of Scottish regiments from the Dutch service. To his correspondents in England William declared his willingness to help them if he were formally invited by those who had sufficient authority to warrant such an invitation.

In June 1688, while the rebellious bishops were still on trial, the Queen gave birth to a son and heir, and an hour or two after the bishops' acquittal seven of the magnates of Church and State signed their invitation to William. Within a few weeks, it is said, half of England was singing or whistling *Lilliburlero,* a soldiers' marching song whose doggerel verses were set to a tune that Purcell may have written. It was a summons to rebellion livelier than the *Marseillaise,* and according to repute sang a king out of three kingdoms.

The invitation to William was reinforced by many resounding names. Prussia and Hanover promised to protect Holland in his absence, and William, assuring his supporters that parliament would be free and law respected—declaring, moreover, that he had no intention of deposing James—landed at Torbay, with an army of 24,000 men, on the 5th November. He had made a gambler's decision, and even the weather favoured him: the gale that blew him into Devon held the English fleet under the Gunfleet Sands off Essex.

James had again refused to call parliament, and lacked the resolution to fight. What England clearly demanded was Protestantism and parliamentary freedom, but James, obsessed by his own purposes, was blind and deaf to realities. He had, moreover, become curiously and fatally incapable of decision. Loyalists and men of goodwill were utterly discouraged by what seemed his moral or intellectual failure, and his stark ineptitude. His Lieutenant-general, John Churchill, afterwards Duke of Marlborough, abandoned him to join William; as did the Duke of Grafton and, a day or two later, George of Denmark and James's daughter Anne, and the Duke of Ormonde. The King who, in his prime, had been so brave—and always obstinate—now faltered, broken in spirit, and when he fled in disguise was so maladroit as to let himself be halted by fishermen and sent back to London. William ordered Dutch soldiers to replace the Guardsmen in Whitehall, and James was made prisoner in his own palace; but he was a prisoner to whom tacit permission had been given to escape, and with unnecessary secrecy he crossed over to France, where his Queen, with her infant son, had thankfully retired before him.

He made fatuous appeals for assistance to the Emperor, the Pope, even to England and the Tory churchmen whom he had so deeply offended. Only Louis XIV was disposed to help him, and the French

King had no more generous motive than to weaken England by detaching Ireland from its rule. He offered to establish James in Ireland, who in March 1689 put to sea from Brest, entered Dublin on the 24th, and with flaccid irresolution awaited his expulsion. He, the soldier who had fought so gallantly under Turenne, had lost all semblance of ability and will. Protestants had fled from the menace of his arrival, with French officers and money to support him; Tyrconnel raised a huge, undisciplined army; and the Protestants of Ulster, who had taken refuge in Londonderry, defied the great force that invested it, and for a hundred and five days maintained their hardy resistance and established a tradition that was to dominate all Ulster's history thereafter.

It is difficult to assess the nature and extent of James's personal collapse—the failure of a man who had been a good soldier and diligent in administration of the Navy—but another winter passed, and he made no effort to train and discipline the army that Tyrconnel had mobilised. His inactivity and impotence were rewarded when he was finally defeated at the battle of the Boyne in 1690. He returned to France and the hospitality of Louis XIV. Any hope of renewed intervention on his behalf was ruined by disaster to a French fleet, and as the empty years went by the court of St. Germain, where he lived in gloom and austerity, became known as the most doleful place in France except the Bastille.

He died in September 1701, leaving, of the eight children born to Anne Hyde, his daughters Mary, who had married William of Orange, and Anne, married to Prince George of Denmark; and of the seven born to Mary of Modena, two who survived him: James Edward, the Old Pretender, and a daughter who died of smallpox in 1712. Of his several illegitimate children the most notable was James Fitz-James—son of Arabella Churchill, sister of the Duke of Marlborough—who was ennobled as Duke of Berwick and became a Marshal of France and a Duke of both France and Spain.

Hapless Queens and Claimants

1

The clouds which had descended on the shining qualities of the royal Stuarts, and hidden them behind the inept and melancholy last years of James II, continued to obscure them during the reign of his two daughters and the lamentable incompetence of a claimant who drifted across the Scottish scene like the rain that descends, too often, to obscure the majesty of the Western Highlands and the gaunt beauty of the Isles. There was, it is true, a recrudescence of Stuart spirit—a revival of James IV's romanticism, of the dynastic intention of Mary, Queen of Scots, of the charm and gallantry of Charles II—when Charles Edward, the Young Pretender, issued his reckless challenge to the Hanoverian throne; but that was defeated by the gathered might of a new world to which embattled clans presented no serious menace.

Constitutional history must here—though very briefly—take precedence, and the remnant Stuarts be recognised as accessories to history; or vain protestants against its inexorable progress.

Of William III it is difficult to write with admiration. His success, though determined by a gambler's throw, was elaborately prepared and ultimately ensured by his opponent's moral failure and intellectual collapse. England acquired an unlikable King who removed from its people their neurotic fear of Catholic conquest, but in recent years few have applauded the manner of his achievement, and no one has found pleasure in remembering him. He was an historical factor in the final establishment of Protestantism, and little more can be said for him. He was a link or bridge between the absolutism of the Stuarts—revived with such brilliant discretion by Charles II—and the increasing absolutism of Parliament or cabinet which a Dutch King, an ailing Queen, and a Hanoverian succession made inevitable.

Stuart blood—the diminishing genes of Stuart inheritance—created that bridge or link. William and Mary succeeded to the throne from which James II had fled because Mary, William's wife, was James II's daughter by Anne Hyde, and heir to the throne; William himself was a grandson of Charles II; and both were Protestants.

Of Mary there is little to be said, not much to admire, no cause for gratification in her memory. On the chessboard of politics she was merely a pawn, sacrificed to advantage and given to a cold husband who, when she proved barren, treated her with the contempt that came easily to a man so callous. The Dutch liked her, William insulted her—he was jealous of her rank, more exalted than his—and her father left her short of money. She was, none the less, a devoted wife who, as Queen, did her duty in so far as she was capable of it, and in her devotion to religion and the Church of England may have found a reward sufficient to herself though unrecorded in history. Charitable by nature, blameless in conduct, of indifferent health, she fell ill in the harsh winter of 1694, and died of smallpox.

William, unmourned, died eight years later, and the succession passed to Mary's younger sister Anne, who was then thirty-seven, and for nearly twenty years had been married to Prince George of Denmark, the younger brother of King Christian V. What is commonly remembered of him is Charles II's verdict: "I have tried him drunk and I have tried him sober, but there is nothing in him." In his life of Marlborough, however, Winston Churchill, with characteristic generosity, records that the Prince "had a reputation for personal courage, and by a cavalry charge had rescued his brother during a battle between the Danes and the Dutch in 1677. He was neither clever nor learned—a simple, normal man, without envy or ambition, and disposed by remarkable appetite and thirst for all the pleasures of the table." And a critic of more charitable temper than Charles II has written that the marriage was "one of great domestic happiness, the prince and princess being comfortable in temper and both preferring retirement and quiet to life in the great world."

Of larger importance than her husband was Sarah Jennings, who married John Churchill, the future Duke of Marlborough; and the supreme irony of the new reign is that after Anne had spent dull years miscarrying and recovering from miscarriage, her brilliant subject went out to win battle after battle in a crescendo of triumph. A military policy of imaginative daring was carried through with unexampled success; by creating a United Kingdom, the Act of Union with Scotland laid the foundation stone of empire; the splendour of Dryden's age was succeeded by the scintillating genius of Alexander Pope; Congreve gave comedy a new, more graceful fame; while the poor exhausted Queen resigned herself to sad memories of the nursery so often prepared and never used.

Between 1684 and 1688 she had miscarried four times, and given birth to two children who died in infancy. A son, William, lived for some years, but during the reign of William and Mary, Anne was disturbed by their lack of amity and found, in herself, a growing dislike for her royal sister who, she said, talked too much. After Mary's death William's authority was weakened, and to assure himself of Anne's goodwill—on whom the Declaration of Rights had settled the succession—she was established in her own court at St. James's Palace, where she suffered six more miscarriages, two more infants died shortly after birth, and finally the little Prince William died. If her marriage did in fact continue to be "one of great domestic happiness," her devotion to George of Denmark must have been truly remarkable.

Her life was drab, of no importance except to the Protestant succession, but her reign was glorious. She made Marlborough Captain-general of British forces at home and abroad, the Dutch accepted him as supreme commander of the allied armies, and in that European convulsion called the War of the Spanish Succession he won early advantage over the French, and in 1704 set out on his great march from the North Sea to the Danube, his infantry footslogging for six weeks at ten miles a day. It was a British army that began the march—English, Irish, Scots, and Welsh—and Prussians, Hanoverians, Danes, and Dutch would join him later; north of Ulm on the Danube he would meet the army of the Empire to whose help he was going. The French had been misled by the unforeseen advance into Germany, but with their Bavarian allies would have an army at least as strong as that commanded by Marlborough and Prince Eugène.

Marlborough had decided that wars could not be won by marching and counter-marching, siege and sally, but only by major battle; and before that battle could be fought there was to be a desperate but necessary assault on the Schellenberg, the hill that covered his projected crossing of the Danube at the fortress of Donauwörth. The long march neared its end, and the army that had moved in interminable procession through a green countryside faced the menace of the steeply rising hill. It was a summer evening, and British troops led the advance. Grenadier Guards and Royal Welch Fusiliers, Royal Scots and Hampshires, conspicuous in their scarlet tunics, launched the attack against furious fire from a prepared and strongly held position, and for half an hour there was hand-to-hand fighting of incredible savagery—French Grenadiers bore the brunt of the attack—before the British, having lost about 3000 men in thirty minutes, fell back to a sheltering dip in the slope of the hill.

Marlborough immediately ordered renewal of the assault, which dismounted brigadiers and colonels led; but that too was beaten back. Then, on the right of the British, the Emperor's Lieutenant-general, the Margrave of Baden, went in with his Germans, with a reserve of infantry that Marlborough ordered up, and with the Scots Greys, dismounted like the reckless colonels who had died. Still the French and Bavarians held most valiantly, but where the wounded Margrave led there was less resistance—the French on the south of the Schellenberg had been drawn away to meet the first assault—and gradually the weight of the attack forced the tired defenders off the hill and down towards the river. Marlborough halted his infantry and launched his cavalry—English, Prussian, and the remounted Scots Greys—in a pursuit as savage as the first attack.

Of the 14,000 men who had held the Schellenberg only 5000 were able to rejoin the main Bavarian army; and in the armies of Marlborough and the Margrave there were nearly 6000 casualties. Of the 4000 British who had been in action 1500 were dead, as many wounded, and Winston Churchill records, with proper respect for the fighting spirit that animated all who served with Marlborough, "The proportion of loss among the senior officers was beyond compare. Six Lieutenant-generals were killed and five wounded, together with four Major-generals and twenty-eight Brigadiers, Colonels, and Lieutenant-colonels."*

The Schellenberg was stormed on the 2nd July. The crossing of the Danube was secured, and Bavaria lay open to the invaders. Marlborough himself was shocked by the cost of the operation, and it contrasts oddly with the sedulous care he had taken to ensure the safety, com-

* Winston Churchill: *Marlborough, His Life and Times.*

fort, and well-being of his soldiers on their long march. But the combination of a skilful, long-plotted strategy with the explosive ferocity of the tactics necessary to secure the river-crossing discloses the inner strength of that courteous and accomplished man, as clearly as the valour of soldiers on both sides reveals the total courage of professional armies, well trained and led by spirited officers, in an age when war was endemic and for the majority of mankind there were few professions available other than arms and agriculture. The assault on the Schellenberg was a prelude to the great battle of Blenheim in August, and Blenheim was followed by the major actions at Ramillies in 1706, Oudenarde in 1708, and Malplaquet in 1709; all of which Marlborough won for his ailing Queen.

Between Ramillies and Oudenarde, England and Scotland found their long-delayed destiny in an incorporating union, unpopular on both sides, but eventually productive of great achievement and an empire whose influence on history has not yet been fully assessed. To enhance the politeness of English life, under its sad Queen, Addison and Steele composed their essays for the *Spectator;* Swift exercised his lambent genius in political pamphlets; Pope gave literature a new brilliance in his *Essay on Criticism;* and Defoe paraded his muscular prose in a *History of the Union.*

A more conspicuous addition to England's scenery was the dome of St. Paul's. Christopher Wren had begun to rebuild the old church, burnt in the Great Fire, in 1675, but the dome and the west end were not finished until 1711. Wren lived until 1723, and his influence on architecture—ecclesiastical, public, and private—lasted longer than he. His assistant, Nicholas Hawksmore, was a vital link between Wren and Sir John Vanbrugh, who began to build the great Yorkshire palace of Castle Howard in 1699, the still larger Blenheim palace in 1705. An unfriendly critic composed an epitaph for Vanbrugh:

> "Lie heavy on him, Earth! for he
> Laid many heavy loads on thee"—

and Pope thought the magnificence of Blenheim would offer little comfort to those who lived there: "For where d'you sleep and where d'you dine?" More typical of domestic architecture in the reign of Queen Anne were relatively small houses characterised by simplicity and the grace of finely calculated proportions.

2

When Anne died, in 1714, the Protestant heir to Britain was George, Elector of Hanover, a grandson of Elizabeth the Winter Queen of Bohemia, and great-grandson of James VI and I. The Elector, who came to his greater throne as George I, was fifty-three. He spoke no English, his ministers knew no German. He had the poor taste to prefer Hanover to England, he had divorced his wife within two years of marrying her, and he was on bad terms with his only son. Before leaving home he had made arrangements to pack the English Bench with Whig judges, and in the new parliament of 1715 there was a large Whig majority. When Jacobites in Scotland and the north of England rose in protest against a Hanoverian king, there were many Tories who saw and relished the prospect of intrigue; and the Tory party paid heavily for its lack of judgment.

On the death of James II in 1701, his son James Edward had been proclaimed at the Palace of St. Germain as King James III and VIII of England, Scotland, and Ireland, and was recognised as such by Louis XIV of France and Philip V of Spain. Neither Louis nor Philip, however, had much favour or influence in England, and not only was their recognition of the boy disregarded by parliament, but it was made high treason to correspond with him: he was only thirteen, and for the next five years subject to the nominal regency of his mother, Mary of Modena. Excluded from succession to the English throne by the Act of Settlement, passed in the year of his father's death, James Edward became the ineffectual sovereign of a court of exiles, the hope and despair of angry dissidents, and the centre of conspiracy frustrated by its own ineptitude.

He was a reserved and melancholy youth, without a trace of the wit and charm and easy kindliness of his uncle Charles II. He was brave, or could exhibit bravery, as his father had done, and in 1708, when the French made an aborted attempt to land in Leith, he was notably calm in the face of danger. The French fleet was surprised by an English squadron, of superior strength, under Sir George Byng, and the French admiral escaped only by good fortune when the wind veered and blew from the southwest. James pleaded to be put ashore, alone, but no one would listen to that audacity. He returned to France in time to fight at Oudenarde, and then at Malplaquet, where he charged—again and again, it is said—with the cavalry of the Maison du Roi, and became so well known to his apparent enemies that after the battle many of Marlborough's officers, with the generosity that so often tempered the brutalities of war, used to drink his health, and soldiers, when he rode by the brook that divided their lines, would take off their hats and cheer him.

But little applause attended his later years, and as if marked by mischance he had the ill fortune of attracting those to his side who were doomed to failure by their own incompetence. After the accession of George I, peaceful and uninterrupted despite the low thunder of resentment that preceded it, there were, beyond question, Jacobite sympathisers throughout the country from Cornwall to Aberdeen; but they had no intention of rising without a promise of success. The Whigs were dominant, the new King was on his throne, and to dislodge an English king—though he spoke nothing but German—was not an enterprise that would recommend itself to sober men unless a leader appeared who had the gift of lighting enthusiasm, a plan and a policy to promote confidence, and a core or nucleus of ardent supporters who could inspire faith in his cause. But in James Edward there was no such fire, and when rebellion broke out in Scotland, and the Pretender's standard was flown on the Braes of Mar, though in England there was much anxiety on the one side, there was no enthusiasm on the other; and in Scotland there was widespread contempt for the Pretender's* champion.

In France Louis XIV, *le Roi Soleil*, had died at the age of seventy-seven. Without him there was no prospect of French support, and without French support there was very little chance for the success of a rebellion. What little hope remained was dissipated, from the start, by its fatuously incompetent leader, the Earl of Mar, known as "Bobbing John." To Scots of the more fiercely patriotic sort he had not endeared himself by supporting the Treaty of Union, and after serving Anne as her Secretary of State for Scotland he had written to George I to seek re-employment. The Hanoverian did not want his service, and Bobbing John, deeply offended, came out as the leader of a Jacobite rebellion without having given thought to the strategy or tactics of

---

* James Edward Stuart, recognised by his Jacobite supporters as James III, was called by the Whigs "the Pretender"; i.e. claimant to the throne.

rebellion, without considering how his rebellion could serve the Jacobite cause.

To the Braes of Mar, however—the broad and handsome country that rises beyond Balmoral and looks up to the shining heights of the Cairngorms—the Royal Standard attracted a great host of Highlanders, some intent on booty, some deeply stirred by loyalty and indignation, by a sense that their old privileges and their old inviolate land were now open to foreign menace; and under Bobbing John the greater number of them did nothing at all for two months. From the west and the north they came—Clan Donald, Camerons, and Mackenzies—Ogilvies and Gordons from Angus and Aberdeen—out of Perthshire Murrays and Drummonds and Robertsons—Macintoshes and Macphersons from Speyside and the Middle Highlands, and most of them, for two months, did nothing.

In October Macintosh of Borlum led fifteen hundred in a wild foray to the south, and in the north of England joined forces with English Jacobites, only to be heavily defeated at Preston in mid-November. On the same day, the 14th, Bobbing John at last led his Highlanders to battle near Stirling, where the Duke of Argyll held a sound defensive position; and at Sheriffmuir, a few miles to the north, there was a scrambling fight that brought neither credit nor victory to either side. Then, towards the end of December, when all hope of success had vanished, the Pretender landed at Peterhead. In many places he had been proclaimed as James III and it was, perhaps, a sense of honour that induced him to come ashore. But there was nothing he could do, and with Bobbing John he re-embarked at Montrose and returned to France, leaving his supporters to pay the bill for his adventure: it cost them nineteen Scottish peerages, forfeited by attainder, and in England the lives of the young Earl of Derwentwater and Lord Kenmure, who were executed.

James was not allowed to remain in France, and found a refuge in Modena, his mother's old home, and later in Urbino, a dull place from which, in 1718, he removed to Rome. There was an abortive plot to enlist the help of Charles XII, King of Sweden, but that came to nothing. Then Spain offered assistance, and at Cádiz a fleet was mobilised, with transports to carry 5000 men; but a storm scattered it, and two ships only arrived in Stornoway, with 300 Spanish soldiers. They crossed to the mainland under the Marquess of Tullibardine, found a few enthusiastic Highlanders to march with them, but were quickly routed in Glenshiel, and the Spanish adventure came to an end.

Then James thought it expedient to marry, and from Poland got the promise of Clementina, granddaughter of its great king John Sobieski, who had saved Vienna from the Turks. There was opposition from England, where the Whigs were averse to any purpose of perpetuating the Stuart line; and the Emperor was persuaded to prevent Clementina's arrival in Italy. She and her mother were arrested at Innsbruck, and a few months later, in the most romantic fashion, rescued from the schloss where they were imprisoned by Charles Wogan, an Irish officer in Dillon's Regiment.

Wogan, who came from County Kildare, had been "out in the Fifteen," taken prisoner, and escaped. He was the first of the Jacobite court to meet Clementina Sobieska—he had commended her sweetness, her discreet gaiety, to James—and sentiment as well as devotion to the Pretender may have contributed to the zeal which spurred his horse along the road to Innsbruck. With him rode Major Gaydon, Captain O'Toole, Captain Misset—all of Dillon's Regiment—and Mrs Misset with her maid Janetta. They went in disguise, and the good girl Janetta, told that their purpose was to carry off an heiress who was in love with O'Toole, agreed to play a dangerous part in the game. At the schloss, while Clementina dressed and gathered her jewels to go off with Wogan, Janetta undressed to take her place in Clementina's bed. From the inn where the others waited they all—all but Janetta—set off for the frontier at two o'clock in the morning, and rode without hindrance until Clementina discovered she had left her jewel-box behind. O'Toole went back to retrieve it, got into the inn by heaving a bolted door from its hinges, found the jewels, and returned to join those who waited so anxiously for him. Then a courier tried to stop them, but Misset and O'Toole filled him full of brandy, and with no more trouble they rode into the papal city of Bologna.

From Innsbruck the girl Janetta escaped without much difficulty, and Clementina's mother avoided tiresome interrogation by opportunely swooning. The Pretender was in Spain, but Clementina was married to his proxy, given by the Pope a state entry into Rome, and received her husband some three months later after a second marriage performed with the papal blessing. There was, however, no happiness in the union brought about with such dashing contrivance. It has been suggested that Clementina was too devoted to her Church to find pleasure in marriage—others have complained that she was a jealous and suspicious woman—but it seems equally possible that the granddaughter of John Sobieski thought her husband a dull dog, which he was; or she may have fallen in love with the gallant Irishman who rode with her from Innsbruck. But she conceived, and on the 31st December, 1720, bore a son who, christened Charles Edward Louis John Sylvester Maria Casimir, eventually became more widely known as the Young Pretender; and four years later there was a second son, Henry Benedict Maria Clement, destined to ecclesiastical dignity as the Cardinal Bishop of Frascati.

Those two sons were Clementina's contribution to the Jacobite cause; and James himself, having begotten them, did nothing more for it. Clementina died young, at the age of thirty-two, and soon after her death James, despite unhappiness with her, began to fall into a premature decline. He withdrew from Roman society—in which papal generosity had maintained him with some grandeur—and devoting himself to religious exercises, became a recluse and gradually a helpless invalid. He lived until the beginning of 1766, but he had been long forgotten and his death was unnoticed. In St. Peter's, however, Canova's great monument remembered him in the cold gravity of marble: the cold gravity that may have alienated the Polish gaiety of Clementina.

It is agreeable to record that Charles Wogan, of Dillon's Regiment of wild Irishmen, was created a baronet for his rescue of the Princess, and after exchanging from the French service into the Spanish, became Governor of Barcelona; from where he engaged in correspondence with his distinguished fellow-countryman, Dean Swift. What a happy conclusion to a life of gallant independence!

3

In the memory of a multitude of people there survives a picture—framed either in sentiment or suspicion—of a pretty, dandified youth in a costume of theatrical extravagance, attached to which is a label bearing the name of Charles Edward Stuart.

That picture is quite unlike descriptions of the Prince that were written by two men who had seen him at close quarters during the fourteen months of his Scottish adventure. The Rev. Dr. Carlyle—

famous for the nobility of his appearance and the social eminence of his friends—saw him in Edinburgh, and wrote, in his *Autobiography:* "He was a good-looking man of about five feet ten inches; his hair was dark red, and his eyes black. His features were regular, his visage long, much sunburnt and freckled, and his countenance thoughtful and melancholy." A year later, when the Prince, after defeat at Culloden, had been living a hunted, fugitive existence in the Highlands and Western Isles, the Rev. John Cameron, sometime Presbyterian chaplain at Fort William, met him in Lochiel's country near Loch Arkaig. He was "bare-footed, had an old black kilt coat on, philabeg and waistcoat, a dirty shirt and a long red beard, a gun in his hand, a pistol and dirk by his side. He was very cheerful and in good health, and in my opinion fatter than when he was in Inverness."

Given the proper circumstances, failure and defeat may more happily preserve a man's name than success; and the legend of the Young Pretender has survived because he failed to achieve a purpose, which was political, in circumstances and an environment that were perfectly designed for the creation of a legend. But the defeated hero of the tale was not a pretty boy in fancy dress; he was a grown man, dedicated with passionate intensity to a major enterprise, whose body endured, without mishap, the perils, hunger, and hardship of a five months' chase through the wildest parts of Scotland. His venture was ill conceived—it had no hope of success and it brought misery to those who supported him—but he himself must be taken seriously because he was devoted to a cause which, though hopeless, was not ignoble, and his personality was so strong and pleasing that he engaged the absolute loyalty of several thousand people.

Born in Rome, in the Muti Palace, he was a strong, healthy child who grew into an active, vivacious boyhood. He gave early promise of grace and charm, and with his youthful passion for golf, tennis, and shooting went a marked disinclination for serious study. He spoke French and Italian easily enough, but showed a stubborn aversion to Latin. Wherever he went he made friends and found ready admiration. He was soon conscious of what he conceived to be his destiny, and trained himself for military adventure by strenuous exercise. He had the requisite physique, the gift of courage, a ready tongue, and the rare ability to inspire devotion. To say that he lacked judgment is not to disparage him, for it was lack of judgment that led him to fame.

It was generally believed that no attempt against England was possible without help from France or Spain, and in 1744 France was disposed to offer help. In the complicated politics of the War of the Austrian Succession France had been committed to war against England as well as Austria, and an expedition was prepared, under the inspiring leadership of Marshal Saxe, to expel the Hanoverian usurper, George II, with an army of 7000 men. But England, as often before, was protected by its weather, the French fleet was defeated by a violent gale, and Louis XV was disinclined for further effort. It was then that Charles Edward showed the remarkable intensity of his resolution; disappointed but undeterred, he made plans for a private invasion of Scotland. His father did not encourage him, Louis XV did not dissuade him, and Antoine Walsh,* a Franco-Irish shipowner of Nantes, gave him active and generous help. Having raised some money —by pawning the Polish crown jewels? That has been suggested, but seems improbable—Charles acquired a modest armament: a few field-guns, fifteen hundred muskets, ammunition, and a thousand broad-swords. Walsh lent him the brig *Du Teillay*, and by discreet arrangement with the French government the old battleship *Elisabeth* was allowed to escort the brig and carry, with his armament, sixty well dressed volunteers.

Elisabeth, however, was engaged by the English ship *Lyon*, and after very bitter fighting, in which both suffered heavy losses, *Elisabeth* put back to Brest and the *Du Teillay* sailed on alone, to put the Prince ashore, with only a handful of supporters, at Loch nan Uamh between Moidart and Arisaig on the west coast of Scotland. The date of his disembarkation was the 25th July, 1745.

His supporters, the "Seven Men of Moidart" as they came to be known, were strange and improbable associates in so reckless a venture. The Duke of Atholl, attainted by the Hanoverian government, had been out in the rebellion of 1715, and as Marquess of Tullibardine had led the little Spanish force that fought in Glenshiel in 1719. He was, by now, nearly sixty and suffered from gout. Aeneas Macdonald was a banker in Paris, Francis Strickland an Englishman from Westmorland, Sir John Macdonald had served for many years in the Spanish cavalry and was about the same age as Atholl. Sir Thomas Sheridan, an Irishman who fought at the battle of the Boyne in 1690, had for many years been in the Old Pretender's service; the Rev. George Kelly, also Irish, born in 1688, was an enthusiastic Jacobite plotter

* John S. Gibson: *Ships of the '45.*

who had spent fourteen years as a prisoner in the Tower; and John O'Sullivan, born in County Kerry, had served with the French army in Corsica, in Italy, and on the Rhine, and was only forty-five. He became the Prince's Quartermaster-general, and his authority was much resented by some of the Scottish Jacobites.

The Prince had already been warned, by Macdonald of Boisdale, that he had better go home; and when, on the 19th August, he raised his standard at Glenfinnan, there gathered beneath it, not the embattled clans in a general rising as he had hoped, but only the Macdonalds of Clanranald, Glengarry, and Keppoch; Lochiel and his Camerons; and the Stewarts of Ardshiel: about six hundred in all. Most of the chiefs were cautious. They remembered disaster in '15, the fiasco in '19, and though none liked the Hanoverian government, they had become reconciled to it. They listened to Duncan Forbes of Culloden, whose character all respected, whose wisdom was widely recognised, and who would have nothing to do with rebellion. It has been said, indeed, that he who defeated Charles Edward was not the Duke of Cumberland, but Duncan Forbes.

But Charles was undismayed, and within the next two or three weeks he had rallied another fourteen or fifteen hundred men. Most of the British army was in Hanover, and in all Scotland there were only between three and four thousand regular troops. Their General was Sir John Cope, who in difficult circumstances made a strategic blunder and allowed Charles to march to Perth, and so to Edinburgh on the 18th September. The Old Pretender was proclaimed as James VIII, and three days later Cope, who had come south by sea, faced the rebels at Prestonpans and saw his regulars demolished in fifteen minutes by a Highland charge.

Charles remained in Edinburgh until the end of October, and there was dancing again at Holyroodhouse. But he would not allow public rejoicing for his victory—they were his father's subjects who had been defeated—and the wounded whom Cope had left at Prestonpans were well cared for, prisoners generously treated. The behaviour of his wild Highlanders was impeccable, the good burgesses of Edinburgh forgot their fears and their daughters waited for the Prince with adoring eyes and fluttering hearts. But in the solid, sensible, Presbyterian Lowlands of Scotland very few declared for him or marched with an army that had grown to seven or eight thousand men when it turned towards

England. They crossed the Border near Carlisle, and advanced as far as Derby.

Charles had expected the clans to rise and greet him; he still believed that thousands of English Jacobites were waiting to welcome him; and again he was disappointed. There were English Jacobites in plenty—Jacobites in theory but not in practice; drinking Jacobites who nightly toasted the King across the water—but except for a couple of hundred in Manchester few put down their glasses to join him. Many of the magnates of the kingdom behaved, like most of the Highland chiefs, with exemplary caution and waited to see what would happen.

The military situation was interesting. General Wade, of long experience but now elderly, commanded an army of doubtful morale at Newcastle. The young and vigorous Duke of Cumberland, with experienced troops lately returned from Flanders, was at Lichfield in the Midlands, and his major responsibility was the protection of London. Its immediate defenders lay in a large but ill disciplined army, poorly officered, at Finchley. Its only claim to memory was created by Hogarth, who caricatured it with merciless relish. London itself, where the Highlanders were believed to be cannibals, was said to be in a state of near panic, and there were rumours that George II was preparing his retreat to Hanover.

At Derby Charles was vehemently intent on continuing the advance, but he was overruled by his Lieutenant-general, Lord George Murray, who had shown military capacity by dislodging Cumberland from Lichfield, with a pretended advance into Wales, and thus opening the road to London. Whether Murray or Charles was right has been the subject of much debate. It is possible that Charles, by rapid movement and another Highland charge, could have broken through the disorganised army at Finchley and occupied London; but would the cautious Jacobites, his livelier sympathisers in North Wales, and the latent opposition to the Hanoverian monarchy then have united in his support? Would an appearance of success have attracted those who, in any age, are attracted by success? The old resistance to a Catholic monarch had lately been disabled by Charles's public declaration that he assented to the Protestant mode of worship.

On the other hand there was the energetic Cumberland, with an army of increasing strength, moving slowly but with menace through the Midlands. There was Wade in the north, with the anti-royalist or anti-Stuart emotion of Yorkshire to support him. There was the Royal

Navy, which commanded the narrow seas and showed no disposition to declare for Charles. There were, above all, an historic distrust of the Stuarts, an ingrained, English disapproval of rebellion—of violent innovation—and a native distaste for the sort of major decision which would necessitate a constitutional change. It is probable, on the whole, that Lord George Murray, vilified though he has been for it, was justified in his insistence that the Jacobite army must turn its back on London and retreat from Derby.

That retreat, though conducted with speed and efficiency, was the prelude to disaster. It need not have been if Charles had had the military gifts of Montrose, or if Murray had had a larger perception of what was possible. They might have withdrawn to Inverness, and made a resolute attempt to gather Highland resistance in such form and strength as would have persuaded the Hanoverian government to offer reasonable terms for peace; or they could have reoccupied Edinburgh and from Scotland's capital appealed for French assistance and compelled, from London, a politic agreement by which—at worst—Charles, in consideration of his withdrawal from the scene, might have secured immunity for those who had supported him.

But Charles and Murray were by now on the worst of terms, and by evil compromise they decided to lay siege to Stirling. That decision led to the ill-managed battle of Falkirk from which Charles emerged as the nominal victor, but with no prize for his victory. So far from profiting, indeed, he was worse off than before. Cumberland, who had lingered in England to repel a threatened French invasion, now hurried north to replace the brutal, incompetent General Hawley, who had been beaten at Falkirk; and the Highland army, depleted as always by success—for the simple clansmen had the ineradicable habit of going home to enjoy the trophies and spoils they had won—was forced to retreat without any strategic purpose other than a dubious hope of recruiting its strength.

That retreat, in January 1746, led directly to the calamitous affair at Culloden in April. The battle there was quickly determined by Cumberland's immense superiority in artillery, by the disciplined efficiency of his army—which included Scottish as well as English regiments—and by his tactical skill, against which the fearless gallantry of half-starved Highlanders, exhausted by ill considered manoeuvre, had no defence. Cumberland would have gained great honour by his victory if he, like Charles when he defeated Cope at Prestonpans, had shown pity for the wounded and clemency to those whom he had beaten. But Charles and his Jacobite army had so shaken Hanoverian England, so shocked and frightened its Whig ascendancy, that Cumberland, brutal by nature, was given license to punish all the accessible parts of Highland Scotland with such sadistic fury as has made his name a thing of evil remembrance even to this day. The violence of his revenge, indeed, has done much to exalt the memory of Charles Edward, and perpetuate the legend of "Bonnie Prince Charlie."

Rescued fom the bloody slaughter at Culloden by his Quartermaster-general, the Irishman O'Sullivan—compelled to flight, for he was no coward—Charles Edward rode southwest and into the wilder Highlands of the Atlantic seaboard. There, and in the Outer Isles, he survived all manner of danger, the most pertinacious pursuit, by reason of his own intrepid spirit, his physical hardihood, and the devotion to his person and his cause of many people, gentle and simple, whom disaster had not daunted. They succoured him in his extremity, when death was the known punishment for sheltering him. There was a price of £30,000 on his head, and in 1746 £30,000 was such wealth, in the Highlands of Scotland, as none had ever known and few could have imagined; but though poverty was native and hunger a recurrent visitor, no one betrayed him. No one entertained the thought of betraying him except a canting minister, of the respectable name of Macaulay, who tried to enrich himself with that monstrous award; and he was defeated by the honesty of his humble neighbours.

The name of Flora Macdonald is pre-eminent among those who gave their service to the Prince, though others did as much as she, and more. There was the old, sea-wise sailor Donald MacLeod who took him, in an eight-oared boat, from Loch nan Uamh to Benbecula in the Long Island through a night of raging storm. There were MacDonald of Kingsburgh and his lady, who sheltered the Prince in Skye; there were the old Laird of Mackinnon and Captain John Mackinnon. There was Captain Donald Roy MacDonald, wounded at Culloden and still in service though his wound had not healed. There was Captain Malcolm MacLeod, who lived long enough to entertain Dr. Johnson and James Boswell with the tale of his adventures; and the schoolmaster Neil MacEachain, who went into French service and became the father of a son who died a Marshal of France and Duke of Taranto. There was Glenaladale, sometime a major in Clanranald's regiment, who, though still suffering from the wounds he got at Culloden, marched with the Prince through the wildest parts of the west Highlands, when redcoats and militia-men were searching every glen and hillside for him. There was Ned Burke, born in North Uist, whose humble occupation was between the shafts of a sedan-chair and whose epitaph recorded the amiable fact that he "preferred a good conscience to thirty thousand pounds." All these deserve honourable remembrance.

The exceptional esteem accorded to Flora MacDonald owes not a little to a popular belief that sentiment—a more familiar emotion than dynastic loyalty—enlisted her help and coloured her association with the Prince. There is, however, no substance in that belief. Their time together was very short, and Charles, ludicrously disguised as a female servant, caused needless anxiety by his refusal to regard either his disguise, or the danger which made it necessary, with sufficient seriousness. He was amused, it seems, by the absurdity of an adventure which, for a little while looked more farcical than heroic; and though to Flora he showed the utmost courtesy—was now tenderly careful of her comfort, now gravely respectful—he was untouched by deeper emotion. She had risked her life by ferrying him from the Long Island of the Outer Hebrides to a hope of safety in Skye; and when, on a night of pouring rain in Portree, he took farewell of her, he saluted her with royal condescension and said, "For all that has happened I hope, Madam, we shall meet in St. James's yet." But she never saw him again.

He seems, indeed, to have inherited no trace of his grandfather's sensuality—no particle of Charles II's amatory genius—and throughout his life was curiously uninfluenced by sexual appetite. The enigmatic Clementina Walkinshaw was certainly his mistress but equally certain is the fact that no great and glowing passion illumined their relationship. In Paris, after his flight from Scotland, he spent some years of puzzling obscurity and became very friendly with the Princesse de Talmond, a cousin of the Queen of France. Madame de Talmond was forty when he met her, and in his letters to other ladies he referred to her as *la vieille* or *la tante;** that she was his mistress as well as his adopted aunt is not impossible, but he seems to have found her useful rather than emotionally stimulating. There were two other ladies in whose house he is said to taken refuge, but they, perhaps, enjoyed a friendship which could not have admitted him, and there is no evidence of intimacy stronger than some letters which he wrote to one of them,

* Compton Mackenzie: *Prince Charles and his Ladies.*

to ask for the loan of English books. The wife he tardily married was unfaithful to him, and had good reason for the ill temper she showed.

Charles Edward—gallant, agreeable, handsomely made—attracted many women, and responded, with enthusiasm, to none of them. Nor is there any record—no hint or whisper—of any perversity in his nature. Brave and vigorous as he was, manly as he seemed, he was devoid of passion. He was moved, and the active part of his life was dominated, by a dynastic purpose like that of his grandfather's great-grandmother, Mary, Queen of Scots. He was as narrowly intent as she on what he conceived to be his destiny, and as little interested in the sexual exercises that maintain life in a dynasty. If Flora MacDonald had been born in time to rescue Charles II from the oak tree where he hid after the calamitous battle of Worcester, he would not have left her without showing some appreciation of her goodwill; but when Charles Edward said goodbye to Flora he remembered, with more honesty than emotion, to repay a small sum of money that he owed her. The royal Stuarts, it may be, were genetically exhausted, and Charles Edward, almost the last of his race, was, if not physically incapable of prolonging it, without the vulgar appetite to do so.

That does not detract from the heroic quality of his long evasion. For five months he was hunted through the Highlands and Islands, and with a high spirit survived recurrent danger and grievous hardship. The French made many attempts to rescue him, the Royal Navy defeated all but the last of them. The ships of both navies, their companies and their captains, showed seamanly skill and a marvellous reserve of courage in their watch and ward over the island waters, or their stubborn attempts to break through a busy screen of frigates thrusting to windward or searching narrow sea-lochs on a perilous reach. And while sailors, of one side or the other, scanned angry skies and the menace of broken water, on the great hills of the mainland Charles and one or two companions, with a guide found by providence or chance, were breaking through the comparable screen of regulars or militia-men who fenced the country from Loch Nevis and Loch Hourn to the gentler slopes that look down towards the Moray Firth.

In August he acquired a bodyguard of redoubtable old soldiers who had taken an oath of continuing hostility to Cumberland and his army, and pursued their private war with ingenuity and some success. They were known as the Seven Men of Glenmoriston—though in fact there were eight of them—and for some weeks they took good care of the Prince, and because they were skilful foragers he lived well on whisky and mutton, butter and cheese and venison, but had to eat his meat without bread; they never found bread. They moved gradually westward again, and at the end of the month, in Lochiel's country, the Prince walked out of danger and into the safety, the relative comfort, of Cluny's Cage. That was "a romantic, comical habitation" which had been contrived for Cluny—Ewen MacPherson, chief of the clan—on a high slope of Ben Alder, a great hill that rises to nearly 4000 feet about twenty-five miles east of Fort William.

He was there when news was brought of two French ships in Loch nan Uamh, and on the 19th September, in the very place where he had landed fourteen months before, he went aboard *L'Heureux* with Lochiel and many of his followers, and before midnight both ships weighed anchor and set sail for France.

Of his remaining years one cannot write with pleasure. He was, to an extraordinary extent, single minded, and because he had been defeated on the only venture that mattered—his personal crusade—his life had been deprived of purpose. So, with nothing left to live for, his life lost dignity. He did not, indeed, admit the finality of his defeat until proof of it could no longer be doubted, and for some considerable time he nursed the hope of returning to Scotland at the head of a French army. There was much popular enthusiasm for him in France, but the King, declining to give him an army, judiciously offered him a pension instead; and when Charles refused his charity, he was arrested and expelled from France.

He still had many friends, and in 1750, when there was a revival of sympathy for the Jacobite cause in England, he daringly went to London and for several days sought assurance of the help he had been promised. He soon found that he had been misled, and went to Berlin to ask help from Frederick the Great. Frederick offered sympathy, but nothing more. Then there was a plot to kidnap the Hanoverian royal family—Charles was insistent that no physical harm should be done them—and in Antwerp a Jacobite agent busily bought muskets. But the plot proved as vain as the expectation of help from Frederick the Great.

In 1752, when Charles was in Ghent, he was joined by the mysterious Clementina Walkinshaw. He had first met her after the battle of Falkirk, when he fell ill and she opportunely appeared to nurse him. Her arrival in Ghent may indicate a devotion undimmed by six years of separation, but some have suspected that she was a Hanoverian spy, sent to seduce him and discover his intentions. Whatever her motive, she became pregnant and bore him a daughter. It was about this time that Charles began to give his friends concern by drinking too much. He had shown, during his Scottish adventure, a fine ability to carry his drink, but a tendency now began to let drink carry him.

Charlotte, Clementina's daughter, was born at the end of October 1753, and for some years Charles and Clementina lived together in the artificial amity that a common addiction to drink may lightly encourage or rudely dispel. He who had survived the pursuit of redcoats in Highland hills was now beset by spies and informers, for his mere existence was still a potential menace to the Hanoverian government of England.

In 1765 he went to Rome to see his dying father—that lamentable old man whose spirit had long predeceased his body—but arrived too late. In Rome, however, his spirit revived, he enjoyed Roman society, and for several years lived a sober, well regulated life. Clementina had left him, or been dismissed, and in 1772, when he was fifty-two, he married the Princess Louise of Stolberg, who was eighteen. It was Louis XV, King of France, who persuaded him that matrimony was his duty—it cannot have been his pleasure—and when duty, reluctantly acknowledged, failed to beget an heir, the elderly husband sought comfort in the bottle, the young bride in adultery. Louise found a devoted companion in the rich poet, Vittorio Alfieri, and Charles fell ill with melancholia. But Charlotte, his illegitimate daughter by Clementina Walkinshaw, came to Florence, where he was living in 1784, and brought him her love, brought him a little comfort, and stayed with him until his death four years later. Poor Charlotte did not long survive him.

4

The Old Pretender's second son Henry, also born in the Muti Palace, was five years younger than Charles Edward, and had the honour of baptism by Pope Benedict XIII. More tractable than Charles, he was a pretty, affectionate child, and by his foolish father was preferred to his robust and independent brother.

At the age of twenty he tried, unsuccessfully, to gain admittance to the adventure of 1745, and later saw a little service with the French army. Early devoted, not merely to the Christian faith, but to the forms and ritual of its Catholic expression, he disliked intensely the frivolity of Parisian society and the friends among whom, after defeat in Scotland, his brother sought solace. He told his father that he wished to enter the Church, his father approved, the Pope applauded their decision, and with a recognition, that now seems remarkable, of royalty's superior claim to God's favour and ecclesiastical authority, he was immediately created a Cardinal-deacon of Santa Maria in Campitello.

Promotion and enrichment soon followed, but Henry was embarrassed by his father's attempt to dictate his spiritual advancement, and tried to escape the interference, to which no Cardinal should be subject, by retiring to Bologna. The Pope repressed his attempt to assert independence, he was recalled to Rome, and new honours accrued. He became Bishop of Frascati in 1761, two years later was vice-chancellor of St. Peters, and the richest ecclesiastic in Rome.

Splendidly accomplished in all his churchly duties, he never forgot the dignity of his blood, and paraded in a stateliness more regal than his elder brother could ever afford. He retained, it seems, an unusual innocence—an ignorance of the world of which Roman cardinals, in the Eighteenth Century, were seldom guilty—for when the Princess Louise discarded her husband, Henry gave her houseroom in his palace of the Cancellaria, though her lover the poet Alfieri, was in daily attendance on her.

After Charles Edward's death in 1788 Henry claimed succession to the sovereignty for which his brother had fought—a bishop, he said, was not invalidated by ecclesiastical office for secular authority—and had a medal struck on which he named himself Henry IX. But the French Revolution, and Napoleon's invasion of Italy, brought calamity to him—he had previously enjoyed the revenue of fat livings in France—and he, the rich cardinal, forced into flight, found poor refuge in Venice in a shabby house on the Rialto. The ultimate indignity—but a resumption of comfort—came when he accepted, from the English government of George III, a pension of £4000 a year, for which, to the British ambassador, he expressed his gratitude.

He was able to return to Frascati where, undisturbed, he lived out the remainder of his life. He lived, indeed, to the age of eighty-two, an achievement matched by none of his family from its earliest days in Scotland. But his death left the dynasty without an heir. He who had so sedulously paraded its dignity, had betrayed an ancient family by his preference for the pomp and celibacy of a cardinal see. The genius of the Stuarts had spent itself, the royal line had reached its terminus. Or so it seemed.

But under different names and heavy disguise the patrimony of Stuart blood had still a diluted reality, and in the course of time another monarch—in whom sentiment sometimes overrode reality—was to rejoice in her inheritance and magnify it by the pride and pleasure with which she took seisin of lands in the very heart of her northern kingdom.

Their Improbable Successor

Leaves From The Journal Of Our Life In The Highlands, by Queen Victoria, achieved a fame and popularity unrivalled by any royal or ruling author since Julius Caesar composed his *Commentaries* on the Gallic War; and in her *Journal* she recorded a sunny afternoon in September 1873 that she spent in a small steamer on Loch Arkaig.

The loch lies in the wild country where Charles Edward, the Young Pretender, had known extreme discomfort in 1746; and with Queen Victoria, aboard the steamer, was Cameron of Lochiel whose predecessor had been one of the first to bring out his clan and join the Prince. Enchanted by the blue and golden landscape, and Lochiel's kilt and plaid, the Queen was also aware of the historic interest of the occasion; as was her private secretary, General Ponsonby.

"As General Ponsonby observed," she wrote, it was "a striking scene. 'There was Lochiel,' as he said, 'whose great-grand-uncle had been the real moving cause of the rising of 1745—for without him Prince Charles would not have made the attempt—showing your Majesty (whose great-great-grandfather he had striven to dethrone) the scenes made historical by Prince Charlie's wanderings. It was a scene one could not look on unmoved.'

"Yes; and *I* feel a sort of reverence in going over these scenes in this most beautiful country, which I am proud to call my own, where there was such devoted loyalty to the family of my ancestors—for Stewart blood is in my veins, and I am *now* their representative, and the people are as devoted and loyal to me as they were to that unhappy race."

The Queen had first visited Scotland in 1842, five years after her succession. She was twenty-three years old, devoted to her husband,

and two young children already promised the busy domestic life with which she would enclose her imperial dignity. With the Prince Consort and their staff she embarked on the royal yacht *George*, and followed by an escort of seven or eight vessels set out from the Thames to arrive at Leith three days later. They were immediately impressed by Edinburgh: "It is quite beautiful, totally unlike anything else I have seen; and what is even more, Albert, who has seen so much, says it is unlike anything *he* ever saw." They travelled through Perthshire, read *The Lay of the Last Minstrel*, and Albert was introduced to deer-stalking. They had been given the warmest of welcomes, and warmly they had reciprocated. That visit was the beginning of a love affair which brought happiness to both of them and transformed the part of Aberdeenshire in which they finally made their home. For Scotland, indeed, it marked the beginning of a new reputation: it was to make Highland Scotland fashionable.

It is easy, of course, to mock the Queen's enthusiasm for the Highland way of life she so exuberantly adopted, and the tartan draperies that she and Albert devised to colour her claim to Stuart blood found little favour with later generations. But their Stuart blood had floated the Hanoverians to the throne of Britain, and Victoria was a grand-daughter of George III, he a great-grandson of George I, whose mother Sophia was the daughter of Elizabeth, the Winter Queen of Bohemia, whose father was James VI and I. Elizabeth, who inspired so much devotion, had in her lifetime enjoyed little profit from it, but her descendants had much to thank her for, and Victoria—never a woman to deny emotion its satisfactions—lavished her affection on the land to which the Winter Queen had given her an hereditary title. Tenuous it was, but she thickened it with the reality of her powerful sentiment.

It was in 1848 that Prince Albert took a lease of Balmoral, on Deeside in Aberdeenshire, and the Queen's first holiday there, in September of that year, immediately persuaded her that Balmoral was the property she wanted. It lies, indeed, in a delectable countryside, a green champaign of river-lands between the superlative crest of Lochnagar on the one hand, the high tableland of the Cairngorms on the other. Deeside had a history sufficient to make it interesting—there were Gordons and Farquharsons in the background, families which never failed to bequeath legends of prowess or sturdy eccentricity—and the climate was good, the air dry and sunny; the Dee was a noble salmon-stream, and on the nearby hills there were stags in plenty for the Prince Consort.

The old castle was rather small and not very conveniently designed, but when Victoria was able to buy what she held on lease, that disability was soon removed. The old castle was demolished, the new Balmoral built, and the estate enlarged by purchase or lease of neighbouring properties. The Queen acquired a Highland home, suitable for her Majesty, and her neighbours, both noble and simple, were delighted by the return to Scotland of a reigning sovereign.

Her humble neighbours were enriched by new employment, and their lives made more comfortable by the better houses that royal proprietors built for them. Increasingly, as the years went by, the Queen showed a remarkable ease, a simple friendliness, in her relations with cottagers, her servants and their families, and on Deeside re-created that habit of genial association with the commons of their kingdom which had distinguished her remote ancestors James V and James III. Of larger importance, as economists value it, was the rising price of land that lay within an ever-widening periphery of the royal establishment; and the fashion for acquiring a Highland residence which was promoted by the royal favour bestowed on Balmoral.

That the creation, throughout the Highlands, of large sporting estates—occupied only for a few weeks in August and September—was not of lasting benefit for the northern counties is now quite obvious; but in the latter half of the Nineteenth Century it created employment, and brought in a seasonal income, when no other source of income existed, and no one had thought, with any longer perspective, of the problem which the Highlands presented. As an interim measure, as a temporary expedient for dealing with a crisis of which the seriousness had not yet been recognised, the sporting estate was of considerable value. On deer forest, grouse moor, and salmon river—in the shooting lodges they built for brief accommodation—English proprietors or their rich tenants maintained a population, small indeed, which the native economy of the Highlands could no longer support.

The Queen and the Prince Consort showed remarkable enterprise, and a hardihood beyond expectation, in exploring the country in which they found such pleasure. In the middle years of the Nineteenth Century good roads were few, and even good roads were rough: twenty miles behind horses was a long journey. But in 1860 Victoria and her husband set out on a September morning, drove to the granite-pinched tumult of water at the Linn of Dee, transferred to ponies and rode through Glen Feshie to the valley of the Spey: about forty miles, twenty on horseback. At six in the evening they mounted a shabby vehicle, "a kind of barouche," and behind "a pair of small and rather miserable horses" drove for three hours to the straggling little village of Grantown. They dined and slept at a small inn where "Grant and Brown were to have waited on us, but were 'bashful' and did not." —Grant and Brown had taken a little too much to drink, and "bashful" is a charmingly sympathetic way of describing their condition.—The next morning, under a wet sky, a steep road led to the bleak and windy heights of the village of Tomintoul: four hours to cover fourteen miles through spectacular scenery. From there, after lunch, they got ponies to ride to Inchory and Loch Builg under Ben Avon, where carriages waited to seat them in rattling discomfort down the narrow road through Glen Gairn. They returned to Balmoral at half-past seven, having ridden or driven round the massif of the Cairngorms: perhaps a hundred miles in two days.

There were other journeys, no less enterprising, and arduous exploration of the rough excitements that lay round about Balmoral: the Forest of Ballochbuie, Loch Muick, and the high ragged edges of Lochnagar. The Queen and the Prince Consort were devoted to their new domain, and entered into happy possession of its wildest parts. Their enthusiasm was unforced and natural, and the Queen's discovery of the Highlands was a major event in her life.

In the life of Scotland it was an event which should not be exaggerated, but must be recognised as fortunate. For a long time Scotland had lived, almost anonymous, in political obscurity. In parliament it was nominally represented by forty-five members, in reality it had been "managed" by a succession of able men who used their power of patronage to secure their own authority through the acquiescence of qualified parliamentary electors who, in Scotland, numbered only about 2600 until the franchise was extended in the reforms of 1832. The most influential of the managers was Henry Dundas, later Viscount Melville, but also known as Harry the Ninth. He died in 1811, and his son Robert succeeded him in his sphere of interest.

The Eighteenth Century had, it is true, sired a cultural renaissance, and the Industrial Revolution had begun its uncharted advance into the future. Between the accession of George III in 1760 and the death of Walter Scott in 1832 the apostles of the Age of Enlightenment fondly called Edinburgh "the Athens of the North"; and Sir Walter, with European fame to reinforce his genius, had created for his readers a new portrait of Scotland, of its people and its scenery, that was more agreeable than anything they had previously known or suspected. West of the Atlantic and east of the Arabian Sea Scottish soldiers and administrators were creating an empire, and since 1746 Scotland itself had lived in peace; and that was a blessing it had rarely known. In the Eighteenth Century its population increased by fifty per cent, its income rose fifty-fold. There was much for which to be thankful, but a nation—and Scotland had never conceived itself as less than that —needs recognition and some of the ornaments, the trappings and trimmings, the visible forms of nationality; and they were lacking.

It is, of course, a complaint still heard in the farther parts of Britain that the enormity of London obscures the vision of those who live there, and in the narrowness of its view, its ignorance of what lies beyond it, the metropolis is very like an overgrown village. A hundred years ago there was much truth in that complaint. The importance of London was manifest to all, the growing importance of the industrial north only grudgingly admitted.

Society was aristocratic, it had its own recognised frontiers, a limited population—no Reform Bill had yet extended the social franchise—and secure in their enormous riches the aristocrats, or most of them, lived in the southern counties of England. Scotland, like the north of England, robustly assured itself that it had no need of titled splendour, that democracy and its equalities were much to be preferred—that homely virtues and honest toil were the true crown of life —but when Victoria and the Prince Consort first sailed into Aberdeen, and drove out to Balmoral, their journey was a triumphal progress.* Arches spanned the road through fifty miles of a delighted countryside —arches of flowers and evergreens, sprouting bridges of thistles and heather, a flaunting display of crowns and banners, an exuberant arch of oats and barley, a fantastical structure built entirely of heavily antlered stags' heads—and the fervour of their welcome so far transcended the normal exclamations of loyalty that it rather resembled the gratitude with which a beleaguered garrison would welcome a column marching to its relief. The people of the northern kingdom were hungry for a sight of royalty, and Queen Victoria had come to their rescue.

* David Duff: *Victoria in the Highlands.*

As surprising as the excitement in Aberdeenshire—perhaps more surprising—was the enormous length at which London newspapers reported the royal visit. They had prepared for it in advance, reporters and artists awaited the Queen's arrival, and columns were filled with picturesque description and admirable drawings. By her daring eccentricity the young Queen had opened the minds of her metropolitan subjects to the fact that her realm extended far to the north of Oxford Street.

As a royal estate Balmoral survived the death of Queen Victoria, and did not lose the favour of her successors. Edward VII cared little for it, but George V and George VI enjoyed its freedom, its forests and its moors, and Queen Elizabeth brings her growing family to the turreted castle that now looks as native a growth as the trees that curtain it. After two and a half centuries Queen Victoria redomesticated the royal family in Scotland. It was her own wish to do so. No social or political pressure turned her thought and fancy to the north. It was a romantic impulse that determined her, a remembrance—real in essence though sentimental in its expression—of the Stuart blood that circulated, however thinly, in her impulsive heart. And what she determined she did with no more backing than Charles Edward had when he landed in Loch nan Uamh to conquer Scotland with the Seven Men of Moidart. But where he failed, Victoria—as wilful as he, but in her own fashion—succeeded.

A Glossary

Many of the apparent difficulties of early Scots writing are due only to an unfamiliar spelling, and disappear when the lines are read aloud.

In the first stanza quoted on page 14, for example, "kest" is quickly translated into cast, "sodayn" into sudden. "Qu" in "quhare" and "quhich" equals the letter w; and many words, such as "pleyne," which means complain, and "lyte" for little, are so close to their modern equivalents that they need no explanation.

In later lines "tho" means then, "takyn" is token, "mo" is more, "seyne" is say, "astert" is avoid, "sike" is sigh, "sely" is not silly but weak or simple, "wote" is knows.

In the next instalment of the poem, however, there are many words whose meaning is less obvious, especially when the royal author makes a catalogue, or bestiary, of the animals that visit him in his dream. Here is a list of obscure or difficult words:

"Lusty" is pleasant; "enbroudin" is embroidered; "maner" is kind of; "blew as lede" is blue as lead; "curall" is coral; "gesserant" suggests a resemblance to chain or mail armour "fere" is mate: "pantere" is panther, though why it should be like a "smaragdyne," or emerald, is obscure; "slawe as" means no more than slow ass, and "druggar beste of pyne" refers to its life of painful drudgery; "nyce" means wanton, not agreeable; the "werely porpapyne" is the warlike porcupine; "percyng" is sharp-sighted; "lufare" is lover, "voidis" means drives out, and "evour" is ivory: the unicorn was said to be loving and gentle in the presence of a maiden, and its horn was an antidote to poison.

"Dress" is rise; "fery" is active; "standar" means standing: the elephant was thought to have no joints in its legs, and so could do little else.

The wily fox is the widow's enemy because it steals her hens; the goat has always been a climber; the elk was a noble target for a man armed with a crossbow; the boar often stands as if it were listening or hearkening; the grease of the badger or "grey" is wholesome for hurts; and hares devour "wortis" or plants.

The verses on page 59 are not difficult. "Blicht" means coloured; "wale" is choice or pick; "prevene" is precede: the line means she was the pick and blessing of humankind. Then, as always, a rois is a rois is a rois.

In the lines from Dunbar on page 62, "spreit" is spirit; "claif" is split; "wox" is grew; "dicht" is made ready.

On page 77, "skaith'd her a puir flee" means did her no more harm than a flea.

Bibliography

In a preface to his memorable study of Queen Elizabeth, Sir John Neale wrote: "For biographical guidance the reader is referred to Dr. Conyers Read's *Bibliography of British History, Tudor Period*, the publication of which saves me from occupying space with a very lengthy list of books."

I have always been ready to accept help from my betters, and I shall follow Sir John's example and refer curious readers to the bibliography I appended to *The Survival of Scotland;* thus refraining from adding to the length of the present volume.

For a book of this sort—much of which is manifestly opinion rather than fact—a bibliography may, indeed, be misleading. I have, for example, my own opinions, very firmly established, about Mary, Queen of Scots; but the substance of what I have written about the Casket Letters comes, very largely, from T. F. Henderson's book about them, published in 1890, and T. F. Henderson's interpretation of Mary's life and character is totally unlike mine. I have also read, with pleasure and instruction, his very informative biography, *The Royal Stewarts;* but what I think of James VI is very far from what he thought.

Either in the text or in footnotes I have drawn attention to sources from which I have acquired some particular piece of information, of which I was previously ignorant; but having once noticed a source I have sometimes tapped it again without the tribute of an *op. cit.* I am deeply grateful, however, to the authors I have mentioned, for I have mentioned none whose work has not given me lasting pleasure as well as timely assistance.

Index

272